Dance Ped
for a Diverse

Dance Pedagogy for a Diverse World

Culturally Relevant Teaching in Theory, Research and Practice

NYAMA MCCARTHY-BROWN

Foreword by TAKIYAH NUR AMIN

McFarland & Company, Inc., Publishers
Jefferson, North Carolina

LIBRARY OF CONGRESS CATALOGUING-IN-PUBLICATION DATA

Names: McCarthy-Brown, Nyama.
Title: Dance pedagogy for a diverse world : culturally relevant teaching in theory, research and practice / Nyama McCarthy-Brown ; foreword by Takiyah Nur Amin.
Description: Jefferson, North Carolina : McFarland & Company, Inc., Publishers, 2017. | Includes bibliographical references and index.
Identifiers: LCCN 2017011482 | ISBN 9780786497027 (softcover : acid free paper) ∞
Subjects: LCSH: Dance—Study and teaching (Higher) | Dance—Study and teaching—Social aspects. | Dance teachers—Training of. | Culturally relevant pedagogy.
Classification: LCC GV1589 .M325 2017 | DDC 792.80711—dc23
LC record available at https://lccn.loc.gov/2017011482

BRITISH LIBRARY CATALOGUING DATA ARE AVAILABLE

ISBN (print) 978-0-7864-9702-7
ISBN (ebook) 978-1-4766-2607-9

On the cover *in front* Magi Ross, *kneeling front row left to right* Janira Bremner, Fania Tsakalakos, Kiera Mersky, *second row* Rhonda Moore, *third row* Cheryl Hinton (photographer Bill Hebert)

Printed in the United States of America

McFarland & Company, Inc., Publishers
Box 611, Jefferson, North Carolina 28640
www.mcfarlandpub.com

To those who unapologetically dance the dances of their ancestors: May you dance on, and may those who watch know that they bore witness to the essence of humanity.

Table of Contents

Acknowledgments   ix

Foreword by Takiyah Nur Amin   1

Preface   6

Part I: How to Create a Culturally Relevant Classroom

One—What Is Culturally Relevant Teaching?   13

Two—Toolkit for Teaching Culturally Relevant Pedagogy   35

Three—Nuts and Bolts: How to Develop a Culturally Relevant
Class Culture   51

Part II: Culturally Relevant Teaching and Critical Dance Pedagogy for Classes Pertaining to the Dancing Body

Four—Culturally Relevant Ballet   65

Five—Culture, Music and Composition Class   85

Six—Critical Dance Pedagogy for Repertory: Two Case Studies
by Selene Carter and Nyama McCarthy-Brown   103

Part III: Critical Dance Pedagogy and Diversifying Content and Approaches to Dance Education

Seven—Reshaping Dance History by Deconstructing Whiteness
by Julie Kerr-Berry   127

Eight—Native American Dance History and Powwow Styles
by Kelly Fayard   154

Nine–World Dance: Retire the Term   169

Ten—From Conservatory Training to Teaching Dance
   in Public Schools: A Cultural Shift *by Corrine Nagata with*
   Liza D. Kroeschell   190

Epilogue   204

Chapter Notes   209

Bibliography   219

About the Contributors   227

Index   229

Acknowledgments

As I come to the close of my time preparing this manuscript, I am struck with gratitude thinking of the many people who have invested energy into this book. I would be remiss if I did not acknowledge the support of countless people, friends, family, and colleagues who stimulated and propelled this work. Dialogues with students and teachers in the field of dance and education inspired many of the ideas developed herein as well as the investigations of my graduate school classmates both at the University of Michigan and Temple University. Sherrie Barr was the developing editor, without whom this text would not present the rigor and balance of ideas it does. Kariamu Welsh was instrumental in sharing insights on Dance Education and the publication process. Mentorship was extended to me by Tommy DeFrantz in responding to the work as well as colleagues Karen Schupp, Stephanie Power-Carter, Selene Carter, and the Mellon Dance Studies Seminar Community of fellows and advisors.

My deepest gratitude is extended to my number one and first supporter, my mother, who spent hundreds of hours reading every draft of every chapter, again and again, often because she was unable to save on her computer or the file she revised did not attach or send when emailed to me. Without complaint or a hint of annoyance, she graciously read, re-read, and read again, providing needed feedback with each revision.

I offer sincere appreciation to each of the contributors to this text: Takiyah Nur Amin, Selene Carter, Julie Kerr-Berry, Kelly Fayard and Corrine Nagata. These individuals generously shared their research and teaching discoveries through the creation of an original essay for this book. Their commitment to the field is evident in their scholarship.

Finally, I wish to extend a special thanks to my students, who taught me the value of critical dance pedagogy and culturally relevant teaching. Without my students this work would not be possible, and it is for dance students everywhere that this work was created.

Foreword
by Takiyah Nur Amin

Whether I am interacting with colleagues at my university, chatting with family members at social gatherings or engaging with friends near and far on social media, I am confronted by one simple, oft-repeated and taken-for-granted refrain. *"The world is changing."*

In the wake of consistent and highly visible protest aimed at racist social policies in the communities of Ferguson, Baltimore, Charleston and across the country, it seems that friends, family and colleagues alike are convinced that we are moving into a new era—a new world, one that requires a reorienting of our relationship to both self and other. As the democratization of information proliferates through online mediums like Twitter, Snapchat, Facebook, and other platforms, the possibilities for growing awareness of social and political change and consequently global action have become increasingly commonplace. I marvel at how quickly information—whether it is an article that synthesizes the commonalities between youth protests in Palestine and the #blacklivesmatter protests in the U.S. or tweets that amplify the lived experiences of native-born black women in Africa—has become a part of not only my regular information "diet" but is also referenced easily by students, family and peers. *Perhaps the world is changing. I remain unconvinced.*

Sure, the social and political landscape around us is different than it was a decade ago. One can point to everything from shifting demographics, rising protests, the toppling of long-standing regimes and changing public sentiment around symbols once believed benign by many to see that yesterday and today are not the same. Still, I am not sure it's the world that is changing as much as our understanding of the complexity around us that is in flux. It feels more accurate to suggest that with increased access to media and information for many and the possibility for communication across perceived boundaries, our ever-changing world requires that we make space for nuance, challenge assumptions, assimilate information once over-looked and engage in the re-making of ourselves to attend to this re-making of our world.

If this is true, how are those of us committed to Dance Education going to equip ourselves to engage students meaningfully as we strive to make sense of the relevance of our practice in this new context? What do we need to do as edu-cators to ensure that this changing world does not leave us behind in a heap of outdated methods and ways of thinking, best suited to some other time and place? How do we help our dance students make sense of living in an increasingly mediated, intensely diverse world, with all of its ambiguity, messiness, unrealized ideals and untapped potential?

An anecdote: I've been teaching in higher education settings for over a decade and in community settings before that. I am always struck when students enter my classroom with a palpable enthusiasm and obvious anx-iety about being in the course. It isn't because of what they've heard about my reputation as a professor or some concern about the syllabus. These students articulate that they are really excited about taking my class and looking forward to the course but they don't "know anything about dance." Once I probe deeper, what becomes apparent is that not "know[ing] any-thing abut dance" means they have not studied and been trained to profi-ciency in Western and historically privileged dance forms. Not knowing modern dance or ballet has become shorthand for not knowing anything about dance at all. These students, quick to dismiss their own embodied experience and cultural knowledge in favor of what they think my university classroom and role as a professor will privilege, has become a sad and all too familiar experience for me as a dance educator. I do my best to disrupt this faulty notion and assure the students that not only are they welcome in the class, they are also encouraged to bring themselves—including their lived experiences with dance and movement—to the course we are endeav-oring through together.

Here's the thing: as dance educators, we have to do more than disrupt this kind of faulty thinking that disregards one's own cultural experience in favor of something deemed of higher value. Sure, many of us may have lived in this field for decades referencing our own training experiences that upheld similar value judgments. Sometimes we've celebrated our own teachers who, no matter how well-intentioned, were in many instances neither considerate of nor committed to teaching in a manner that held an emancipatory ethic or even considered the possibility that the movement vocabularies of their students—across race, class, gender, sexuality, region, and nation—could be of merit, except as the occasional accent to the "serious" work of their classrooms. Even some of us who champion bringing forward less lauded movement vocabularies and their attendant philosophies into our classrooms need to do a better job of considering how to value the lived, embodied knowledge our students carry and how it connects with and can inform whatever it is we are endeavoring to share with them. *If, in fact, the world is changing, we have to do a better job of equipping ourselves and our students to live in it.*

Dance Pedagogy for a Diverse World: Culturally Relevant Teaching in Theory, Research and Practice is intended to help those of us committed to Dance Education do better—in our research, our thinking and our teaching. This book focuses on the implications of culturally relevant teaching—*an approach that enables students to relate course content to his or her background and cultural context*—in the dance classroom. With an emphasis on practice that is theoretically grounded and informed, this book is a critical intervention that will assist dance educators in re-shaping their approach to and the content of both text-based and movement courses in dance. First articulated by Gloria Ladson-Billings in the late 1990s, culturally relevant teaching endeavors to ensure that students can maintain a sense of cultural integrity and relevance while succeeding in academic settings.

An admission: I've been fortunate in my career as a dance educator to engage with scholars in the field of education more generally who are deeply familiar with and conversant in the work of Ladson-Billings and other champions of culturally relevant teaching, including Geneva Gay, Lisa Delpit and the late Asa Hilliard. I have learned much from education colleagues about critical pedagogy and approaches to culturally relevant teaching. Still, when I mention that my field is dance studies and ask them to help me connect the dots between the approaches they celebrate and the specific contexts of a dance classroom, most of them have been at a loss. Similarly, when I am with dance colleagues, especially those who teach courses that are movement-based, and try to enjoin them in a conversation about bringing culturally relevant teaching to their classroom, I am met, more often than not, with blank stares or with a suspicion that I am an interloper, seeking to undermine their classroom authority or make them teach dance as if it is some other discipline. These experiences have left me confused, frustrated and resigned at various moments in my career, convinced that my own interests as a dance educator in critical pedagogy in general and in culturally relevant teaching in particular are misplaced or unnecessary. It's made me think about leaving Dance Education behind on many occasions.

This book endeavors to address the frustrations mentioned above that I and others, I am sure, have endured since formally entering the Dance Education field many years ago. And I know I can't be the only one who is glad to have this resource to connect the dots between the intricacies, norms and social mores of Dance Education to the theory and practices offered by culturally relevant teaching, grounded in research from the field of education.

Dance Pedagogy for a Diverse World deftly deals with prickly questions raised by race, class, nationality, gender and sexual identity, diversity and appropriation in the classroom in a straightforward, uncompromising tone. This is an especially important text in that it doesn't let dance as a discipline off the hook, blindly celebrating the field as a bastion of equality and access where all are valued and welcomed with open arms. Divided into three parts, this book makes plain the assumptions that persist in the field— about everything from "technique" to the appropriateness of terminology like "World Dance"—and provides thoughtful ways for addressing many of the deficits that persist in our discipline.

Part I centers the work of author Nyama McCarthy-Brown and focuses very clearly on culturally relevant teaching as a transdisciplinary approach to teaching that engages a range of methods. Grounded in her own narrative, McCarthy-Brown shares experiences as a dance student and later as a dance educator that lead her to exploring culturally relevant teaching as her pathway in Dance Education settings. McCarthy-Brown takes readers through her experiences, sometimes funny, sometimes painful, with dance that for many will be sadly familiar and for others will foster an awareness of the ways in which students move through learning in our field when their culture isn't valued, and the implications this has for their learning. Additionally, seasoned educators will find useful resources and sample assignments—I am especially struck by McCarthy-Brown's Auto-biographical Movement Poem, for example—that can be easily adapted to a range of teaching contexts.

Part II hones in on physical and creative practice. This section includes chapters on how to actually create a culturally relevant classroom that fosters connection with students, specific insights on culturally relevant teaching in dance and an exploration of using this method specifically while teaching ballet, arguably the most celebrated of all Western and historically privileged dance forms. Selene Carter and Nyama McCarthy-Brown coauthor a chapter that offers two excellent models of how to use critical dance pedagogy in repertory courses: one focuses on differently abled dancers and the other centers of issues of race. Each chapter could easily stand alone and be shared for workshop or training sessions with pre-service teachers.

Part III brings in the voices of other dance educators to demonstrate the application of critical dance pedagogy and culturally responsive teaching in a range of contexts. Julie Kerr-Berry's contribution is especially noteworthy as she shares selected teaching strategies meant to facilitate an antiracist engagement in dance history courses. Kelly Fayard's exploration of Native American dance history is especially helpful and a distinguishing feature of this text in that it considers how to bring in the oft-overlooked legacy of indigenous peoples into dance history conversations that are traditionally dominated by other discourses. McCarthy-Brown provides sensible and compelling arguments in this section regarding issues of cultural sensitivity to be considered and addressed in composition courses as well as the need to interrogate the term "World Dance," an orientation to dance that often reinscribes cultural hierarchies in the classroom as normative. Corrine Nagata's discussion of shifting from teaching in conservatory contexts to working in public school settings lays bare some of the challenges and assumptions that using a culturally relevant approach can help navigate.

Nyama McCarthy-Brown points us to what's possible in our Dance Education classrooms. Her book not only gives us access to the kind of thinking that has been central in education settings more generally for over two decades but provides a pathway for application in a range of dance settings. What is perhaps most compelling is what this book, with its forthrightness and clear agenda, makes plain: as dance educators, we have no excuse for foregoing approaches that value, embrace and operationalize the best of what our students bring to the classroom. Moreover, we have the responsibility to challenge assumptions and practices in our field that reinscribe hierarchies, which foreclose opportunities and impede learning. As a field, we have in this book an invaluable resource that not only makes clear where we've been but just how much further we can, and must, go.

Takiyah Nur Amin is an assistant professor of dance studies and a member of the affiliate faculty in the Department of Africana Studies at the University of North Carolina at Charlotte. Her research and teaching interests include Black performance and aesthetics, twentieth-century American concert dance and pedagogical issues in dance studies.

Preface

Race and My Relationship to Dance

"How do you identify?" "What are you?" Growing up bi-racial, I often heard these questions. I understand the curiosity some people had about my appearance as I too have puzzled about the race of many people. Still today, some people identify my ethnicity while others see my ethnicity as a non-issue, either because I am a person and that is all that matters, or because I am clearly a person of color and that is all that matters. Yet as a young girl growing up, I remember being happy to claim that I was half white, hoping that I could also claim some of the white privilege that my white friends had. Now, as an adult, I identify my race as African American. I have come to believe that race is not a choice of identity but rather a construct that is socially decided. This is to say that the way the world responds to us has a great influence on how we experience the world. I cannot opt out of being an African American any more than I can opt out of being a woman. However, it would be equally false not to acknowledge my connections to white culture. I was raised by a single white woman. Although I embrace my Irish, English, and German heritage, my personal daily experiences in this world have been most impacted by my being a woman of color. To be sure, my culture and ethnicity are tied to my mother and her lineage in countless ways. Yet the way that the world has treated me and continues to treat me has had a great impact on who I am.

As a child I did not have the language to identify what I was experiencing, but I experienced great racial affinity, segregation, discrimination, and prejudice in and around dance. I remember playing outside my house as a child, making up dances with other neighborhood children. I danced with my dad and sisters on Saturday mornings while we watched *Soul Train*

6

and mimicked ways to "get down." In these instances, I experienced and embodied an African American aesthetic that I was implicitly discouraged from nurturing later while studying Western-based dance forms such as creative movement and ballet.

By the time I entered the School of the Arts High School in San Francisco, I felt like I had to transcend my class, race, and body in order to succeed in dance. Financial limitations led me to free dance classes through the local Recreation and Parks Department; these classes became a lifeline for me as a child. Yet as I grew older, there were many inferred messages that the only type of dancing that was important was the dancing studied in studios and performed on stage by thin people. Other dance forms were "nice" and "fun," but one would not be chosen to perform without "technique"—and a thin body. For me, this was the beginning of those ever-present whispers that equated one's dance ability with Western training, ballet in particular. So I traded in dancing with my community and family for taking classes at dance studios and working to get a better extension.

I continued to feel limited by my family's financial resources and my black fat body. By the time I was seventeen I felt like I was too far behind to catch up with what was then considered "good technique." So I shifted gears, went off to college, and majored in political science, with hopes of pursuing law. As it turned out, dance called me back after college, but that's another story.

My early encounters with dance began thirty years ago, and yet I still see race operating in the same ways. Although African-derived dances such as hip-hop are gaining wide mainstream acceptance, these dance forms remain on the fringes of conservatory training. When I look at dance in my community, it still reminds me of Beverly Daniel Tatum's book *Why Are All the Black Kids Sitting Together in the Cafeteria?* I see white companies here and black companies there. Yes, there are exceptions, and yes, some people mix it up, but these are, by and large, anomalies. Dancing continues to be a raced experience.

In writing and compiling this text, I want to engage in a conversation about a Dance Education that considers how a culturally informed approach to the body and movement can support student learning. My purpose is not to address segregation in dance directly, although that may be a bi-product of the text. Through this book I seek to give teachers strategies for students in the twenty-first century. I hope that as a result more students will have positive experiences in dance and develop limitless ideas of where dance can take them.

How I Came to Believe Culturally Relevant Teaching Can Address Challenges in Dance Education

In 1998, I took an urban education course. The course proved life-changing. I was introduced to culturally relevant teaching and learned how connecting teaching methods and course materials to students' cultures can enhance student achievement. I filed all that I learned away, not realizing how useful my new insights would become to me in the near future.

In 1999, I began teaching dance in a public inner-city high school in Oakland, California, to a diverse community of African American, Latino, and Asian students. I saw my work as valuable, offering students opportunities for artistic expression through daily dance classes. I purposefully created safe spaces that connected to the culture of my students. One way of doing this was to bring in local guest artists representing diverse backgrounds that reflected the students' cultural roots. I expanded their dance experiences using community resources that allowed them to see themselves in all the dancing we did together. I brought in modern dance students from the University of California, Berkeley, and dance specialists from the local community college, who happened to be Asian. We attended performances together, seeing the San Francisco Ballet's *Nutcracker* and local dance companies lead by African Americans—Savage Jazz and New Style Motherload. The local companies developed relationships with students and the school that lead to student internships and performance opportunities. I featured students' Mexican folkloric dancing and hip-hop in our dance concerts. My intent was to validate the cultural background of all the students. This was my first and best teaching experience as a dance educator in a public high school.

In hindsight, I realize that this teaching experience was chronologically closer to my general education teacher training studies (promoting culturally relevant teaching) and well before my graduate dance training studies that were Western-based and historically privileged. I now recognize that my goals for my students in Oakland affirmed their cultural roots. For me, their culture and lives in Oakland, California, were always to be at the center of their Dance Education experience. Unfortunately, my approach to teaching dance changed after I left the Bay Area to pursue graduate studies in dance.

After earning my MFA from the University of Michigan, I relocated to Atlanta, Georgia, where I was charged with starting a dance program in a small performing arts high school, Carver School of the Arts. This was to be a premier arts high school with a conservatory model. Western-based dance technique through the idioms of ballet and modern dance was the curriculum focus. I was young, excited, and determined to succeed. The school, preparing to open in a very short period of time, was not conducting auditions until a few weeks before the beginning of the term. Because we needed a certain number of students in order to open the school, most applicants were accepted into the program. My students were all African American from inner-city Atlanta. Because few had access to previous formal dance training, I would be starting from scratch. My goal was clear: train the students in widely accepted Western and historically privileged dance forms, and spend as little time as possible on "other" forms.

I had my work cut out for me. My students, excited to be dance majors, were all deficient in the one thing the program focused on—Western-based dance techniques. So I took the approach I had been taught and focused on ballet and modern. It was only a matter of weeks before the students became disgruntled and disruptive. The more I pushed for what I believed to be the needed high standards for dance, the more the students acted out with incorrigible behavior. I shot down every request made for hip-hop music and hip-hop dance instruction. I said, "You already know hip-hop, let's learn something new." The students were intuitive enough to know that eliminating their dance aesthetic was not going to work for them. They already had a dance form they were tied to and which embodied their culture. This form gave them confidence and motivated them to study dance. The students were not interested in the dance training I was offering.

I was well-intentioned, but I was wrong. I allowed mainstream Western dance aesthetics to cast a shadow over the gifts and values of my students' dancing. My students had entered into the dance program because of their love for dance. By limiting their opportunities to Western-based dance instruction and assessment, I had alienated their cultural affinities and aesthetics. In essence, I did not see or value what my students possessed and had to offer. I focused on their deficiencies as I implemented traditional assessment systems that preferred Western-based knowledge and embodiment. These methods alienated my students just as much as the dominant culture-based general education curriculum tends to do.[1] For these inner-city students, my class had become yet another example of the American public school system that silenced and diminished African American artistic expression. As I reflect on this time in my life, I consider how ridiculous was my rationale that students already proficient in hip-hop did not need to further develop those skills. What dance teacher would discourage students from studying ballet because they had already achieved competency? None. The study of any dance form, if there is to be consistent growth or even maintenance, is a daily practice.

When dance majors began dropping my program, I started questioning what I was doing. Why would these kinesthetically intelligent individuals, with a professed love for dance, leave the discipline of dance? It was time for me to critically examine my teaching pedagogy and curriculum. In identifying my use of authority over the curriculum as a form of colonialism, I quickly recognized how damaging my teaching practices were in that they were alienating and disrespectful to the embodied dance knowledge of students. I needed to redirect my focus as a dance educator and develop tools for myself and other dance educators as well.

There is a wealth of research and literature on culturally relevant teaching and critical pedagogy that offers valuable insights for dance educators.[2] Utilizing more than fifteen years of teaching experience and research, I have adapted many culturally relevant teaching and critical pedagogy strategies to dance and share them herein. I hope to equip dance educators with culturally responsive tools to create productive learning environments for dance students, not only valuing the dances that belong to the students and their cultural groups, but also exposing them to new dance forms, and heightening student achievement.

How to Use This Book

This book is about culturally relevant teaching in dance and critical dance pedagogy. Culturally relevant teaching is a method of teaching that adapts instructional tools and content to relate to the cultural affinity of students. Critical dance pedagogy asks students and teachers to investigate questions about the systems of power that dictate who performs, when, and where; who receives Dance Education, when, where, what genre, what levels, with what types of resources (i.e., studio space, dance attire, and quality of instructors); who is included in Dance History; who is pictured in our textbooks; who is funded; who is excluded from the main concert stage; and who decides the value of dance. Ultimately, critical dance pedagogy questions who is supported in learning dance.

Once CDP Is Applied and Issues Are Illuminated, Then What?

Culturally relevant teaching can act as a response to questions of power around the design of Dance Education teaching methods—CDP. CRT provides practical solutions to address issues of inequity that often come forth when critical dance pedagogy is applied to Dance Education and Dance Studies in our classrooms. Culturally relevant teaching offers possible remedies to the inequities often identified. CRT is specifically designed to support students often excluded and marginalized.

Diversifying our dance curriculum is a particular strategy to respond to inequities in Dance Education that are uncovered through CDP. By diversifying our curriculum, educators provide students with multiple perspectives of dance; it is an approach that can be utilized with all students of all ages and all genres of dance.

Which Strategy for Which Students?

Culturally relevant teaching is designed for students outside the dominant culture, because the vast majority of curriculum was not created for this demographic.

Critical dance pedagogy is most effective with high school and college students, as they possess developed critical thinking skills.

Diversifying curriculum is essential for students of all ages and demographics. The chart below shows which pedagogical approaches are appropriate for certain age groups and cultural backgrounds.

Population	Pedagogical Approach		
Age	*Culturally Relevant Teaching*	*Diversification of Curriculum*	*Critical Dance Pedagogy*
K–8	✓	✓	
High school	✓	✓	✓
Higher education	✓	✓	✓
Cultural Background			
Students from the dominant culture		✓	✓
Students outside the dominant culture (often students of color and international students)	✓	✓	✓

One

What Is Culturally Relevant Teaching?

The Problem

Imagine you are ten years old and just enrolled in a dance class at school. You are excited because you know how to dance. This is one class you know will be fun and you can walk in the door with confidence. You arrive on the first day with a wide smile. To your surprise, you are told that your idea of dance attire is ... different. Your idea of talented dance movement is ... different. Your idea of musical accompaniment is ... undeveloped, and your current dance ability is ... at level one. You are told that the dances you know are "great, fun, and cool" and are encouraged to practice these dances at home or on the playground as you will not be able to practice or perform them during class. On the other hand, you will be learning dances that are highly valued and appreciated in the dance world. And, if you work hard, you may even earn the privilege of performing these dancers for your family, school, and community. Although these dances will be new to you, and do not reflect your culture, they will enhance your dance skills and give you legitimacy as a dancer. Now, aren't you excited to learn?

This book is a response to the scenario outlined above, one that has been and continues to be manifested in a multitude of ways throughout this nation and the world. To give just one example, I learned of a similar story when conducting research at the University of Cape Town in South Africa. There I met a South African teacher of dance who told me that he was spotted in his rural community "dancing in the bush." He was subsequently given opportunities to learn Western dance forms. After being appropriately trained in Western contemporary dance, he was then told,

13

"*Now* you are a dancer." He was so insulted by the notion that he was nothing up until he was taught the white man's dance aesthetic that he quit contemporary dance completely.[1] Similarly, I can recall numerous times when I have been made uncomfortable by comments friends and colleagues made while watching a dance concert, and singling out African American males, gifted in vernacular movement: "Look at him dance, all he needs is some technique, I wish I could get him in a ballet class." I interpret these comments as "If I could teach him a more legitimate form of dance, one that is aesthetically pleasing to me, then he would be more valuable." In contrast, I cannot recall one instance where a ballet or modern dancer was evaluated and noted for his or her lack of an Asian or African dance form. The hierarchy of dance is clear.

As dance educators who seek to build multicultural communities and embrace pluralism, we cannot risk our students thinking that we seek to de-legitimize their cultural aesthetic. This text exploring research, theory, and practice of culturally relevant teaching can be a resource for all dance educators who wish to counter such hubris.

Dance, Social Constructs and Privilege

Dance is a cultural experience. It is a racial experience. It is a gendered experience. It is a kinesthetic body experience. All of this is to say that one's experience in dance is reflective of his or her demographic and dance environment. When I walk into a dance class I am immediately aware of my culture, race, and, at times, depending on the class, my age. I presume men have a heightened awareness of gender within most dance classrooms. Gay, transgender, and queer people have a heightened awareness of whether or not the space is welcoming or hetero-normative. In order to be successful in any given environment, one has to find ways to communicate—to understand and be understood by those in power. For some individuals this is an easy process of assimilation, for others it is a matter of "code-switching," and for still others it is a challenging puzzle that never fits together. To be sure, those outside the dominant culture have a heightened awareness of their differences and know the embodiment of their culture(s) will call attention to their differences.

Students outside the dominant culture find ways to navigate their journey, as do the departments that serve them. As an African American woman, I have been privy to a number of conversations with African American dancers expressing challenges they have met in mainstream Dance

Education. I have also noticed that in most of the dance departments I encountered throughout my experiences in higher education, there was a scarcity of African American dancers, yet, at the same time, the schools boasted an African American dance group of some kind. In further investigation of this phenomenon, I learned that many African American dancers feel marginalized and undervalued in the larger dance programming of the dominant culture. Culturally focused dance organizations often develop in schools where there is a lack of culturally relevant dance offerings.

I interviewed a graduating senior who explained that she directed her energy away from the mainstream departmental programming and toward an African-based dance company throughout her four-year experience. She sought mentorship from African American female graduate students in the company, recognizing that these individuals would be her lifeline throughout her undergraduate experience. She noted that when she talked to her African American undergraduate peers who were not in the African-based dance company, they spoke of feeling alienated, excluded, and marginalized by limited performance opportunities in the department. She did not share their experience. She attributed her different experience to the mentorship of the African American graduate students in the dance company to whom African American students outside the company did not have access. She also spoke of her own cultural, ethnic, and racial challenges when performing in department dance concerts that were separate from the company. She was not equipped to do her makeup and described often feeling "discarded" when she did not know how to apply makeup. Not surprisingly, her white counterparts were not equipped to assist her. Although similar experiences of being at a loss in connection to hair and makeup existed when performing with the African American company, those were less embarrassing and somber because she did not feel as isolated. She was not the only one who needed assistance. Equally relevant, she was not singled out as different because of the make up needed to flatter and enhance a darker complexion. Finally, there was no awkward silence around what to do with her hair.

I share the above anecdote to draw attention to the need for culturally relevant and sensitive experiences in dance and to bring attention to the types of privilege white students have backstage. To not have to worry about whether you can find the right foundation color for your skin is a privilege. To know that your castmates, teachers, and backstage helpers will be equipped to help you with your hair is a privilege.

What Is Culturally Relevant Teaching and Critical Dance Pedagogy?

Theoretical Frames and Historical Background

The discussion of teaching approaches in this book reveals a transdisciplinary approach to the multifaceted practice of teaching dance. Menah Pratt-Clarke defines transdisciplinary as "the use of multiple theories, methods, approaches, frameworks, and disciplines to understand, strategize, and implement transformative initiatives in society."[2] This explanation becomes a framework for the chapters in this book by which the contributing authors examine and explore pedagogical questions of power. While culturally relevant teaching, in tandem with critical dance pedagogy, are the focus of this text, a transdisciplinary ethos highlighting critical theory, critical race theory, critical pedagogy, feminist pedagogy, gender studies, and social justice is also embraced. With each particular theoretical lens, the questioning of power in classrooms is evidenced throughout, as each author approaches this questioning from her own particular perspective. Power, however, is key: power in the classroom, power in the school, power in the community. And, finally, who has the power; how is it being used; who are the powerless? These frames come together to best identify, subvert, and dismantle oppressive systems of education by questioning power structures, a query that undergirds social justice in education.[3]

The frameworks featured in this book may ensure that students historically marginalized by way of culture, race, class, gender, sexual orientation, or limited physical abilities are empowered and not oppressed through education. These frameworks recognize the systems of power that govern educational settings in the United States and understand that these systems do not support all students. Traditional teaching methods, identified by Paulo Freire as "the banking model," where the all-knowing teacher deposits information into the student, must be questioned.[4] Notions that students will "wear" the movement of their teacher encourage a disembodied and inauthentic learning experience. Ultimately, the scholarship highlighted in this text is committed to power shifting and empowering students who have been relegated to the margins.

Culturally relevant teaching, a term coined by Gloria Ladson-Billings in the 1990s, is a method of teaching that relates to the cultural background of students while also going beyond using content to which students can relate.[5] The concept is featured throughout this text because of its accessibility and focus on application. Culturally relevant teaching embraces a teaching method that relates to students' communication style and tone, learning style, and cultural beliefs. Ladson-Billings discusses the term as a pedagogy that "empowers students intellectually, socially, emotionally and politically by using cultural referents to impart knowledge, skills and attitudes."[6] As scholarship on it has flourished, so has its descriptive terms. For example, these methods are also referred to as culturally relevant pedagogy and culturally responsive teaching.

Culturally relevant teaching was initially developed in response to education researchers finding consistent patterns of lower performance for students of color than for those students from the dominant culture.[7] Culturally relevant teaching and culturally responsive teaching were developed to address the needs of underprivileged students who were not achieving on the same scale as children who identified with the dominant culture. Multicultural education specialist James Banks articulated the need for culturally relevant teaching in his seminal work forty years ago when he wrote: "[E]ducators should respect the cultural and linguistic characteristics of minority youths, and change the curriculum so that it will reflect their learning and cultural styles and greatly enhance achievement. Minority students should not be taught contempt for their cultures."[8]

As the need to relate curriculum to students remains pedagogically pertinent, Banks' scholarship continues to hold relevance today. One reason for the disproportionately low number of students of color in mainstream dance programs is culturally alienating teaching methods. Culturally relevant teaching helps to combat such alienation by building student confidence and self-esteem. Without culturally relevant teaching and diversified curriculum, students experience cultural deprivation, which also can be an overwhelming obstacle for students feeling alienated each day of their schooling experience. Educators need to consider the often irreparable damage done to students' esteem of their culture and self when both are diminished through an educational approach that fails to value them.

Geneva Gay, a prolific education scholar specializing in culturally responsive teaching theory and research, highlights the ongoing poignancy of these challenges in our educational systems. She has characterized the attributes of such pedagogy as follows:

1. It acknowledges the legitimacy of the cultural heritages of different ethnic groups, both as legacies that affect students' dispositions, attitudes, and approaches to learning and as worthy content to be taught in the formal curriculum.

2. It builds bridges of meaningfulness between home and school experiences as well as between academic abstractions and lived sociocultural realities.
3. It uses a wide variety of instructional strategies that are connected to different learning styles.
4. It teaches students to know and praise their own and one another's cultural heritages.
5. It incorporates multicultural information, resources, and materials in all the subjects and skills routinely taught in schools.[9]

Within this structure of culturally responsive teaching, students can be affirmed in their culture and learn how to affirm others in theirs. Dance educators, as teachers in the arts, have an opportunity to make a significant impact if we value the artistic and cultural expression of students—and utilize their cultural knowledge as a conduit for learning.

Critical Dance Pedagogy

Critical pedagogy is an activation of critical race theory in systems of education and is conversant with culturally relevant teaching. As Barry Kanpol states: "Critical pedagogy is a cultural-political tool that takes seriously the notion of human differences, particularly as these differences relate to race, class, and gender. In its most radical sense, critical pedagogy seeks to unoppress the oppressed and unite people in a shared language of critique, struggle, and hope to end various forms of human suffering."[10]

For the purposes of dance educators, I submit the term critical dance pedagogy (CDP): an application of critical pedagogy (teaching approach that examines systems of power) to the dancing body. Thus, CDP examines who gets to dance, in what spaces, with particular considerations of race, class, and gender. Unlike culturally relevant teaching, which was designed for students of color, CDP is a pedagogical approach that works well with various demographic configurations, including the homogeneous. Students are challenged to investigate power systems, structures, and relationships as they impact dance, dancers, and dance forms. Admittedly, white students often resist such examinations of power structures because they are often faced with the unpleasant realities of privilege.[11] I have found that it is important to highlight the opportunity those with privileges have to make significant change and highlight some of the changes that have been made historically due to those with power widening spaces for those without.

Issues of social justice are at the heart of culturally relevant teaching and critical dance pedagogy. In 2009, Secretary of Education Arne Duncan proclaimed education as a fight for social justice in a speech at the University of Virginia: "I believe that education is the civil rights issue of our generation. And if you care about promoting opportunity and reducing inequality, the classroom is the place to start. Great teaching is about so much more than education; it is a daily fight for social justice."[12]

Understanding that education is an issue of social justice that goes beyond the rights of access and extends to content and delivery is not new. Editors of *Rethinking Our Classrooms* describe a social justice classroom as "grounded in the lives of our students; Critical; Multicultural, anti-racist, pro-justice; Participatory, experiential; Hopeful, joyful, kind, visionary; Activist; Academically Rigorous; and Culturally sensitive."[13] Thus culturally relevant teaching and critical dance pedagogy are components of a social justice educational framework.

> *Culturally relevant teaching was designed for students whose cultural background is not aligned with the dominant culture. Thus this approach works best when serving students of color.*
>
> *Diversifying content is a great approach that expands the educational experience for all children. Similarly, critical dance pedagogy is amenable to all demographic class configurations. The latter two methods do not depend upon utilizing student culture when delivering content.*
>
> *Student-centered classrooms remain a tenet in all of these approaches.*

In opposition to culturally relevant teaching, many dance educators feel that dance is open, welcoming to all, and, by its creative nature, relevant to all humanity. I argue that social constructs of race, class, and gender permeate all aspects of society, including Dance Education, and must be challenged consistently, with all resources possible. In addition, I have met many people outside the dominant culture that felt uncomfortable, devalued, and rejected within Western Dance Education programs. The difference in experiences, between those who have a vested interest in maintaining the system and those alienated by it, draws attention to the Western culturally informed structure of Dance Education in the United States. This is demonstrative of how privilege often goes undetected by those who hold it.

From a historical standpoint, education theory, research, and practice that is culturally relevant has been developing in general education (K–12) for decades.[14] Unfortunately, the arts, and more specifically dance, has taken limited interest in this pedagogical approach. For decades dance educators have exalted theories and ideas of inclusion and acceptance of all individuals. Dance education pioneers like Alma Hawkins, Margaret H'Doubler, Richard Kraus, Sarah Chapman, Brenda Dixon Gottschild, and Judith Hanna have all written about teaching culture through dance in some configuration. Yet these scholars did not address these issues in their teaching methodologies. In 1992, dance educator and scholar Sarah Hilsendager presented this issue at a National Endowment conference, stating: "The majority of university programs emphasize ballet and modern genres, 'which are Eurocentric in both content and teaching approach.'"[15] Although her statement demonstrates an understanding and recognition of a problem that existed more than twenty years ago, the issue of diverse content continues to be a point of discussion in the field of Dance Education because little attention has been paid to developing teaching approaches to meet the needs of students from a variety of cultural backgrounds.

Folk, ethnic, world, and global dance forms have been present in dance departments in higher education since the 1960s.[16] However, such diverse dance forms are typically positioned on the fringes of the curriculum, utilized as supplemental material content and rarely substantial. The inclusion of diverse dance cultures has been invaluable to the dance community. But the purpose of culturally relevant teaching is to serve students from culturally diverse backgrounds through the use of student culture as a teaching tool. Although diversifying content is very important, it does not address culturally informed learning modalities.

From a theoretical perspective, some dance scholars have taken on the task of expanding social justice dialogues to Dance Education. Critical race theory, feminist theory, gender studies, and critical pedagogy have informed the discourse of Dance Education through the writings of scholars such as, but not limited to, Sherry Shapiro, Sue Stinson, Doug Risner and Sherrie Barr.[17] In their 2010 article "Moving Social Justice: Challenges, Fears and Possibilities in Dance Education," Risner and Stinson explore issues of social justice in Dance Education and identify student resistance to multiculturalism in the classroom.[18] They present scholarship that exposes racist practices that support homogeneity in Dance Education. While Risner and Stinson make a compelling argument for calling out Eurocentric bias in dance and teaching students to seek diverse voices for an expansive understanding of dance, they also provide an applicable teaching model for dance educators.

The Body as a Carrier of Culture

Cultural clashes in the dance classroom are common. The body is our instrument, it identifies us and we identify with our bodies. Our body contains us, it is the package that holds us together for better or worse. But it also displays cultural signifiers such as age, race, gender, size, physical abilities and disabilities, and, at times, religion; all of these signifiers are inscribed on the body. Sherry Shapiro explains: "The body in feminist and postmodern theorizing comes to be seen as the personal material on which inscriptions or particular discourses of the culture have become embedded. To read the body in dance education is to see the values of the culture from whence it comes."[19]

This way of seeing the body, as Shapiro notes, is in contrast to Western traditions of dance that focus on "size, shape, technique, flexibility and life (that is of the body)."[20] But in dance we cannot escape the body—our instrument—even though it can prompt personal and external judgment provoked by these inscriptions. Overcoming the marginalization brought on by social constructs and stereotypes often active in a subconscious realm of covert discrimination is challenging. Students who regularly experience discrimination have a heightened sense of awareness, i.e., students of color, LGBTQ students, and students with non-normative bodies. Negotiating discrimination is a component of their daily educational experience and becomes a part of their identity.

The desire to homogenize persists and easily extends to our gender norms and hetero-normative society. I often have heard whispers along the lines of "What a beautiful dancer, he just needs to butch it up." In response, I ask: What if we presented a range of possibilities and interpretations of masculinity and femininity? What if we were not bound to the binaries of traditional gender constructs? What if the embodied cultural markers of students were embraced? Dance educators and dance makers often ask the dancer to come forward as a blank slate, free of movement accents. However, I believe that dance educators must recognize, honor, and uplift each student's cultural embodiments as primary and significant, to be worked with, not overcome.

Culture and How We Make Sense of the World

All people have cultural backgrounds. Many people identify with multiple cultures, fluent in the cultural practices of several groups. Culture is a collection of social systems, customs, rituals, traditions, and ordinances that groups of people practice, share, protect, and develop. As an individual from the United States, I practice a number of customs specific to this country. I live in a country with a representative government. "The Star Spangled Banner" is the national anthem. Public school education is an accepted component of this country's democracy. The United States is considered the home of apple pie, the lindy hop, jazz, and hip-hop. Although Americans hold diverse opinions on each of these various cultural signifiers, there is wide recognition of their existence and how they function in American culture. This cultural knowledge of signifiers provides a shared cultural experience.

Dance Culture

At the heart of all cultures are customs which people practice for the benefit of the community and historical preservation of the culture. Groups of dancers are no different as they also maintain cultures. Within traditional Western-based concert dance culture I understand that one should remove one's street shoes before entering the studio space. However, for members of a social dance community, this may or may not be the case. Traditional Western concert dance culture also has spoken and unspoken ordinances on attire, the appropriate time for talking, treatment of the space (i.e., no eating or gum chewing in the studio), and rules about use of equipment (such as "No leaning on the barres"). Yet cultures are not stagnant; they shift over time. For instance, the shoe rule, in many dance studios, has relaxed to make space for hip-hop dancers with sneakers. In this way cultural practices evolve to meet the needs of group members. That is to say, culture is everywhere and ever-changing.

> "Dance, as an embodied understanding of ourselves, can connect to a moral and ethical pedagogy that not only honours the life of the child but also makes possible a new way to envisage being human"—Adrienne Sansom

The Application of Culturally Relevant Teaching to Dance

Culturally relevant teaching, recognizing and building on the cultural knowledge of students, is applicable to all subject areas, including dance.

Yet for this approach to be effective in dance, dance educators must be aware that all dance is culturally informed. Although the instructor may feel comfortable in a modern warm-up where dancers walk around the room and explore space, it does not mean students experience that same comfort level with this exercise. In instances where students are unable to see themselves in the curriculum content, they often feel as if they do not belong and disengage from their learning. There must be an awareness that what is ordinary for the instructor may be out of the ordinary for students. From that place of understanding, instructors can find ways to build bridges to their course objectives.

Culturally relevant teaching strategies are illuminated in the work of Mary Stone Hanley, in particular the pedagogy model Culturally Relevant Arts Education (CRAE).[21] Hanley writes of this model as a form of social justice, the act of inclusion that counters the marginalization of minorities and embraces cultural diversity. Hanley provides the following examples of CRAE:

> When activities are about the transformation of injustice and are arts based—such as films or plays generated by artists that address a community problem, adolescent spoken word poets who work with younger children teaching them to speak power through poetry, or muralists who record a community's struggles and triumphs or who remedy urban blight with color and form—the artists are engaged in CRAE.[22]

Similar creative practices can be employed in dance. Choreographers can work with students to develop a piece that addresses a community problem; dance students can embody poetry that advocates for social justice; dance educators can select music from communities that are outside the mainstream and work with scenic designers and costume makers to develop culturally relevant art spaces. Such activities give voice to those with little agency to be heard. As educators, we decide what is important for students to learn. If we do not shine a light on the people and communities outside the dominant culture we fail our students and perpetuate a lie. It is a lie to think that only the dominant culture is worth our study and contains artistic techniques of value.

In her text *Culturally Relevant Arts Education For Social Justice*, Hanley explains that culturally relevant approaches "affirm the learner's power to produce knowledge" and "challenges prejudice of any kind."[23] She highlights the need for this type of instruction in the arts, where creative process often begins with the artists' lived experience. Building on the scholarship of Diane Friedlaender and Linda Darling-Hammond (2007); Gloria Ladson-Billings (2009); and Geneva Gay (2010), which focuses on culturally relevant pedagogy, Hanley asserts, "artists are empowered by their cultural knowledge, enabling ownership of learning, which stimulates intrinsic motivation, curiosity, and imagination."[24] She goes on to state:

> Meaning making is the core of education, if it is to be relevant and useful; without relevancy and usefulness, learning is vacuous and alienating, and resistance becomes a factor as learners try to reestablish their agency.[25]

Student dancers who currently do not see their culture reflected in the curriculum would experience a more affirming education if they understood and believed that the goal was to add to the cultural knowledge they already possess as opposed to trying to overcome or change it.

Cultural Relevance Informing Curriculum: Global Perspectives

International research on culturally relevant teaching has yielded substantial affirmative findings. The research indicates that student learning and creativity flourished when teachers were equipped with the skills to shape learning experiences in a culturally relevant manner.[26]

In *African Dance Education in Ghana*, Ofotsu Adinku presents a conceptual framework for Dance Education and a proposal for planning curriculum.[27] Esteem-building is noted as an integral component of Dance Education in Ghana. Teachers are encouraged to build esteem through teaching content that connects to and uplifts tribal culture and tradition as well as national culture. Adinku's text succeeds in tapping into African principles of learning and is designed to meet learning objectives of a Ghanaian university dance department, an educational system that admittedly greatly differs from that in the United States. Insight into ways dance departments can be structured to honor cultural values in regard to dance, cultural heritage in the arts, and dance in particular, is embedded in the learning objectives. Within this system, recreational, ritual, and social purposes of dance are valued on the same level as theatrical performances with all forms holding significance for local communities.

In the late 1980s, the New Zealand physical education curriculum was reshaped to be culturally responsive to the Maori culture. The new approach was to engage physical activity through *Te ao kori*, a concept that frames how the Maori culture understands the world of human movement.[28] Traditional, sports-centered curriculum for physical education was dismantled and physical education goals were reconfigured to a *te ao kori* framework. The significance of culturally relevant teaching tools in physical practices is evident in these and similar dance research findings.[29]

More recently in New Zealand, Elizabeth Melchior examined the shift in dance curriculum from a teacher-centered, disembodied approach wherein the teacher gives students specific movement vocabularies and technique to an embodied, student-centered approach that focuses on process.[30] Her research is supported by the scholarship of Kerry Chappell who writes, "learning is an active and social meaning-making process, rather than a transmission of activity."[31] Melchior's findings also support Paulo Freire's anti-banking educational model. Moreover, data affirm that culturally relevant teaching positions teachers to provide students with a student centered, embodied movement experience.

Understanding the cultural kinesthetic orientation of students is a valuable resource for educators. Kyra Gaunt's *The Games Black Girls Play: Learning the Ropes from Double-Dutch to Hip-Hop* provides insight into the kinesthetic cultural expressions of African American females.[32] The cultural and gender-specific ways of knowing movement described by Gaunt can deepen the way educators understand African American female students, their body language, and the cultural foundations which inform the composition work of these students. The focus of Gaunt's work is music and body and connects directly to dance within the black community. Gaunt's multifaceted discussion of expressions of the black female body offer resources to dance educators in regard to sensitivity to cultural heritage and practices connected to kinesthetic ways of being and choices of movement. These factors are integral to the way that black students experience Dance Education and explore their fundamental knowledge of movement. In terms of curriculum design, these are issues of which dance educators and practitioners should be aware of, as this information opens up a context in which one can consider how all people encompass movement styles related to their culture(s). In learning more about students' kinesthetic cultural expressions, educators can find pathways to engagement and culturally relevant teaching.

The research on CRT in dance, although limited in quantity, supports my argument for these teaching methods. This pedagogical approach increases student confidence, engagement, and achievement.

Culturally Relevant Required Reading

One way to make curriculum culturally relevant and diverse is through required readings. In 2011, I conducted research on the effectiveness of culturally relevant and diverse required readings with college dance students.[33] The data emphasizes the value of students seeing themselves in the content, being able to relate to course resources, and in turn having greater success in their educational experience. Students feel included not simply by the good intentions of the teacher, but through concrete examples and resources utilized to support learning objectives. The importance of students—in particular students who have been systematically and historically marginalized and excluded—feeling included in multiple facets of the course cannot be overstated.[34] Further, diversification of resources is of great significance to homogeneous learning communities as well. If we as a society do not want any single group of people to think themselves superior, then we must provide them with diverse resources and evidence of a wide spectrum of humanity in the world.

Culturally Relevant Teaching and the Teacher

Dance educators have an opportunity to forge a classroom culture that not only recognizes students' culture, but also incorporates such culture into the curricula. That means teachers develop customs, language, artifacts, and rituals that students can collectively experience as a springboard to create a culture within the dance class. It is likely that most teachers already do this in some form.

Although education is culturally informed, curriculum may not be culturally relevant if educators do not make a conscientious effort to make it so. One way of doing so is for dance educators to take an active role in adapting curriculum. In a 2011 study on diversifying dance curriculum, I found that many teachers and administrators had the desire to diversify curriculum, but lacked the models and resources to put action behind their good intentions.[35] Culturally responsive education scholar Geneva Gay asserts, "Intention without action is insufficient."[36] It is not enough to acknowledge that systems are unjust and discriminatory. Even though you may not have the power to make change on a national level, you can change the educational experience of students in your class. To be sure, students often do not have enough information about the field of dance studies to construct their own curriculum. Yet it is important to empower students whenever possible and work with them as partners in their own education.

Within the context of culturally relevant pedagogy, it is the teacher's responsibility to research students' culture and seek out resources to share with the class. The teacher may ask students from this cultural background if they feel what has been presented is accurate in their experience, or if they think something has been misrepresented or left out. Some students like to share information about their culture and will feel valued at your request that they share and that you acknowledge that they are the expert of their culture. Others may feel that it is not their job to teach the class. Be prepared to move forward with the information you have gathered whether or not the students display an interest. Ultimately, students already know about their own cultures; this information is for you to use as a bridge to student success, while simultaneously sending a message to the class that the students' culture is valued and worthy of your class time.

When the class is composed of a white community, learning about other cultures is still important. In fact, it may even be more important. In these instances, diversifying course content or employing critical dance pedagogy would be good teaching approaches. Without engaging issues from multiple cultural perspectives, students run the risk of believing that their culture is the only culture that matters. Some or all of these students will move forward in life and come into contact with people from diverse backgrounds. They need to understand how to engage and interact with people who do not look like they do. While one could argue that this is not the job of the dance teacher, I would argue otherwise. Teaching students how to navigate their space in a diverse world is the task of all educators. Additionally, dance teachers have the special privilege of guiding students through an embodied learning experience that is non-verbal, body related, and can be transformative in its impact. This is a unique and personal component inherent in dance training.

Supporting Students' Culture in the Classroom

In the text "I Won't Learn from You," Herb Kohl explains not-learning—wherein a learner intuits that his or her personhood is at stake and sabotages an opportunity to learn. "Not-learning tends to take place when someone has to deal with unavoidable challenges to her or his personal and family loyalties, integrity, and identity. In such situations there are forced choices and no apparent middle ground. To agree to learn from a stranger who does not respect your integrity causes a major loss of self. The only alternative is to not-learn and reject the stranger's world."[37]

Kohl's theory speaks directly to issues Ruth Gustafson describes in her research about African American students failing in music education and my personal experiences teaching Western-based dance forms in an African American community in Atlanta. In contrast, teaching methods that are designed with students' culture in mind, and are student centered, can empower educators with information that will maximize learning and allow students to flourish within a context that honors their culture.

> *The issue of non-learning has also been a growing challenge for students from competition dance backgrounds, as many try to negotiate dance programs in higher education settings. Recognizing their dance community as a cultural group to which they are closely tied could be very effective in supporting a positive educational environment for these students.*

Cultures bring people together, and the people who practice a given culture are often identified as a "community," such as the Jewish community or the gay community. A given culture may also contain sub-cultures. For example, in addition to my affinity to cultural practices of those from the United States, I am also connected to the African American community, the Generation X community, the feminist community, and the dance community. Within the dance community there are countless sub-cultures as well. I am a member of the traditional Western dance community as well as the salsa dance community and the black dance community. Membership to one community does not negate membership to another.

It is possible to develop a dance class culture and community that supports students' membership to multiple communities (dance or otherwise). Through the course of an individual's life there are some communities to which membership will be a constant. These communities will provide lifelong engagement, a means to connect and relate to other members and the world. Being a member of an ethnic or religious community is often a lifelong membership. Membership to the LGBTQ community is another example of membership to a group that is related to an individual's identity as opposed to a time in their life. Some communities only will be a part of people's lives for a limited period of time, like their high school community. That is not to say that high school culture is not important. On the contrary, it can be quite significant. No matter the length of time one is involved in a particular community, its culture should not alienate, marginalize, conceal, deny, or denigrate another culture from which students come, to which they will return, and of which they may always be members.

Cultural Diversity

Dance educators have the power to nurture and support students' connection to their kinesthetic cultural heritage in addition to teaching

Western dance or other dance forms; one does not have to displace the other. Diversity speaks to difference. Each person can bring difference to a class in some way; some differences are more apparent or significant than others. For most, diversity in skin color will have a greater impact on how one experiences life than diversity of hair color. Here, for the purposes of this text, the term diversity is specifically used to describe cultural diversity. A culturally diverse group is a group of people within which at least three or more different cultural backgrounds are represented (culture grouping extends to ethnicity, sexual orientation, religion, competition dance, and so forth). Grouping is fluid, and students may belong to more than one group. Again, as an example, I am a woman, American, African American, White, Irish, German, Yankee, bi-racial, Christian, middle-class, and educated. Some group membership is monumental to the identity of a person, while other affiliations may mean little.

For some, ethnic identity is significant; this is more often the case with people of color whose daily experiences are often impacted by racial prejudice. For others, grouping by gender (male, female, transgender, or gender queer) or sexual orientation may be of greater importance. Still there are some who think of themselves as individuals, and whether they have cultural affinities or not, they focus on how they experience the world as individuals.[38] It is most important to consider how each student would like to be seen and acknowledged.

Often within a group of learners from the dominant culture, individual students may be uncomfortable with questions about their culture. Some feel as if they do not have a culture. It is common for people, especially those of the dominant culture, to feel as though their daily practices are just normal practices. The misconception that only people perceived as "others" possess "culture" must be challenged. Raymond Williams addressed this issue in his seminal 1958 essay, "Culture Is Ordinary." Although it's common to accept one's daily activities, tools of use, food, and technology as simply ordinary life and not as a "culture," this sensibility is a dangerous ideology. First, it is false because everyone holds a culture. Second, it falsely agrees with those who adopt the idea that their culture is the default and primary culture of significance with all other cultures being different and "other." Historically, separating a dominant group from a group of others has led to many incidents of discrimination against those categorized as other. A class with students from diverse backgrounds offers exciting opportunities for all present to learn from one another. I encourage educators to acknowledge and highlight the various cultures of all students.

It is important, in instances where the teacher is incorporating one, some, or all of the students' cultures into the course, not to expect or ask the student(s) to educate the class. I encourage teachers to research their students' culture. Pose general questions to the class about their culture, or ask them to fill out surveys or respond to written questions; however, do not single out students. It should be an opportunity for students to share, not a responsibility. If you do research on your own, you may ask students if, to their personal knowledge, your findings are accurate. This places the students in the expert position on the subject of their culture. In addition, it signals to them that learning about their culture is important enough for you to take the time to do the research.

Cultural Capital

Pierre Bourdieu's contributions on cultural capital are noteworthy for any dialogue centered on culture and education. In his theory of how inequity is reproduced, Bourdieu developed the term cultural capital to reference implicitly and explicitly learned skills that position people in a stratified society.[39] Implicit lessons take place in the home and directly impact how social class is replicated through each generation, whereas explicit lessons take place at school or in a structured educational setting. Implicit lessons are more powerful as these are often multifaceted and ever-present.[40] Over the past three decades Bourdieu's theory has been expanded and used extensively in education research with its focus on how stratified societies stay so because of inherited cultural capital that ensures one's boundless or limited opportunities that regularly appear in embodied, objectified, or institutionalized states. Today, cultural capital can be seen as the resources people are given to help them move forward in life. Cultural capital is essentially a survival kit and varies with each educational environment.

Cultural capital is something everyone possesses. Rachelle Winkle-Wagner describes cultural capital as a hand of cards. Different cards constitute a strong hand in different games, depending upon the rules of the particular game. Similarly, the cultural capital that may negate someone's success in one game or environment can ensure his or her success in another game or environment.[41] Thus, cultural capital is contextual; what is valued as capital in one community may be worthless in another. When traveling to a new place and entering a new culture, adapting to that culture is paramount to one's quality of life in the new community. In order to succeed in the environment one must learn the socially preferred tastes in music, art, and food.[42] In the United States, most people who have cultural affinities outside the dominant culture will develop cultural capital in the dominant culture while they maintain their inherent cultural affinities. U.S. cultural capital is necessary to excel in the educational system or the workplace. Cultural currency, in any given community, allows one to "talk the talk and walk the walk." Without this ability an individual may find him or herself excluded by cultural power brokers from the inner circles of the group.[43]

Cultural capital extends to dance, and can be readily evident in dance aesthetics. When students are evaluated through a Western-informed filter of what valued dance is, a Eurocentric hegemonic ideology is being applied. As a result, some students conclude that the embodied knowledge, the cultural capital that they possess, is not sufficient to move forward. What is challenging to grasp for many, students, teachers, and educational administrators alike, is that to relinquish or neglect one's own cultural capital has ramifications that impact their relationship with all those with whom they share culture. It is possible to negotiate cultural capital in multiple currencies. However, it is a challenging balance to achieve and maintain,[44] especially as advancement in socio-economic status is tied to the cultural capital of the dominant culture. It can be particularly difficult for young people who may not understand the complex and mutually exclusive cultural codes.

It is now painfully clear to me that my interest in attaining cultural currency in the dominant culture of the dance world alienated me from the black community. More specifically, my studies in Western dance techniques alienated me from African American vernacular dance, an embodiment of my cultural history and a means of relating to other members of the black community (particularly black people outside the world of dance). As a bi-racial woman raised by a white woman and treated by society as a black woman, my inability to relate to the black community was a loss for me. At times, I was unable to learn, thrive, understand, value, or share the treasures of my cultural heritage. On many occasions, I was excluded and unable to participate. Simply stated, I could not get out on the dance floor and "get down" with my people. Kinesthetic cultural experiences were uncomfortable to me and I was embarrassed regularly due to my inability to embody African American vernacular dance. It seemed that white, black, Hispanic, and Asian people all expected me to embody a kinesthetic prowess for African American vernacular dances. However, my ballet and modern dance teachers implicitly communicated to me that my cultural dance affinities and aesthetics would hold me back if not shed. These teachers communicated this by uplifting students who embodied Eurocentric dance aesthetics and awarding such students all primary performance roles and scholarships. As a result of these loud but unarticulated messages, I lost cultural currency within my community in exchange for cultural currency in Western dance forms.

Dance Stereotypes

Just as societal stereotypes are present, dance stereotypes are active within dance schools, programs, and departments. There are assumptions such as all dance students need ballet; white students are more suited to ballet than black students; students of color are more suited to urban forms. Such notions often impact the dance forms students are encouraged to study and dance curricula designs at large. "All men in dance are gay" is a stereotype that serves to maintain a narrow and limited understanding of masculinity and male identity throughout our society. The stereotype that all black people can dance is alive and well, and not only is it untrue, it discounts the years of training that dancers invest in their particular dance form in order to be proficient. All of these ideas are stereotypes that impact, either subconsciously or consciously, the way we educate students and even the ways in which students learn. These stereotypes support a learning process constructed through a hetero-normative, dominant cultural lens that marginalizes and harms students.

Ballet is ensconced in American culture as high art. Ballet is not bad, but it has been used as a tool for white supremacy. I cannot count the number of students I have met who have been told, "You are a great dancer, all you need is technique," which is code for "ballet." What is actually being said is that they need to lay their artistic practice of dance aside and embrace a Eurocentric dance practice in order to obtain legitimacy in the world of dance. This ideology begs to be unpacked and hip-hop provides a way to do just that. The suggestion that a hip-hop dancer needs "technique" ignores the technical training and kinesthetic intelligence exhibited in this genre. Hip-hop technique is steeped in African dance aesthetics and African American vernacular movement. To suggest that such a dancer is in need of technique is to suggest that hip-hop is void of technical value. In addition, the inference that every dancer needs ballet training is as misguided as the suggestion that every dancer needs African dance training. Western-based dance forms can enhance one's dance skills, but the idea that all dance hinges on any single dance form is inherently erroneous. If such a premise were true it would mean that Indian Classical, Polynesian, Irish Step, Middle Eastern, and Israeli dance (and the list continues) held limited learning value as a dance form.

> *If you see stereotyping among your students, consider it as a valuable teachable moment. Address stereotypes directly. Asks students to explain the stereotypes, how they operate, and if they can think of any examples. Challenge students to investigate how stereotypes can be harmful. Asks students to consider what happens when stereotypes go unexamined.*
>
> *When we ignore the implicit micro-aggressions of prejudice we support systems of oppression.*

Culturally Informed Assumptions

As humans we are taught to read other people. This can be a benign act of identifying a smile, or the pain in the eyes of a child who has fallen down. Our ability to read others helps us to understand others each day, and to be understood. Yet, it is all too common that someone misreads another person. While teaching at a private, predominately white school in New England, I found that a number of African American students would downplay their dance prowess to counteract being "read" and assumed to be great vernacular dancers. They shared concerns that in addition to the challenges of being accepted in a predominately white and intellectual community, now they would have to overcome being stereotyped as a dancing body—and possibly dismissed as less intelligent. To avoid such readings, some students would understate movements; choose not to dance full-out; or dance in a mechanical manner to avoid embodiment of an Africanist aesthetic "groove." Instead, these students would exhibit a held upright orientation and movement that contrasted to earthbound bent knees. For the reader, these "readings" are ways of understanding the world; as one looks closely, it becomes apparent that readings are inherently culturally informed. To be sure, those outside a particular culture often lack the knowledge to read a person or situation. Misunderstandings can impact an educational process.

Examples of such misunderstandings can be found in education literature. In explaining the need for culturally relevant pedagogy, education scholar Lisa Delpit describes a scenario in certain Native Alaskan communities where children are taught not to speak to adults. Some teachers, in an effort not to put pressure on these students, respond by not engaging them. However, within the context of mainstream education, Delpit documents how these interactions—or cultural clashes—have been misinterpreted as non-verbal behavior, addressed by placing these students in special education classes.[45] Ruth Gustafson also provides insights into such misinterpretations.[46] She discusses how often African American children perform poorly in music classes because of a disconnect between Western methods of music education that require the student to listen to music without kinesthetic response.[47] Within the African American culture, music and dance are often experienced simultaneously, and to disengage movement from music is problematic to learning for many of these students. These examples support my findings that culturally relevant teaching can make a significant difference in student success.

Conclusion

In considering the research, theory, and lived experiences of people outside the dominant culture, dance educators can reshape foundational dance pedagogy and curriculum to be more student centered and culturally relevant for the variety of educational environments where students learn to express themselves through kinesthetic movement.

Culture is a lifeline for all people. Meaning is made through cultural informants and reference points. These cultural informants act as building blocks that people use to develop an understanding of the world. Thus culture has a significant impact on the lens through which the world is seen and understood. Research findings indicate that students learn more when pedagogy practices are culturally relevant. Culturally relevant teaching values culture and is rooted in the belief that all children deserve to be educated through a lens to which they can relate. It is about being included, by way of cultural referents, rather than excluded. It is about valuing your students' cultural heritage and, therefore, valuing your students. The more educators know about their students the more effective they can be. Culturally relevant teaching expands the possibilities for dance educators to reach all students, and, in so doing, develop the creativity of students as well as their physical well-being.

Two

Toolkit for Teaching
Culturally Relevant Pedagogy

Students learn best in an environment where they feel safe, welcomed, and appreciated. Culturally relevant teaching[1] helps to cultivate a welcoming space that will heighten students' success and enjoyment in the learning experience. By incorporating students' culture into the learning process, a teacher demonstrates respect, appreciation, and value for that culture.

Throughout this text a variety of strategies and suggestions are offered to dance educators. However, there is no one-size-fits-all when teaching through a culturally relevant lens. First and foremost, the pedagogy must relate to the students in the room. You will have to employ trial and error tactics as many things might not work well the first time around. Some strategies offered in this text may be perfect for your student population and others may not be a good fit. Some may work with one class and not the next and vice versa. These are challenges embedded in the profession of teaching. I encourage you to let your classroom be a laboratory and regularly try new approaches. Even when new strategies are not successful, students will appreciate your interest in trying to improve teaching practices. Experience is the best resource; the more you try new strategies the more you will have a sense of what kinds of exercises and resources succeed with your students.

What Is Culture?

Culture is a system of customs agreed upon by a group of people. Culture provides groups of people with a unifying approach to experience life.

Culture encompasses practices and structures that support basic functions of daily life, such as clothing and housing, often particular to the geographic location in which the culture is situated. Culture also includes customs that provide order and safety for a community of people, such as time parameters for age-appropriate events, regulations to implement the use of car seats and seatbelts, styles of eating, cooking, language, and fashion. Moreover, "culture provides us with a blueprint" for how to live.[2] The work of education scholar Ruby Payne explores one such blueprint through the "hidden rules" of the classrooms, in which codes of conduct serve as cultural systems that a group maintains to sustain their culture.[3]

Many people think of culture in relation to the expression of arts: aesthetically informed costumes, theater, music, dance, and visual arts. Because dance is one of these cultural expressions it is likely that many students will have had some encounter with dance in their home community. If they have not, this may be a reflection of limitations or restrictions on dance within their culture. All people possess culture. Yet some students have not figured this out. In instances when students are unable to identify and share their cultural characteristics and customs with the class, you may have to conduct some research. If this is the case, consider it a learning opportunity for you and your students and an opportunity to illuminate your students' cultural heritage. To be sure, it should not be a covert operation. Let your students know you are interested in them and want to know more about their culture.

Discuss cultural movement affinities in your class. You can share examples of traditional African-derived dance characteristics, European-derived dance characteristics, Hispanic-derived dance characteristics, Native American-derived dance characteristics, and Asian-derived dance characteristics. Ask students to describe or demonstrate the dancing they have seen in their homes, families, schools, places of worship and communities. All responses to these inquires, even when students say, "We don't dance," can provide information.

It is important to note that college and university students can also gain something from exploring personal cultural backgrounds. In 2014, at a small, private liberal arts college in the Northeast, my students and I were given the opportunity to do a short residency of six classes with Urban Bush Women. Each class focused on the students' culture. The experience reminded me of exercises I had throughout my time in K–12 in-service professional development. These university students had an overwhelmingly positive response to the work. Initially, however, there was resistance from students who felt that they did not have a culture. But as the residency progressed, each student was able to identify things from their culture, how they inherited customs from their mother's or father's family, or how they had adopted American cultural practices that differed from their family. When sharing gifts from their culture, one student observed that his family culture had instilled in him a belief in non-violence. I was enlightened in that moment because I realized my family had given me that belief as well. Explorations in individual cultures are valuable for all students of all ages.

As discussed in chapter one, there is a dance culture: customs and practices that individuals committed to dance engage in. Within this culture, there are many sub-cultures: salsa, contemporary dance, classical Indian dance, Polynesian, bhangra, ballet, tango, and so on. Each sub-culture maintains practices that are specific to the heritage of that dance form or local dance community. Its members practice specific customs regularly and identify in significant and personal ways with the dance form. It is all too common for educators outside a dance sub-culture to underestimate the cultural ties students have to particular dance communities. Most dance educators recognize the problems with preferring a particular aesthetic. Yet an issue that must be addressed is that some fail to acknowledge some dance cultures as just that—a culture. I have witnessed this most often with hip-hop and Western competition dance, but I am sure it extends to other dance forms as well. A dance educator decides that a dance form has little artistic merit and is dismissive of the form, and as a result, implicit and explicit comments are given that make students feel devalued and alienated. The dance aesthetic of the dance educator must not exist above all others. Instead, an open space where all aesthetics are welcomed and valued equally must exist.

Reasons to Implement Culturally Relevant Teaching

Culturally relevant teaching is applicable to all educational settings. Consider the following reasons to implement culturally relevant teaching practices.

1. Hegemonic aesthetic dominance/supremacy blossoms in the absence of culturally diverse curriculum.
2. Preparing students with culturally diverse resources empowers them to engage with a diverse population in the future.

3. Students have a visceral need to see themselves reflected in the curriculum.
4. Students who have felt disempowered in educational structures need to see their culture valued in an educational institutional setting.
5. Students feel empowered when they have a voice in their education.
6. The choice not to provide an educational experience that relates to the students' culture is to reinforce the dominant culture and suppress the culture of students.

The culturally relevant strategies you elect to implement will depend upon your specific teaching situation. The particulars of your teaching assignment will determine the modifications you will make to suit your class culture and curriculum. I have crafted courses that were culturally relevant in every way I could think of when teaching high school students in under-served urban communities. In contrast, my courses in higher education are often comprised of more white students who are accustomed to the dominant culture. In these instances, I employ critical dance pedagogy as well as diversify course material. Students in higher education have made an investment in an educational system and structure that usually includes an interest in acquiring traditional Western dance practices and knowledge. Yet they also benefit from diverse course material that offers a pluralist lens through which to view the world they are preparing to enter.

Multiculturalism vs. Cultural Relevance

Curriculum cannot be culturally diverse if it does not reflect diversity. There is a difference between using teaching methods that relate to students' culture and teaching students dances from a range of cultural backgrounds. Both are valuable. Multiculturalism, or diversifying curricula, means to expand content with a variety of material that comes from different experiential lenses, which may not directly relate to students' cultural background. For example, one might include Polynesian and Mexican folkloric dance with a student population that is Caucasian and African American. Curriculum diversification is an excellent and valuable practice for all students and teachers, but it is not culturally relevant pedagogy.

Culturally Relevant Teaching

Diverse Course Content

In looking at the above diagram you can see that culturally relevant teaching and diverse course content can overlap. However, the two domains are largely different in their objective and outcome. Culturally relevant teaching focuses on the culture of students in order to meet the learning needs of all the students in the classroom and diverse course content helps students to have a greater understanding of the diversity in the world in which they live.

Within the context of a higher education dance program curriculum, it is common to see one or two courses that provide diverse perspectives—most commonly, a World Dance course. Diversity of this nature speaks to culturally diverse content. Unfortunately, this approach to diversity confines diverse perspectives into relegated topics and content, suppressing the need for diversity in all courses. In a 2011 study on cultural diversity in college dance departments, I found disparities between the diversity embraced by language in department literature and mission statements and the embodied diversity expressed on the concert stage. Ideally, programs with a true commitment to cultural diversity would find ways to express this commitment through the artistic medium of dance. Thus, a dance concert within a culturally diverse dance department should present artwork with a range of cultural influences as opposed to a monolithic dance aesthetic. Unfortunately, I found that dance productions on the main stage of many of these institutions reflected a Western-based dance aesthetic. When one aesthetic is continually embodied and presented, students get the message that it is the valued aesthetic within that space. Further, I argue that the isolation of diverse content into specific courses, as opposed to integrated throughout the educational experience, results in a disembodied and cursory understanding of diversity in dance.

Goals

For many dance educators, each class, course, semester, and school year is focused on a series of goals, most often both short- and long-term. Dance education goals look different depending on the educational setting. The educational goals in a conservatory training program are different from those in a liberal arts setting. Similarly, goals for a K–12 population will differ from goals in higher education programs. Within these different settings there are also varying needs for diversifying curriculum. In some dance settings it is apparent from the moment you enter the studio classroom that you will have to modify the curriculum either because of the disconnect and barriers between the students and content or ability level of students. In other settings, the majority of the students may be totally invested in the course material as is and the dance educator may feel little motivation to take time from class preparation and teaching to diversify curriculum. In a space where all seem invested in the material it is important to be aware that students who are not members of the dominant culture, or for whatever reason might feel disconnected from the content, may not feel empowered to express feelings of marginalization or alienation from the content. If you teach in a diverse community and find little diversity within your class, it is worth considering why. Is it possible your teaching methods and course content alienate students who are from outside the dominant culture? (Questions to consider when developing culturally relevant teaching strategies can be found at the end of the chapter).

> *Culture comes in many forms. There may be aspects of your students' culture that are generational and some may refer to technology or pop culture. Reaching students through pop culture can often bring students with culturally diverse backgrounds together, i.e., Facebook; Twitter; or current pop stars, authors, and actors.*

Where to Begin?

When the new school year or semester begins, teachers have the opportunity to set expectations for students. The first two weeks are critical in establishing the type of learning environment you will provide. This is also an opportunity to place all of your students on the same page. Even a seemingly homogenous group of learners is diverse in a number of the ways.

As the leader, you have the power to create community among this group of students. Giving students a distinct class culture is one way to put them all on level footing. Some of your students may not possess as many years of dance training as others. Providing common experiences for students each day gives them something in common—a shared cultural experience that can build confidence and community and does not draw attention to differences.

An exercise where some students flounder and others flourish is not a shared experience. Consider offering strengthening or flexibility exercises that stretch each student to their maximum potential and can be performed as a community, taking the spotlight off any one particular student, or a celebratory phrase where all students flourish together, this could be a line dance or contra dance—there are many possibilities. These make for common and positive experiences.

Historically, many school communities utilize the power of the arts as a unifying activity. Few things compare to the sense of unity that develops when people are invested in a production. Engage students in a class goal and try to replicate this feeling of community on a class level. Young students will often take to being a part of "Mrs. Johnson's class" and some teachers may be able to build cohesion through this sense of belonging to the class community. In particular, students of color and those whose family structure relies on extended family and kinship often thrive when they feel the teacher cares about them.

Getting to Know Your Students

The first step to designing a class culture attuned to one's students is getting to know them. However, getting to know one's students is a process. The student and teacher relationship, like any relationship, has peaks and valleys; it can change significantly over the term, or it may change very little. Both parties have an impact on the development of the relationship. That stated, the teacher is in a position of authority and responsibility. The relationship cannot flourish without the teacher's ability to create a solid foundation for students.

1. Focus on the process of getting to know your students, and be an active participant in the journey.
2. Make a plan to get to know your students over the length of the term (semester, school year, etc.).

The more information you gather in the beginning of the year, the more you have to build on for the duration of the course. Although it is challenging, I like to spend one to two weeks focused on developing class culture, particularly in K–12. Some students resist as they want to "dance" and move their body immediately. However, all students can feel the benefits of a cohesive learning community. In fact, arts education researchers suggest that a teacher's knowledge of how students learn and who they are can be more valuable in the classroom than the subject knowledge of the instructor.[4] When students see you taking an interest in them and their lives, they will invest more in you and the course material.

Surveys

Surveys have value as a tool to understand your students. Surveys are most useful with elementary students who cannot articulate descriptive responses to inquiries about their culture. A short survey or questionnaire can be a good starting point to learn more about them. They can tell you quickly to what region, neighborhood, culture, or religion students feel connected. For example, questions about places of worship, stores their families patronize, dress, language, food, holidays, family activities/celebrations, and family/birth order may be informative. Ask students how birthdays are celebrated in their family. Some may say that birthdays are not celebrated in their family. This information is valuable and may help you to navigate space around the birthdays of other students. Some students may describe a birthday with cake, singing, and candles. You can identify these practices as customs and explain how they are components of their culture. The responses to the survey can serve as an effective example of culture and customs for students having a hard time identifying cultural practices. (A survey sample is located at the end of the chapter.)

Survey questions can yield a gold mine of information. Who is influential in each student's life? How does the student spend his or her free time, and what does he or she desire? Responses to these questions can help you find potential motivators for student learning. The question about influence can be especially useful if you have a student struggling in your class as this person could be a motivational resource. Knowing what students like to do can provide information that could be used as a bridge for student learning. For example, if students share that they play basketball every day after school, they may relate to dance movement that is grounded in nature or similar to guarding when on defense. Or they may express a desire for a feeling of buoyancy and enjoy jumps. This information can also assist you when you are searching for an image that will assist students in their dancing. You may find that they respond well to images of an elongated arm and hand extended toward a basketball hoop.

Despite the value of surveys, there is a risk of oversimplification. Surveys cannot provide an understanding of individuals or explain how they see themselves in the world. For example, on a questionnaire I always identify myself as an African American. One reason for this is that when I was a child, teachers told me that I was black and should check that box. In fact, I am bi-racial, raised by a single parent, in a white household. I identify with the dominant culture in a number of ways. However, if a teacher were trying to understand my ethnic identity through a survey, little would be revealed. If you decide to use surveys, they are best used to begin a dialogue that is followed up with additional opportunities for students to share more descriptive personal information.

Many cultural retentions and customs that students may experience in their homes are not necessarily explained to them as cultural customs or practices. As a result, they may or may not identify the practice to you as a cultural custom. At times they may not even have the cognizance to relate the culturally relevant experience you provide them to familial experience. Many people are unaware of their cultural affinities. Yet they may *feel* more comfortable with the activity and you may see them perform better in the space. For example, many do not realize that they have a specific, culturally informed response to music, often to be still and listen, or to rock, sway, or physically keep the beat. As you learn more about your class community, share your discoveries with students so they too can be cognizant of their movement affinities.

Caring

Caring is an essential component of culturally relevant teaching. Teachers must demonstrate their sincere care for students. All students want to know that the authority figure leading them through their educational experience cares about them. However, for ethnically diverse students, who often have a heightened sensitivity to discrimination and at times distrust mainstream institutions, there is an even stronger intrinsic need to feel that their teachers care about their well-being. Geneva Gay explains how caring is a significant component of the work of a teacher.

> It is manifested in the form of teacher attitudes, expectations, and behaviors about students' human value, intellectual capacity, and performance responsibilities. Teachers demonstrate caring for children as *students* and as *people*. This is expressed in concern for their psycho-emotional well-being and academic success; personal morality and social actions; obligations and celebrations; communality, and individuality; and unique cultural connections and universal human bonds.... Students, in kind, feel obligated to

be worthy of being so honored. They rise to the occasion by producing high levels of performance of many different kinds—academic, social, moral, and cultural.[5]

Numerous education scholars, including Gloria Ladson-Billings and Carmen Mercado, have brought forth research on the power of caring as a component of effective teaching for students of color.[6]

I asked many students who their favorite teacher is and why. I cannot count the number of students who noted in their response that their teacher cares about them. I was aware of this ideology when I was teaching middle school English in Oakland, California, and years later while teaching high school social studies in Atlanta, Georgia. I remember how, in both settings, which predominately served students of color, students would come in each morning and announce to me, "I did your homework, Ms. McCarthy-Brown." To that I would say, "You mean, you did *your* homework." These exchanges made it clear to me that were it not for my relationship with students, they would not have made the investment in the assignment and their education. Although I have at times wished that student success were not intertwined with feelings, I think it would be negligent to discount the value of a caring, reciprocal student-teacher rapport.

Addressing Gender

Today, the Lesbian, Gay, Bisexual, Transgender, and Queer (LGBTQ) (Q can also stand for questioning, especially with youth) community has become a great presence in many communities and schools. One way to open your class environment to transgender and gender non-confirming students is to ask students what their preferred pronoun is: he or she (gender specific pronouns) or ze, zir, or they (gender non-specific pronouns). This can give you information about how students identify in terms of gender. I had a transgender student struggling to understand how they wanted to be recognized who chose to use the pronoun *they* in their first year as my student. At that time, they wanted to be acknowledged as having both a male and female identity, hence *they*. In my second year of instructing this student, the student transitioned from female to male and wanted to go by the pronoun *he*. It was important that his community, including me and the students in my class, acknowledged and supported his choice of gender, regardless of the gender he was assigned at birth.

Even in a class where everyone uses the traditional preferred pronouns *he* and *she*, it is a good practice to give students the opportunity to select the pronoun you will use for them. While such a practice may seem odd to a room of seemingly hetero-normative students, it is rare that all students actually are heterosexual. The act of opening the space for other expressions of gender tells students that there are more possibilities in the world than the binary social constructs with which we have been traditionally confined. In addition, it provides students with tools and an experiential point of reference that might be useful to them in their future. If you asked students to share their preferred pronoun, a student who did not choose to announce a non-normative identity could decide not to, but he or she would know that you are open to seeing as he or she prefers. I have also known educators who express their openness to preferred pronouns in their syllabus and refer to students in the plural or as "ze" (instead of he and she) throughout the document and in the classroom in general.

Critical Dance Pedagogy and Gender

A critical dance pedagogy approach to Dance Education requires questioning and reflection on teaching practices. Here are points for consideration as they relate to gender constructs within your dance community. Does your dance program service a small or large number of males? Why or why not? Do you actively recruit or lower admission standards for males? Do male students perform more? Are male students required to take less technique in order to perform more? Do the male students in your program perform hereto-normative gender roles on stage supporting a monolithic construct around masculinity? Moreover, do you seek out male students to perform in hetero-normative roles in order to uphold the historically preferred paradigm of what acceptable gender roles are, even if the roles are marginalizing to all students? Encourage critical engagement of how dance relates within various social contexts. Consider how you might modify some of these questions and pose them to your students.

For some students in the LGBTQ community, dance class is one of the few safe spaces that they have in their life. This may be the only community where members can truly be themselves. In these instances, your support of their relationship to the community as a whole may be of great significance to your students.

Often there are resources on your campus or in your community that can help you make connections to the LGBTQ community if you want to be an advocate of your students. If there are no resources, maybe it's an opportunity for you to create some.

Obstacles to Culturally Relevant Teaching

There are ways in which culturally relevant teaching can be challenging. No teaching method is perfect. The following are some areas of concern and how they can be navigated.

Decentering Power: "I am not an expert on my students' culture"

Some educators are leery of referencing a culture to which they themselves are not connected. In essence, teachers may feel they do not have the knowledge, agency, standing, or chutzpah to draw upon a culture of which they have little or limited knowledge. Most likely, the teacher's knowledge is less than their students'. Yet this challenge can be overcome. *Allow yourself to be the student.* Acknowledge that you are not an expert. Empower your students with the opportunity to teach you about their culture. This should be an offer, not a requirement. Ultimately, your cultural fluency is not your students' responsibility. While some students do not appreciate being put on the spot and asked to share personal aspects of their culture, some students love to share and feel valued when the authority figure of the class takes an interest in their cultural heritage. This process shifts the balance of power and creates a more student-centered class.

Be transparent. Tell students you are interested in their culture because you would like to make their learning experience as relevant to their lives as you can. Let them know that you will try to incorporate what you learn about their culture into the classroom when possible. Also let them know that you are learning and if you have misunderstood an aspect of the culture, or if their experiences are different than what is presented, request students to kindly let you know. If you are honest about your process and end goal of student learning, students will appreciate your efforts and you.

Multiculturalism: "My students identify with more than one culture"

Many students identify with multiple cultures. How does a teacher know which culture to focus on? If a student identifies with multiple cultures, then there are multiple avenues to reach this student. Select the culture that most students in the class can identify with but also incorporate cultures that have less representation in the room too so that no one feels left out. You may have to learn about several cultures and bring multiple cultural referents into the classroom. You and your class will be the richer. Keep in mind that students from the smallest culturally represented groups are probably left out the most. If you have a student who has three cultural identities, and you connect to one, that one connection *is* viable. The goal is to relate to the student in order to boost the transmission of knowledge.

Lecture Styles

One of the main ways to adapt teaching to students in a way that is culturally relevant is to use examples from students' culture. For instance, if you are using visual examples, photos or videos, try to use examples with which students can identify. If most of your students are Dominican, try to find a visual of a Dominican doing the action you are demonstrating. If you are unable to find such a visual, create one with your students, or explain to the class your experience in trying to find one and the need for more diversity in this particular area. This is one component of culturally relevant teaching that can enhance a lecture. If you invest time in learning about the students' culture up front, then those cultural referents can be incorporated throughout lectures or the course (relating course material to cultural practices, foods, dance styles, or events—referencing a quinceanera for Chicano students can be very effective when explaining European-derived dance characteristics of partner dancing and creating spatial patterns). This information can be then used to build bridges throughout the course curriculum. The students' cultural lens stands at the forefront of teaching pedagogy.

Conclusion

Culturally relevant teaching is a method of teaching that is time intensive. Over time, your students' cultural affinities may change, so too must your teaching methods. It is about creating a class culture that meets the needs of the students in the room. It requires teachers to let go of familiar canons and the way their teacher did it. It is experimental, a process of learning about the culture of all students, and rewarding at every stage. The learning can go beyond understanding the ethnic culture of students and extend to other dance cultures, like competition dance, hip-hop, or capoeira. In addition, your students' cultural ties and ways of looking at the world may be informed by a religious culture or the LGBTQ community.

Culturally relevant teaching requires teachers to be open to whatever students describe as *their* culture—even when they are not equipped with the skills or language to identify it as such.

Multiculturalism is an important component of most curricula in the United States. Multiculturalism or diversity in curriculum is not the same as culturally relevant teaching. Culturally relevant teaching focuses on the culture of the students in the room. This can be challenging when teachers may be faced with numerous cultures in one room or students who identify with more than one culture. In such instances, the number of cultural referents may need to expand. Yet, if one student can relate to material through two cultural lenses, you can focus on one. The goal is to relate course material to students and boost achievement; if that can be accomplished through the use of one cultural lens, that is sufficient.

You need not be an expert on all of your student's culture. This is also an area that will likely improve over time. To be sure, the more you know, the better. However, if you approach students with transparency, "I want to learn more about you so that I can help you learn," you will find many students eager to share with you and excited to teach you something. Culturally relevant teaching is an ongoing process of learning about your students and learning how to relate course content to their lives. You do not have to be an expert on your students' culture to find things in their culture that relate to your coursework.

Questions to Consider When Developing Culturally Relevant Teaching Practices

What are the values of your class? General and specific.
1) *Technical development of physical practice*
2) *Creative exploration*
3) *Collaborative processes*

Long-Term Goals?
By the end of the course students will be able to...
  1)
  2)

Short-Term Goals?
By the end for the first unit or first week students will be able to...
  1)
  2)
  3)

What do I know about my students' culture?
  1)
  2)

3)
4)
5)

How can I incorporate student culture into my course?
1)
2)
3)
4)
5)

Suggested Questions for a Survey

1) Who is the most important person in your life? Explain why.
2) What do you do every day after school?
3) What are three things you would like to learn in dance this school year?
4) Where is your family from?
5) What do you do on the weekends?
6) Who do you spend time with on the weekends?
7) What kind of job or career would you like to do when you are an adult?
8) What is your favorite subject in school and why?
9) Do you ever dance with your family? If so, tell me about it?
10) Do you ever dance in your community? If so, tell me about it?

This is a possible question for middle school, high school, or college/university
11) What is your preferred pro-noun (he, she, they, ze, zir, or another)?
12) Are you a member of any groups, clubs, or communities that are important to you?

Pop culture currency can be valuable in the classroom too
13) Do you use social media? If so, what kind?
14) Who is your favorite performer (music)?
15) Who is your favorite dance artist?
16) Who is your favorite author?
17) What is your favorite TV show?
18) What is your favorite movie?

Suggestions for Teachers to Learn More about Their School Community at the Local and District Level

Community knowledge is powerful. As you move forward and want to advocate for opportunities and resources for your students or yourself, or find partners in your advocacy pursuits, you will find that the school community can be a great resource.

Ways to Get to Know Your School Community Checklist
1. Attend faculty meetings; find out which teachers are active and potentially partners for advocacy of student success.

2. Interdisciplinary instruction is a wonderful way to show students how different areas of study are related. Connect with departments that you feel relate well to your student population and look for ways to collaborate.
3. Invite teachers from other disciplines to guest teach or collaborate with you in your class. Offer to return the favor in your colleague's class.
4. Observe other teachers in the building. Select teachers to connect with depending upon the needs of your students in particular years.
5. What resources are available to students after school? Are there tutoring programs? Does the school have a big sports or arts community? If not, look for a way to contribute to your school community by filling this void—ideally enlisting the support of administration, other faculty, and parents.

Ways to Get to Know Your School District Community Checklist
1. Survey your school community. Take a walk around the community, notice the neighborhood, its economic condition, and resources. Are there stores, churches, community centers, residential areas? If so, what kind of stores or churches are present? How is the neighborhood configured? Does this configuration connote an under-resourced or an affluent community?
2. How does the weather impact the community? For instance, does everyone stay indoors half of the year and consequently have less contact with others? Or, are people out and about taking part in physical activities?
3. Attend school board meetings. Learn what the local school district is working on, what issues are important to attending community members, and who makes up the board and participants of the meeting (parents, teachers, administrators, or community members).

Three

Nuts and Bolts

*How to Develop a Culturally
Relevant Class Culture*

This chapter is designed to provide practical information that will assist you in creating a culturally relevant classroom. The material is especially intended for culturally relevant teaching methods in dance technique classes.

The Culture of Your Class Designed by You

Each teacher creates a classroom culture. Most teachers create a traditional studio classroom culture that resembles the culture with which they are most familiar. Teachers structure implicit and explicit guidelines on how to enter and exit the room, how the class will begin and end, how to address the teacher, procedures for students who arrive late, expected sequence of the class, where to stand, how to stand, what to wear, and often how to style one's hair. All of these procedures are customs that are implemented, established, reinforced, or dismantled by the teacher.

The culture of dance classrooms varies even though similarities among specific genres of dance can be found. For example, in an African dance class many female students wear lapas, African print fabric traditionally tied around the waist. There are also rituals around where the drummers sit, when and how they are addressed, as often "dobalè" or "kabiesi" (demonstration of respect extended to the drummers) is practiced before and at the end of class. Throughout class other acknowledgments are made to the drummers with dancers often joining in with clapping or audible calls to encourage and affirm the rhythm. Most ballet classes use a barre for a large

51

portion of the class; students wear specific dance attire; there is often a piano accompanist for music; and sometimes rosin is used for pointe shoes on the floor. Yet even within these prescribed dance cultures there are ways a teacher can create an individual class culture. An individual class culture has rituals specific to the given group of students that provide a common experience for all the students in the room, regardless of personal culture and history, to share. This is an opportunity for teachers to unify students through a shared class experience and culture.

The extent to which a class is diverse is usually not within the control of the instructor. Parents, administrators, economics, and local demographics have more to do with the diversity of a class than the teacher. However, instructors have the responsibility of creating a safe, accepting space for all students, including those marked with difference of any kind, such as body type, gender non-conforming, disability, nationality, culture, or religion. Addressing diversity can be challenging, whether your classroom is homogeneous, diverse, or has one or two students with different backgrounds, special needs, or identify as gender non-confirming. Students can be connected to a myriad of affinity groups. Highlight the commonalities among students, as well as geographic locations. Most students share commonalities as sons, daughters, sisters, or brothers. School or city sports teams can also be useful in encouraging commonalities as well as geographic location. To be sure, every student in the room is a student of yours. The classroom experiences you create for all of your students facilitate a common lived experience. Students can relate to each other through the exercises that everyone does together and the challenges they share as well as the enjoyment of the music and movement.

Seasoned educator Harry Wong developed an excellent framework to help teachers establish new procedures to support the class culture[1]:

1. Explain procedure/new custom
2. Rehearse procedure/new custom
3. Reinforce procedure/new custom
   a. Remind students of the procedure/new custom
   b. Offer multiple opportunities for students to experience this new practice

Ideally class procedures should be established at the beginning of the year. (You can implement new structures, expectations, and routines later i. he year, but it is more challenging.) As a teacher you must consider all e varying logistics that students will need to navigate while in your om. Decide how you will handle issues such as those listed below before ol year begins, so that you can teach students the culture of your classroom at the beginning of the term. Additionally, you may find that one or several of these questions can be transformed into a ritual of some kind.

1. Students arrival—What will students do once they arrive to class, but before the class has begun? Do you need to provide students with a task to complete while you take attendance? Will students do an organized stretch sequence or stretch on their own. Will they review choreography from the previous day?
2. Dressing for class—How long do students have to dress? Where will students dress? What is the consequence if students are not dressed? Can students participate if they are not dressed, or are partially dressed?
3. Tardy students—Will there be a consequence? How should students enter? Will you document tardiness?
4. Early dismissal—What is the procedure if students need to leave class early?
5. Bathroom and water breaks—What do students do if they need to go to the bathroom or get water? Can they go whenever they want? Do they need to ask permission? Do they need a pass? Will you give breaks periodically or at a specific time?
6. Rosin—Where is it located and who replenishes supplies? Who cleans the area?
7. Question in class—Is there a designated time in class for questions? How do students signal to the teacher that they have a question? Do they raise their hand?
8. Class dismissal—What is the procedure for class dismissal? Is there a bell for dismissal? Do you close with applause or an alternative reverence?

Rituals

There is a unifying power in the practice of "rituals," or regularly practiced events or movements. Many think of rituals in a religious context; however, my suggestion here is a non-secular activity. Many dance classes begin with a specific movement or exercise. A ballet class often begins with pliés. Similarly, most classes close with a *reverence* of some sort. One could also call them customs, routines, or daily practices. Rituals can be daily, weekly, or however you choose to pattern them. All classes have rituals whether these practices are identified as such or not.

I suggest you create a ritual to begin and end your class. The best rituals to establish a unique sense of community are those that are particular to your community of learners as opposed to a generic ritual that is experienced in most dance classes. For example, in many Western-based dance classes, students remove their shoes, enter the room, make adjustments to clothing, and move to the dance floor. Students then stretch and chat until the class begins. This pre-class activity can be considered a ritual. What the teacher is doing during this time often establishes the energy for the class. Teachers who draw in at this point, maybe to take attendance, often inspire students to focus on their own physical needs before class or review material from the previous class. In contrast, I have had teachers take this time to work the room with smiles, hugs, and warm greetings. The latter behavior can inspire students to engage with others in a friendly matter. This can be useful in a community of learners who struggle with working together or where there are members of the class with a language barrier. Students often talk and engage with their friends before class. However, if the teacher is greeting everyone it inspires students to greet and engage with *all* their classmates. To extend this into a ritual, one could create a rhythm played on the body, a song, dance, chant, gesture, or movement to symbolize a greeting and entry into the dance space, and use it to include every student.

The teacher shapes the culture of the classroom. A teacher can shape the energy of the class around the needs of the students. If students have challenges working together, structure the course around doing so. Create warm-up exercises that require a partner or several partners. When students perform movement in lines across the floor, refer to each line as their family, with whom they must stay connected; all the lines moving across the floor comprise the village. Conversely, if students need to develop skills for independent practice, create class activities that draw students into personal, physical investigations of their own movement and bodies. This is challenging because if you are a new teacher or have never worked with a particular student, you do not know how to shape the class to student needs. This is one reason I advocate for a "getting to know you" unit in the beginning of any class or course.

One way to infuse a dance class with culturally relevant pedagogy is to restructure the class format to incorporate diverse ways of interacting. For example, if you serve students who have a connection to Chinese culture or Buddhism, you may choose to begin or end each class with a meditative practice. Such a ritual could include movement in a tai chi fashion or maybe a meditative moment of stillness. One might also consider a walking meditation or a moving meditation. Keep in mind that such a movement practice would need to be simple and repetitive in order for a meditative state to be achieved. In creating a ritual like this you can connect to the culture of some students, share a new cultural experience with other students and build upon your class culture.

Another possibility would be to connect to the traditions of the African American community. Within this culture, circle formations are used in many African-derived dances, dating back to the Big Apple, Ring Shout and other plantation dances, and even further back to many dances from West Africa where the slave trade was most concentrated.[2] Circular formations also resonate for many Native American students who have familiarity with powwows and other traditional ceremonies. Instead of facing students toward a mirror and the teacher for center floor exercises, some of these exercises could be done in a circle. This would provide a certain familiarity in structure to many African American and Native American students and offer a new experience to other students. Teachers would not have to change their entire class structure. They could do one exercise in the circle or many. Another option could be for an instructor to create a closing ritual in a circle to end class. Such a ritual could also be used to begin class.

In observing world renowned dance educator and artist David Dorfman's classes, I noticed opening and closing rituals. In the beginning of each class, he gathered all students and asked them what they would like to work on that day. He listened to the requests from a number of students each day. He used their requests as a thread and highlighted opportunities to work on these things throughout the class. For example, a student stated that he would like to work on how to get into inversions. Each time he offered an opportunity for students to develop a skill used in this maneuver, he would bring attention to it. This functioned as a student-centered daily ritual wherein Dorfman supported students' developmental goals. In closing class, Dorfman led students in a short gestural sequence which he explained to me was inspired by the work of David Zambrano.[3] The sequence physically embraces the past behind them, the present they are standing in, the community that surrounds them, and future in front of them. This sequence served as a closing for the class in lieu of a *reverence*, or one could interpret it as the *reverence*.

Names and the Act of Naming

Names are an expression of culture. The way in which names are decided is also cultural. In some settings, you can give students special names, perhaps a dance name. Maybe it's a tradition that each senior receives a dance name. This can be a fun custom depending on the context and community of dancers. In some settings it would be inappropriate and awkward, so know your audience. With all of the suggestions in this text, you have to consider your school population and community before you adopt a custom. That said, I like the custom of naming exercises.

Most Western dance practitioners understand the ballet term *en croix*, literally meaning "on the cross." For dancers, the term indicates that a given exercise will include a leg movement, with the working leg extending to the front, to the side, to the back, and again to the side. Similarly, I like to create an exercise or sequence of movements and name it something special. One could name the movement after anything, maybe a flower or a pet. One of my favorite exercises as a teenager was one my teacher named, with the help of the class, "Uncle Fred." This contributed to creating a culture, language, code, and regular practice specific to the students in the room and gave us a shared experience and means of communication. Such names symbolize a shared understanding and can be one tool in unifying a group that may otherwise have little in common. I often utilize the teaching tool of creating names of exercises with and for my students. Currently, my students hold one of my floor combinations, "Cousin Felix," as a favorite. They light up and look at each other knowingly every time I call for it, and in many cases, when a student requests it.

Movement Affinities

All dancers have movement affinities, the ways in which one loves to move. These are the movements we gravitate to; we come to life when we are asked to perform them. They are also often the movements and physical sensations that brought us to dance in the first place. If you learn what types of movements excite your students, you can design exercises and movement phrases that incorporate some of these affinities. You may also be able to deconstruct the feeling they get from a specific movement or genre and show students how they can find similar sensations in other movements and genres.

You can identify your students' movement affinities in many ways. Often the age of the students and type of dance teaching setting will determine how you approach this matter. Most elementary school students have a limited movement history. They are also especially open to learning new movement. These students are often most comfortable with pedestrian movement: walk, run, jump, hop, skip, chassé, roll, freeze, throw, and kick. You can build on all of these movements as you focus on exposure to new movement. For these learners it is about the development of their movement history and vocabulary. With older students or those with a dance background, you may want to allow them to improvise for one minute and examine what type of movements your students are repeatedly drawn to.

Do students gravitate to the vertical plane, sagittal plane, or horizontal plane?

The vertical plane is similar to making snow angels, in an upright position. The sagittal plane, similar to the motion of riding a bicycle, walking or running. Finally, the horizontal plane moves parts of the body from right to left or left to right.

Two questions to consider in regard to movement are:

1. Do students prefer rhythmic or melodic phrases?
2. Do students enjoy movement that travels or do they prefer to stay stationary?

Another way to examine students' movement affinities is to teach three phrases, each one with a focus on a different type of movement, and identify which students gravitate to which phrases.

Ask students about their preferences. Let them know that it is not always possible to focus solely on what they like. But let them know that what they like is important, that you are interested in their preferences, and they will have opportunities to do movements they enjoy. When you get to know your students' movement affinities you can combine movements they enjoy with new movements that may challenge them. This is an overarching goal of culturally relevant pedagogy—*utilizing the familiar to support acquisition of what is unfamiliar.*

Dance Accents

It is widely accepted that dance is a language. It is a means to communicate and hold shared understandings through the body that can serve as a point of commonality. As a language, dance highlights movement that reveals one's dance background and history. When teaching students dance forms that have a cultural orientation different from their own, educators must remember all that dance can communicate. For example, when I am teaching Western-trained dancers an African-derived dance form and vice versa, I am reminded that the physical orientations of these dance forms,

European upward and African toward the ground, are in direct opposition. Even when dance students are able to replicate the leg or arm movements, there is often an embodied difference. I identify these as "dance accents," and, like language accents, they are challenging to overcome. Allow students to embrace their dance accents and celebrate the embodied histories they carry. Once students are confident in their movements, find opportunities to encourage the acquisition of a new way to move—a new movement accent, if you will. This requires movement analysis on the part of students. They must first recognize the wonderful informed intricacies of their current movement and how it differs from the new movement being offered.

Improvisation

Improvisation is often taught with the idea that this learning experience will place students on equal footing, rather than students being evaluated on their movement affinities. I have found this idea of aesthetic equality rarely works within a Western-based dance context. Although improvisation is utilized in many cultures throughout the world, within a Western-based dance context, a clear Western-desired aesthetic remains. In this context, improvisation can be off-putting to many students of color as well as students without formal dance training, wherein their previous dance encounters were more communal and less focused on the individual in motion. Their unease also has a great deal to do with music choices or the absence of music that can occur in improvisation classes. For many African American, Native American, and Latino students, dance is culturally interdependent with a musical experience. As a result, when students are asked to dance to silence, or to ambient noises, they are instantly placed outside their cultural orientation for dance movement. Within a Western context, improvisation is also often structured about an image or sensory experience, such as light or vibration. This too is a departure from the context of improvisation in many cultures wherein improvisation focuses on storytelling or concrete actions.

There are differences between European music audiences, who generally sit still and are silent, and audiences of African music, who participate by contributing audible sounds, applause, or an embodiment of the rhythm.[4] These differences in no way indicates that improvisation is not a valuable teaching tool, but that it should be utilized with a full understanding of its cultural reference.

For dance educators using improvisation, consider the following examples for incorporating music. Select several different pieces of music. Include at least one with a distinct rhythm pattern so that students whose orientation to dance is aligned with rhythmic accompaniment will not be alienated during this experience. As all music is culturally informed, be mindful with music selection and open yourself up to multiple possibilities for musical accompaniment.

For some students, their orientation toward improvisation is that it is a communal experience—one that usually takes place in the company of others. This stands in opposition to a Western training context where the focus of improvisation is on oneself. One possibility that can address students whose understanding of dance is tied to a community experience would be to frame the movement experience in a way that focuses on interaction with others or one other. Try improvisation exercises in a circle or encourage eye contact and physical interaction. This would make the experience more communal and less focused on the individual—which will be more comfortable for some students.

One common improvisational movement score often used is the *Body Orchestra*. It allows students to explore relationships between movement and sound. Below is a description of the *Body Orchestra*.

1. Divide the dance class into two groups, A and B.
2. Group A develops a rhythm using their bodies as their only instrument.
3. Group B creates a movement phrase to the rhythm of group A.
4. Alternate roles with group B creating music and group A creating a movement phrase.

In this improvisation exercise, students are able to create their own movement while being supported by a rhythm that comes from them as well. This exercise is student-centered in that students drive the content of the music and movement. It can also address issues of rhythm and community.

Another approach to improvisation is to highlight a culturally informed dance form that relates to students in the class. Teach a workshop on the dance form or present a guest artist who teaches that form. Then ask students to use movements and ideas from the workshop in an improvisation exercise. Suggest that students tell a story utilizing some of the movements featured in the workshop. If students feel uncomfortable moving in a new aesthetic, encourage them to stay the course. This experience can develop their compassion for when they encounter others who struggle with movements in which they possess confidence.

Contact improvisation brings forth cultural issues around touch.

Instructors planning to teach contact improvisation should consider diverse cultural orientation around touch. Some students find the idea of touching other students to be a great challenge. Once encouraged, they can overcome this challenge and find a great sense of accomplishment. However, there are students that never overcome this challenge nor do they become comfortable for numerous reasons. Be caution around issues of touch in the studio dance classroom. Concerns relating to culture, previous negative experience around touch, and fear around gender identity and sexuality can emerge.

Autobiographical Movement Poem (AMP)

Embodied storytelling can be a powerful means of expression for students. It is an opportunity for students to share their stories within an educational space wherein they might typically feel invisible. In *The Need for a Story: Cultural Diversity in Classroom and Community*, editors Ann Haas Dyson and Celia Genishi encourage educators to utilize student storytelling. They suggest teachers listen to student stories with sensitivity. Dyson and Genishi assert that teachers can "exploit the power of those stories for bringing children and their diverse experiences into the classroom and forging new connections among students and teachers."[5]

I begin many dance courses with an autobiographical movement poem. It is an opportunity to see how my students like to move and for them to share a story about their lives or families. This assignment can be framed in a highly structured or loose manner. I find that experienced dance students can handle it in an open format while students without formal dance training are often more successful with structured guidelines.

> *Many students without formal dance training have a limited dance vocabulary so a lot of their movements tend to be literal. Although literal movement may not be aligned with your long-term goal for students, it is important to accept students where they are in the beginning of the course.*

Sample Guidelines: Elementary School

Complete the following sentence with a movement for each word.

(Teachers select the sentence that will work best for your students, or select all three if they are older.)

1. My favorite food is _____ (5 movements).
2. My favorite time of day is _____ (7 movements).
3. The most important people in my life are _____ (9 movements).

Each student performs his or her AMP twice, once in silence and once narrating the movement. If you have a large class you may limit your students to one of the above questions.

This exercise works best if the teacher can provide students with an example and perform the first AMP. Perform your AMP twice: first as a non-verbal movement sequence, and second, as a narrated movement sequence.

Show and Tell

Show and Tell is another version of the Autobiographical Movement Poem for elementary students. Students bring in an item or photo from home or a picture from a magazine. They then create three to five movements that explain how this image or object relates to their lives.

Sample Guidelines: High School/University

Option A) Use your body to share three facts about yourself.

Option B) Create a story about your life with your body; include a beginning, middle, and end (the end may indicate life now/in progress).

Option C) Create your autobiography with a dance. Please include the following: jump, gesture, turn, touch the floor (in some way), travel, and repeat a movement.

It is often helpful to give students a time limit on their poem, no more than one minute is a good start.

After students perform their poem once, have them repeat the dance while they talk the class through the movement. Each student shares with his or her body and words. When not performing, each student gives attention to their classmates. It is a time when individual voices and listening as a community are valued.

Rubric for Autobiographical Movement Poem (AMP)

(This rubric is a guideline for students, as this assignment is not graded other than being a component of class participation.)

Students are encouraged (but not required) to ground work in their personal culture.

Assessment Criteria	*Needs Improvement*	*Acceptable*	*Proficient*
The AMP is centered on a **theme**, experience, stage in life, or evolution of a process.	AMP communicates some sense of a theme, experience, stage in life, or evolution of a process.	AMP communicates a theme, experience, stage in life, or evolution of a process.	AMP communicates a clear and identifiable theme, experience, stage in life, or evolution of a process.

Assessment Criteria	Needs Improvement	Acceptable	Proficient
The AMP makes **connections** to the individual's culture/family/or a group with which they strongly identify.	Movement that is generic and not clearly connected to the performer or a given culture, family, or group.	Demonstrates a connection between person and a specific culture.	Demonstrates vivid connection between person and a specific culture. AMP includes artifacts from the individual's culture/family/or group with which they strongly identify.
The AMP incorporates conventional **choreographic tools** such as, but not limited to: levels, spatial patterns, gesture, repetition, use of time, and dynamics in movement effort.	AMP incorporates one or two conventional choreographic tools.	AMP incorporates three or four conventional choreographic tools.	AMP incorporates five or more conventional choreographic tools.
AMP works within **time** parameters.	AMP is longer than a one minute and a half, or less than thirty seconds.	AMP is between 30 seconds and one and a half minutes.	AMP is between 30 seconds and one and a half minutes.

If time permits, students will analyze this rubric and investigate whether it privileges some dance genres over others; if it does, students will be given the agency to reform the rubric.

Autobiographical Movement Poem Collaboration Rubric

Once all members in the class have created an AMP, students can work together to create a collaborative piece. The integrity of each group member's autobiographical sketch must be preserved while developing a cohesive collaboration.

Imagine a student represents each of the shapes in the diagram to the right. Note they are all connected to create the final picture, but each shape's full identity is preserved.

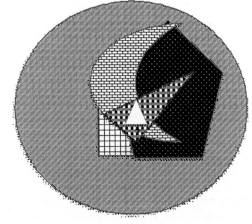

Sample Rubric

Assessment Criteria	*Accomplished*	*Not Accomplished*
All five members are active in process and presentation.		
The composition study is between one and three minutes long.		
Elements of five different individuals are represented in the collaboration.		
Students demonstrate a respect for the individuality of fellow members. (This should be incorporated into the composition study.)		

Personal Dance History

A Personal Dance History is a great opportunity to collect multiple histories and highlight the idea that there are multiple stories, truths, experiences, and ways of understanding the world. Create a chronological timeline to chart historical dance figures. Ask students who should go up on the chart. This gives students a valued voice and allows students to see the artist they value included in their learning experience. Then insert students into the continuum of significant dance figures, literally placing each student on the continuum of dance history. This illuminates the idea that what we do today is the history of the future.

Diversifying Higher Education Curriculum

Higher education is a challenging space to diversify because of the Eurocentric ethos entrenched in the structure of most institutions in the United States. However, educators who take on this challenge have a great impact on the field. Because many students are future teachers, this teaching/learning setting is integral to impacting the field of dance and future generations.

There is little focus on diversifying curriculum in higher education. Rarely does a department hold in-service training, providing tools for instructors to diversify curriculum, as is common in many K–12 educational settings. Educators who take on diversifying curriculum in higher education often travel this path with little support. Typically, the focus in higher education is diversifying the faculty and student body.[6] The assumption here is that the once the faculty and student body have been diversified, everything else falls into place. In actuality, once programs get diversified in number, retention then becomes an issue because the curriculum, pedagogy practices, and atmosphere are often not culturally responsive and cultural clashes are experienced in the classroom. Ideally, curriculum, pedagogy practices, and atmosphere would begin to shift and become more inclusive before faculty and students grow in number. This approach would enable a school community to meet the needs of new members of the community upon their arrival. Although faculty members in higher education often have to pursue the journey of diversifying course material on their own, they maintain a great deal of autonomy in their classrooms, and can be quite effective.

Conclusion

Whether you decide to incorporate your students' cultural music and movement affinities or create rituals that reference their culture or allow students to name exercises, there are countless ways you can build a class culture around your students. Real diversification of curriculum requires more than good intentions; it requires action. Get involved in learning who your students are and show them how your course material is relevant in their lives.

Four

Culturally Relevant Ballet

In a study I conducted in 2011, I found that ballet instructors in higher education dance departments were often challenged by the charge to provide students with historical and social context around the dance form.[1] The struggle to make ballet culturally relevant became apparent when teachers responded to my question about cultural relevancy with comments like "That is not necessary in my class, I teach technique." To be sure, little inspiration can be found in looking at a company photo of the New York City Ballet or ballet photos in many dance history textbooks. American ballet remains an institution that has, for whatever reason, been unable to diversify in ways that would reflect the vast diversity of this country. This chapter is designed to be a practical resource for dance educators of a variety of levels, providing myriad ideas that can expand cultural diversity in the teaching of ballet as an art form.

In exploring how one can make relevant a privileged and aged European dance form to students from diverse backgrounds of the twenty-first century, I considered the ways in which ballet has transcended boundaries of nation and class. Ballet is a world-renowned classical art form, originating in Europe, with roots in the Italian Renaissance court. It further developed in France where the language of ballet was established. Ballet also has a historical and world-renowned presence in Russia. The United States, although a comparatively younger nation, also has notably contributed to the development of the ballet tradition.

British cultural theorist Angela McRobbie explores the socio-cultural complexities of ballet in "Dance Narratives and Fantasies of Achievement."

She describes ballet as simultaneously holding positions of low or high art depending upon who has the privilege of awarding status.[2] That is, placing ballet at a low art level is in comparison to opera or Western classical music and high art in relation to other genres of dance. In either placement, McRobbie asserts the capacity of ballet to be an expressive tool for a range of cultures and communities: "Ballet … a spectacle for virtuoso performance, a part of the 'national heritage,' a showcase for other national identities, and an opportunity for promoting international relations."[3] Many students of color, as well as youth strongly connected to popular culture, perceive ballet as a Eurocentric dance form and find identifying with it challenging. Yet when students are encouraged to examine McRobbie's ideas about ballet through investigating issues of high and low art in dance, and in particular ballet, opportunities for national identities and issues of class can be explored.

Ballet can be connected to the national and cultural heritage of many throughout the world. This can be a challenging idea for many who consider ballet a Eurocentric dance form. However, ballet flourished in Cuba, China and Japan as well as a number of other countries outside traditional Western territories. An interesting ballet, which could be the subject of inquiry into ballet as an expression of national and cultural identity, might be the Chinese ballet *The Red Detachment of Women* (about a peasant girl from Hainan Island and her rise in the Chinese Communist Party). In considering ballet's position in various countries' ideas of cultural imperialism, culture for export and cultural appropriation can be examined. The lesson to be learned from such discourse is that there is no universal experience, reading, or perspective on ballet.

Students might also be interested in examining how the ballet form has traveled throughout the world and compare this examination to that of hip-hop. It would be helpful to keep in mind the institutional mechanics by which ballet travels through the world and whether those mechanics permit or curtail cultural diversity. Another possible vein for exploration is the idea of ballet as cultural imperialism, considering how, for example, the Royal Academy of Dance aims for standard technique and curriculum and has offices all over the world. These topics are rich with opportunities to relate ballet to students' own cultural dance forms while also uncovering ways to better relate to ballet as a classical art form.

Ballet Dancers of Color in the United States

Through research and critical thinking processes, students can explore the dancers of color who have made significant historical contributions to the dance form. A small amount of historical background information is provided on numerous ballet dancers of color in the U.S. This information is intended to be a seed that might inspire research projects and lesson plans that can expand student knowledge of ballet dancers of color.

Ballet companies in the U.S. and Western Europe are overwhelmingly white. Many if not all of the dancers featured had to deal with explicit racism as they worked to achieve their goals in the art form.

Native Americans

The "Five Moons," as they are affectionately known among the Native American community of Oklahoma, are five Native American ballerinas: Maria Tallchief, Marjorie Tallchief, Rosella Hightower, Yvonne Chouteau, and Moscelyne Larkin. Each ballerina has roots in Oklahoma, is a descendent of a Native American Nation, and went on to found or direct an educational institution of ballet.

Maria Tallchief was born in 1925. She was the daughter of an Osage tribal chief, Alexander Joseph Tall Chief.[4] Arguably she achieved the greatest mainstream success of the "Five Moons" with her accomplishment of being the first American to attain the rank of prima ballerina, an honor achieved while performing with the New York City Ballet. At NYCB, she worked closely with George Balanchine. Her expressive artistry was well paired with his innovative choreography. She had a full dance career with numerous accolades before founding the Chicago City Ballet in 1981.[5] Maria died in 2013.

Marjorie Tallchief, Maria's younger sister by two years, followed her older sister's lead into ballet. Marjorie made her professional debut in 1944 at the age of seventeen when performing as a soloist with Lucia Chase and Richard Pleasant's Ballet Theatre. She was invited to join the Colonel de Basil's Original Ballet Russe as a soloist in 1945 which helped to establish her as a professional ballet dancer. In 1956, she was invited to be a leading ballerina with the Paris Opéra Ballet. Marjorie went on to serve as director of dance for the Dallas Ballet in Texas; the Chicago City Ballet in Illinois; and the Harid Conservatory in Boca Raton, Florida, where she still resides.[6]

Rosella Hightower, born in 1920, was a native of Durwood, Oklahoma, and of Choctaw ancestry. She joined Ballet Russe de Monte Carlo in 1938 when she was in her late teens. In 1947, John Martin, dance critic for the *New York Times*, recognized Rosella for a performance of *Giselle*.[7] In the 1960s she opened a dance school, Ecole superieure de danse de Cannes, in France. She passed away in 2008.

Born in 1929 and a descendent of the Shawnee Tribe, Yvonne Chouteau has been committed to the dance art form for most of her life.[8] At the age of fourteen, she was the youngest dancer accepted into Ballet Russe de Monte Carlo. Although Yvonne was born in Fort Worth, Texas, she was raised in Oklahoma which became a place of great achievement for Yvonne. She and her husband, dancer Miguel Terekhov, founded the Oklahoma City Civic Ballet and the first accredited dance department in the United States at the University of Oklahoma in Norman.[9] Most recent accounts place her residence in Oklahoma.

Moscelyne Larkin was born in the mid–1920s. Her mother was a Russian ballet dancer and her father a Shawnee-Peoria Native. Like her contemporaries, she danced with Ballet Russe de Monte Carlo. Moscelyne went on to marry a dancer, Roman Jansinski, and settled in Tulsa, Oklahoma. There, the couple began a ballet school and company, the Tulsa Civic Ballet, also known as the Tulsa Ballet Theatre. Moscelyne died in 2012.[10]

Visual artist Mike Larsen immortalized the "Five Moons" in a historic Native American mural painting, "Flight of Spirit," featured in the Great Rotunda of the Oklahoma State Capital. It is a beautiful piece of art, rich with symbolism and cultural history. Positioned as a testament to the Native Americans of Oklahoma, Larsen's mural expresses the twofold experience of many Natives in the United States. On the one hand, Natives have experienced a tyrannical national system; on the other hand, the white man's dances have been shared, and, in turn, embodied to the point of high achievement by the Five Moons. As images of this mural can be found online, excellent opportunities for students to read about the painting and learn more about the Five Moons and their culture exist. Detailed biographies of each of these Native American ballerinas can be found in *American Indian Ballerinas* by Lili C. Livingston (1997). For younger dancers, there are numerous books and biographies about Maria Tallchief.

African Americans

Examining the work of Arthur Mitchell, the first African American principal dancer with New York City Ballet, offers teachers another platform to expand and diversify ballet curriculum. George Balanchine choreographed the Pas de deux from Agon for Mr. Mitchell (as he notably prefers to be called) in 1957. He first performed it with a white dancer, Allegra Kent. While the piece was performed in theaters, it was almost a decade before a black man partnering a white women was permitted to be broadcast on television.[11] Once he left New York City Ballet, he went on to become co-founder and artistic director of Dance Theatre of Harlem (DTH) in 1969.[12] DTH was created during the civil rights movement as a positive artistic response to the assassination of Dr. Martin Luther King. The company has trained and employed more African American ballet dancers than any other training center or ballet company in the United States and likely the world. One of Mitchell's accomplishment at DTH was his creative commission of *Creole Giselle* (1988). *Creole Giselle* was choreographed by Jean Coralli, Jules Perrot, and Marius Petipa and restaged by Frederic Franklin. It is an adaptation of the classic *Giselle*, originally choreographed by Jean Coralli and Jules Perrot. In contrast to the European setting of the classic, it is set in a community of freed blacks in Louisiana in the 1840s.

Marion Cuyjet was a dance pioneer. In the late 1940s, she owned the first black-owned business in downtown Philadelphia, a dance studio in which she was instrumental in developing the first African American ballerina for a mainstream ballet company.[13] Her primary protégé was Delores Browne who went on to study at the American School of Ballet, New York City Ballet, work with Anthony Tudor, and dance with the New York Negro Ballet.[14] Cuyjet focused on widening opportunities for African Americans as she was acutely aware of colorism in American society. She focused resources on "brown skinned girls," asserting that the light-skinned girls would get opportunities.[15] Interestingly enough, Cuyjet was a very fair complexioned woman and would often pass for white in order to secure resources and opportunities for her students.[16]

Fun facts:

Joan Myers Brown, founder and artistic director of Philadanco, and Judith Jamison, former artistic director of the Alvin Ailey American Dance Theater, were students of Marion Cuyjet at the same time.[17]

There were African American ballet companies in the U.S. before Dance Theatre of Harlem: the American Negro Ballet Company 1937 and New York Negro Ballet of the late 1950s. Both companies were short lived.

In 1955, Raven Wilkinson was the first African American ballet dancer to be invited to join a white mainstream ballet company, Ballet Russe de Monte Carlo. This was a silent yet monumental moment, one that had to be kept hidden. Wilkinson's ability to be a company member depended upon her ability to travel with the company. Segregation laws at that time made it illegal for her, or any African American, to travel and share the stage with a white dance company. The fact that Wilkinson was a light-skinned African American woman and able to pass for white as the company traveled through the South was critical. If identified as an African American, she and the company could be in great danger. She danced successfully with the company for a number of years, although there were several troubling incidents, including one in which she was exposed during a tour in the South and the entire company was confronted by the Ku Klux Klan. Company officials decided to send Wilkinson North until she could join the company safely. Not long after such racially tense incidents of the late 1950s, she was encouraged to leave the company. She eventually left to dance in Europe for a time before returning to the United States in the mid–1970s.[18] Wilkinson performed character roles with the New York Opera until it folded in 2014.

The Houston Ballet, based in Houston, Texas, disrupted the color lines in ballet when it appointed Lauren Anderson to principal ballet dancer in 1990. In 1983 Anderson joined the company where she developed her career. She performed as one of the only African American principal ballet dancers in the world in a predominately white company until she retired in 2006.

Following in Arthur Mitchell's footsteps, Albert Evans was the second African American ballet dancer to join New York City Ballet. He was an immensely talented performer who joined the company in 1988, was appointed to soloist in 1991, and became a principal dancer with the company in 1995. Evans retired from performing in 2010 but stayed on as ballet master until his death in 2015.[19]

Desmond Richardson achieved a successful career in ballet in addition to his accomplishments in other genres of dance. Among his numerous credits, he was a company member with the American Ballet Theatre and the Alvin Ailey American Dance Theater and has been a cast member in several Broadway productions. Richardson's work as a choreographer has been widely acclaimed and in 1994 he and Dwight Rhoden founded Complexions Contemporary Ballet Company.

Misty Copeland is the adored and famed black ballerina of the twenty-first century. She began dancing at the age of thirteen, considered late by ballet standards, and went on to join the American Ballet Theatre (ABT). She focused her career on breaking the color barrier entrenched in the esteemed, world-renowned ABT. She achieved her goal to be the first African American principal dancer with ABT in 2015. This promotion, made by company artistic director Kevin McKenzie, was a historic moment in dance history. Her success has been widely publicized as many in the U.S. have been fascinated with the long-awaited disruption of racist hiring and promotion practices in ballet in the U.S. She personally shares her story in her autobiography, *Life in Motion: An Unlikely Ballerina.*

A critical dance pedagogical approach to curriculum can inspire rich explorations of diversity in ballet throughout the world. When students are provided with multiple examples of diversity among performers, students have the opportunity to see the possibility of pursuing the art form themselves. Ask students to examine the pre-revolutionary National Ballet Company of Iran or the Tokyo Ballet. More diverse representations of ballet can diminish the marginalization that often comes when ballet students and teachers have a monolithic lens. It tells a new truth of ballet, one that is accessible to many cultures. Sharing information about these ballet dance pioneers expands the story of a seemingly elitist dance form to include people of color. For some students these stories will bring possibility and encouragement to embody this world-renowned classical dance form.

Cross-national and cross-cultural exchanges also offer interesting subjects for students to examine. In studying diversity in top tier ballet companies in the United States, one will notice there are few Asian Americans. Most of the Asians in such companies were born overseas, as is also the case for Latino ballet dancers, many of whom were born in Spain, Cuba, or U.S. territory, Puerto Rico. Thus while it is challenging to find Asian and Latino ballet dancers in the U.S., there are many Asians and Latinos performing ballet in other countries. There are well-known ballet companies in Asia, Cuba, and Puerto Rico that have dances in their repertory that could be compared to some of the classic ballets. These countries also maintain established schools of ballet. This allows ballet companies in places that lack diversity among their ballet students (like the United States or South Africa) to acquire trained ballet dancers from other countries to diversify their dance companies. For example, South Africa has established a racially integrated national ballet company, Joburg Ballet, largely by importing their dancers of color from Cuba.[20]

Ballet, Storytelling and Culturally Relevant Teaching

Many popular classical ballets are known for the stories they tell. The phenomenon of storytelling can be identified as a cultural expression. Examining the storytelling aspect of ballet can offer a unique gateway to understanding for those who might otherwise feel culturally alienated from the dance form. In Dorion Weickmann's essay "Choreography and Narrative:

The *ballet d'action* of the Eighteenth Century," she describes how narrative ballet that tells a story developed. Weickmann notes three factors as facilitating the birth of *ballet d'action*. First, enlightenment ideas that allowed dance to be accepted as an independent art form. Second, the technical development of the dance form. Third, the separation of the performer from the audience, which allowed artists to develop a standard of professionalism. In the eighteenth century when it emerged, it was a departure from the court dance entertainment aligned with *grand ballets. Ballet d'action* grew to form the storytelling and narrative ballet widely recognized today.[21]

As *ballet d'action* evolved in the eighteenth century notions that ballet could express the "beauty of the human condition"[22] grew. Full dances that featured the physical positioning of the king and ballets about monarchs and mythical gods decreased while plots with "human conflicts, sentiments and souls"[23] increased.

Historically, the storytelling aspects of ballet have been exploited to support racism in casting. Alvin Ailey described Agnes deMille's outlook on casting as follows: "Does one really want to see a black swan among thirty-two swans in Swan Lake or a black peasant girl in Giselle? It's historically inaccurate."[24] He countered her sentiment with the idea that what we create in the theater is all fantasy. None of the dancers in *Swan Lake* are actually birds. African American ballet dancer Aesha Ash faced similar issues as a member of the NYCB corps when, performing as swans, dancers were told to powder up before going on stage.[25] These behind-the-scenes narratives can be valuable teaching tools. Moreover, framing the use of storytelling as a source of cross-cultural understanding can expand students' appreciation for ballet as well as their understanding of humanity.

The idea of ballet as a storytelling art form can be utilized for marginalized students who hold a cultural orientation that values storytelling. Native Americans and African Americans tell the stories of their culture and community, be it through music, dance, or oratorical expression. Stories carry our culture: what we like to do, what we like to eat, where we go, what we are afraid of, and what we value. Offering students the opportunity to tell their own story through dance may not only be a fun activity, but it can also be an opportunity to get to know more about your students' culture. In addition, storytelling can be a link to bring Eurocentric dance aesthetics into a space of cultural relevancy for students. "We all have a basic need for a story, for organizing our experiences into tales of important happenings.... Through stories, teachers learn of their children's cultures, of their diverse experiences, and of their connections to family and friends."[26] This is also an opportunity for students to see themselves, their ideas, and their values in the curriculum.

Native American culture offers excellent examples of storytelling as utilized for preservation and transmission of cultural history. Stories have carried the beliefs, values, courage, humor, and history of Native American tribes for hundreds of years. As a result, learning through stories can serve as a reference point for students. More pointedly, the sacred value of storytelling within Native American cultures should always be acknowledged.

Many African Diasporic cultures have been preserved through the art of storytelling and oral histories. This is often noted in reference to the scarcity of written documentation as cultural artifacts. In *Talk That Talk: An Anthology of African-American Storytelling*, editors Linda Goss and Marian Barnes address the expansive inclusion of storytellers in the African American culture: "past and present, these folks have gone by many names. Today they are called preachers, healers, teachers, comedians, blues singers, poets, dancers, rappers, painters, liars, and historians."[27]

Share this expansive idea of storytelling with your students. Ask your students if they know any stories, ask them if they are storytellers, ask them to try and become a storyteller of ballet.

Similar ethos about storytelling is found in Mexican folklore and traditions, often referred to as *cuentos*. These are short stories, sometimes fables, legends or folktales, and although many have been published, the history of cuentos is rooted in oral narratives.[28]

As dance educators, we can ask students about their relationship with storytelling, highlight the cultural context therein and relate such stories to the classical stories in ballet. It is possible, depending on the age of students, that they know of some stories that are also performed as ballets, such as *Romeo and Juliet*, *Sleeping Beauty*, or *Cinderella*. Build upon these connections and create ballets that share a story in class. Although I referenced the storytelling traditions in African and Native American cultures, all cultures and all peoples have stories. If we listen to our students' stories, we will gain an understanding of their culture and their hearts.

Addressing Gender in Ballet

Gender can be challenging to directly address in any class. Gender is a culturally informed social construct of how people assigned at birth as girls and boys should behave. Sue Stinson has brought forth research that examines how gender is implicitly taught through many dance classes.[29] For example, most students of dance have heard directions such as "Boys over here, girls over there" or "Boys do this combination, girls do that combination." For many who were taught the chivalrous implicit heteronormative messages of ballet, binary gender constructs are part and parcel of ballet training. However, I would like to offer some suggestions for teaching dance in a ever-changing society, and one that currently is making requests or demands for gender neutral learning spaces.

Possible Strategies

1. Address students as "dancers" instead of "boys" and "girls" or "ladies" and "gentlemen."
2. Tell students of the gendered traditions of ballet class so that students are knowledgeable of historical traditions, but do not insist on practicing them. For example, tell students that in traditional ballet dance classes, the men perform exercises as a group, last. This is done out of courtesy and often because the music gets slower for their jumps as many men levitate in the air longer than women.
3. Encourage all students to perform petite and grand allegro phrases at a faster tempo and then repeat at a slower tempo. Or allow students to select at which tempo and group they would like to perform the phrase.
4. Explain to students traditional dance attire along gender lines and offer them the freedom to wear whatever they like within the boundaries of either traditional female or male ballet attire—with the purpose being to see the line of the body.
5. When showing films consider sharing performances that offer alternative or multiple expressions of gender.
6. Share Mark Morris's *The Hard Nut* and Matthew Bourne's *Swan Lake* as alternative ways to perform gender. Ask students what it means to perform gender. Ask students if there are gender nonconforming movements. Ask students to consider why these dances were created. Ask students to describe the differences between gendered movements in ballet. If they are beginning students you may want to show them a pas de deux performance. Ask students to explain what purpose these differences serve and if they are needed.

For some these suggestions are nothing new, for others they might seem radical. Some educators will make these shifts in their dance classes in response to student needs, while others will make shifts proactively. However you chose to structure your class in regard to gender, it is an issue you will have to address at some point.

> *For university students in Dance Theory courses, I strongly recommend* Reworking Ballet: Counter-Narratives and Alternative Bodies *by Vida L. Midgelow. This book offers text to explore with students that addresses the body, homoeroticism, queerness, cross casting, cross dressing, and symbolism.*

Application of Culturally Relevant Teaching for Technique Class

Suggestions for Music

Consider varying your music for ballet. Western classical music can limit your ability to reach students. Some educators feel it is an abomination to pair ballet with music other than classical. Yet I argue that if you want to break students out of their paradigm, show them you can do the same. Use music from all over the world and from diverse genres. Try Duke Ellington's *The Harlem Nutcracker*, Bach by the Brazilian Assad brothers, or a Celtic selection by Bill Whelan for petite allegro or barre combinations. Adele, India Aire, Norah Jones, and Alicia Keys can bring a more contemporary flare to your class exercises. Tango music is also a great choice for beginners because many of the more commercial options have strong musical accents. It can also inspire emotion and a special connection to the music. Different music can educate students about multiple music options as well as musicians from divergent parts of the world. Additionally, it is an opportunity to blend ballet with diverse music providing a multicultural experience of fusion. When students are in a relaxed groove with a phrase or sequence, introduce or re-introduce some traditional Western classical music to expand their understanding of ballet and its historical relationship to music.

Suggestions for Developing Community

Rituals

Develop rituals: routines done on a daily, weekly, bi-weekly, or monthly basis. This will help to build a class culture and customs that include all members of the class. (See chapters 2 and 3 for more information on rituals in the dance classroom.) Some examples follow.

Salutation. Consider beginning class with a movement salutation, a greeting. This might be a 16-count port de bra sequence with a temps lié or demi-plié. A simple narration to the movement can be taught to connect to cultures that hold great value in storytelling. For example, "I pick up all the goodness I can gather for the day and spread it around the world." For this sequence I might begin, feet in first position, cambré forward, stand up, bringing arms to first position, tendue back, port de bra (carriage of the arms), around the body, bring arms up to high fifth position, open arms to second position, while closing legs back to first position.

Beginnings and endings. Punctuate the beginning and ending of classes with a communal movement/gesture, movement sequence, sound, song, saying, or affirmation. Selecting something that relates to students' culture or something they helped create can demonstrate to students the teacher's interest in "seeing them" within the curriculum and class structure.

Circles. This deconstructs traditional Western Dance Education structures. Teach students about the traditions of the circle "hoda" or "rueda" as used in cultures such as Brazilian capoeira, Cuban salsa casino, African dance, or Native American ceremonies. Use the structure of the circle to create your own class ritual. This could be an opening stretch, a cool down at the end of class, or a closing reverence.

Some ballet movements that can work well in a circle include tendue, rond de jambe, faille, glissade, passé, temps lié, plié (in any position), chassé (side), sauté, port de bras, and bourrée.

Movement sequences for children with a partner. Find a partner and create a shape with your partner (one person reaching into a high level shape and the other person reaching into a low level shape). This could be open creative time for students or reinforce port de bra shapes in the arms. Change partner and repeat. You could also do something as simple as take hands as a class in a circle, take a deep breath together (or several) and recite a daily affirmation.

Ballet combinations for any age. Give a name to certain exercises or patterns. Similar to "en croix" when an exercise is executed to the front, then side, then back, and finally to the side, when you create a new movement pattern give it a name like "Sand Dune" or "Tiger Taps." Sand Dune may be tendue four times to the front, three times to the back, two times to the side, one posse, plié and relevé. Give the students the opportunity to come up with the name of the pattern as a class. This becomes a system of communication exclusive to members in this class community; it builds affinity within the class. Its participants, in addition to traditional structures, inform this culture.

Language

Consider counting in your student's native language (when applicable). You can also learn some basic directional words to use in class with students. Allow students to teach you these words. This de-centers the power structure of class. It communicates that the students hold valuable information, worthy of the teachers' interest and use. My colleague used this strategy to engage Xhosa children in South Africa as they counted in Xhosa.

Age-Specific Content

Content for Any Age

Seek out culturally diverse versions of classical stories for your ballet classes/repertories; write culturally diverse stories for students to perform; allow students to write their own stories; or revise classic stories with twenty-first century characters. When students can see themselves in the content, they can invest in the work in a healthy and authentic manner.

When giving dance students a place to share stories, ballet class offers a unique opportunity to draw comparison. Allow students to tell their story with ballet vocabulary. One way to excite students about the content is to encourage them to direct an aspect of the content or to place themselves in it.

Expand your offerings for reading about and watching ballet. Below is a list of reading material that can widen the representation of dancers of color in ballet. There are also movies like *Mao's Last Dancer*, which chronicles the life of a young Chinese boy who is trained and groomed to become a ballet dancer, or documentaries like *I'll Make Me a World*, which shares firsthand accounts of Raven Wilkinson and Delores Browne, two of the first African American ballet dancers in the U.S. Sharing such texts with students can widen students' ideas of who gets to embody the ballet form. In addition, if you have students of color in your class, the images you share with them ideally will include people who share similar ethnic backgrounds.

Suggested Readings for Elementary School Ballet Students
- *Firebird* by Misty Copeland
- *Tallchief: America's Prima Ballerina* by Maria Tallchief

- *Who Is Maria Tallchief?* by Catherine Gourley
- *Maria Tallchief: The Story of an American Indiana* by Marion Gridley
- *Dancing in the Wings* by Debbie Allen
- *Sugar Plum Ballerinas* (series) by Whoopi Goldberg
- *The Barefoot Book of Ballet Stories* by Jane Yolen and Heiddi E. Y. Stemple (includes a story of a South Korean folktale, "Shim Chung: The Blind Man's Daughter")

Content for Middle or High School

Consider what books, videos, and music you are using in your class. Are you utilizing a diverse range of resources? For example, if teaching classical ballet *Creole Giselle* can be used instead of, or and in conjunction with *Giselle*. An excellent resource for Creole Giselle is Carrie Gaiser's "Caught Dancing: Hybridity, Stability, and Subversion in Dance Theatre of Harlem's Creole Giselle."[30] Gaiser examines issues of race, appropriation, cultural identity and binaries thereof. Another excellent selection for comparison and contrast of a traditional classical work is Rennie Harris's adaptation of *Romeo and Juliet* titled *Rome and Jewels.* Have students compare and contrast different versions so they are presented with multiple perspectives and interpretations. Obtaining alternative versions of classical dances on video is often a challenge. However, you can collect dance reviews from classical ballets and contemporary versions such as *Rome and Jewels,* which would provide students with primary sources from these performances to examine. Anna B. Scott has written an excellent analysis of the production in her essay "What's It Worth to Ya? An Adaptation and Anachronism."[31] Scott provides rich movement description, sequencing of the story, and insights into symbolism that are ripe for class discussions. Another approach would be to allow students to re-create a classic and have students compare and contrast the versions they created. When you feel restrained by limited resources, creating resources is always an option and it is also one way to ensure that what is created for your students will reflect your students' culture.

Suggested Readings for Middle or High School Ballet Students
- *Taking Flight: From War Orphan to Star Ballerina* by Michaela De Prince
- *Maria Tallchief: America's Prima Ballerina* by Larry Kaplan and Maria Tallchief
- *American Indian Ballerinas* by Lili C. Livingston

- *Life in Motion: An Unlikely Ballerina* by Misty Copeland
- *Mao's Last Dancer* (Young Reader's Edition) by Li Cunxin (movie also available)

These books are also ripe for cross-curricular projects with Social Studies and Language Arts.

Content for High School and College

Seminal texts for upper level students are "Digging the Africanist Presence in American Performance" by Brenda Dixon Gottschild and "An Anthropologist Looks at Ballet as a Form of Ethnic Dance" by Joann Kealiinohomoku. Gottschild's text explores the impact of the African aesthetic in American ballet. More specifically, Gottschild examines the work of George Balanchine as he was developing the ballet aesthetic for the New York City Ballet. At the time, he was in dialogue and collaboration with African American choreographers and dancers. As a result, he created an aesthetic that was influenced by African aesthetics.[32] Kealiinohomoku's work explores criteria for ethnic dance forms and argues for ballet to be embraced as an ethnic dance form. Both texts are excellent in offering students the opportunity to consider a different cultural perspective of ballet.

Suggested Readings for High School and College Ballet Students

- *Joan Myers Brown and the Audacious Hope of the Black Ballerina: A Biohistory of American Performance* Brenda Dixon Gottschild
- *The Black Dancing Body* Brenda Dixon Gottschild
- "Dance Narratives and Fantasies of Achievement" in *Meaning in Motion* by Angela McRobbie.
- *Mao's Last Dancer* (Young Reader's Edition) by Li Cunxin
- *Reworking the Ballet: Counter-Narratives and Alternative Bodies* by Vida L. Midgelow

Representation

Unfortunately, resources of Asians, Native Americans, and Latinos in ballet are scarce. I often go to the roster of ballet companies and can usually find several dancers of color. Currently, on the San Francisco Ballet website, Asian dancers Frances Chung and Yuan Yuan Tan can be found. In general a search of several company rosters can usually find a handful of dancers of color. These examples can offer students the opportunity to see themselves in a discipline that does not, by and large, feature dancers of color. You can also call attention to the lack of dancers of color in text form and send students out on a scavenger hunt. If you have a diverse class, and have a hard time finding examples of ballet dancers that look like your students, you may want to have students participate in their own photo shoot. Then you can use these photos to decorate the studio with dancers that look like the students you teach.

Research Projects and Other Assignments

The following suggestions could be developed into full units, research projects, or project-based learning assignments.

1. Examine the promotional photos of the most reputable ballet companies in the United States. Do these photos represent the diversity of the United States? Can this organization serve as a cultural ambassador of the United States? What values are being upheld, what stories are being told in these promotional images?

2. Compare and contrast DTH's *Creole Giselle* with the classical *Giselle*. Consider original choreography and restaging, adjustments to the story, costuming, and reviews from both productions.

3. Obtain the *New York Times* dance review, written by John Martin, of Rosella Hightower's 1947 performance in *Giselle*. Then locate supporting primary sources from the time to gain an understanding of the socio-political context.

4. Write a review of Misty Copeland's *Life in Motion: An Unlikely Ballerina*.

5. Write a critical response to Mike Larsen's "Flight in Spirit" mural. Describe the artwork; examine how issues of race, class, and gender are presented; and explain whose culture is being represented?

6. Read *Taking Flight: From War Orphan to Star Ballerina* by Michaela De Prince, write your own dance autobiography, and compare your autobiography in ballet to De Prince's.

7. Select a ballet dancer to research; write a biography of that person's experience in ballet.

8. Research the founding and closing of the American Negro Ballet Company from the 1930s. Locate primary sources about the company and its dancers and director.

9. Examine ballet dance in Cuba; training and performance experiences and opportunities, and the work of Alicia Alonso.
10. Explore ballet dance in South Korea. Identify the two major ballet companies. Examine how South Korean ballet repertories compare to American repertories?
11. Research dance reviews of Ballet Hispanico and create a theme around the company's artistic development since their founding in 1970.

Scavenger Hunt

An online scavenger hunt can be a great in-class project or a homework assignment. It is an excellent way to diversify curriculum, call students' attention to a lack of diversity in a given area, and develop students' research skills. Identify what you want students to learn and create a worksheet that will guide them through a mini-research assignment. These are best when created by the teacher to bring students into the content material being studied. I like to use them with students to get them excited at home about what we will learn in class the next day. Then students come to class with questions, ideas, and things to talk about—without using class time for viewing and online searches.

The following is a list of organizations and companies, most of which have online resources, that may help you create a scavenger hunt of your own:

- Stories of the Ages: Graceful Heritage—The Five Native American Ballerinas
- Black Ballerina Documentary
- Ballet Hispanico
- Joburg Ballet (South African ballet company which comprises a racially diverse company utilizing a number of Cuban born dancers of color)
- Universal Ballet (based in Seoul, Korea)
- Imperial Fernando Ballet Company (based in New Delhi, India)
- Ballet National de Cuba
- Dance Theatre of Harlem
- Ballethnic Dance Company
- The National Ballet of China
- The National Ballet of Japan
- The Tokyo Ballet

- Reiko Yamamoto Ballet
- Miyashita Ballet
- Matsuyama Ballet
- Black Ballet
- Cairo Opera Ballet Company
- Les Ballets Persans (formerly The Iranian National Ballet Company)
- Ballet Nacional do Brasil

Assessment Considerations

There are countless resources for diversifying academic work in reading and writing, which can be applied to dance. Similarly, composition work offers numerous opportunities for problem solving, and as such, does not have the challenges related to assessment for technique class. For these reasons this section will focus on the assessment of dance technique.

As discussed throughout this book, the dancing body is a conduit of its environment and culture. Each body in motion carries a movement history, physical actions that the body is familiar with as a result of repetition. Most fundamental to the movement history of most bodies is the action of walking. In terms of dance, each dancer holds a particular movement history and language. Educators should recognize that each student's ability to execute movement depends in part on the student's ability to learn, and apply information; but also previous movement history.

Assessment depends greatly on the teaching philosophies of the teacher and the educational institution. Thus, in this section many suggestions will be provided, yet each educator must consider what will work best for their students and school community.

Goals for Objectivity

Objectivity in assessment is a continued struggle for most educators. We try to create and utilize the best systems to be as objective and fair as possible. In artistry the challenge can be overwhelming as at times it seems impossible to tease out aesthetic values when evaluating movement. However, clarity and transparency in the teacher's desired outcomes is directly tied to the objectivity of the assessment process.

Use of Rubric

1. Create a rubric. List and describe five skills of which you want students to demonstrate competency or mastery.
2. Share the rubric with students well before the day of assessment so that they can come to the assessment prepared to succeed.
3. Give students the opportunity to ask questions about the rubric or get feedback on their execution of skills before the assessment. If you do not have time to give each student individual feedback, ask students to videotape each other and complete a pre-assessment self-assessment or peer-assessment. Students can complete a mock-assessment with self or peer assessment rubric to help prepare them for the class assessment.

Here is an example of a rubric for tendus. I selected an exercise that is used in Western dance forms because I want to demonstrate how a teacher can provide an objective assessment in a Western dance form, in which students of color have historically been less successful. This rubric is designed for beginner students, it intentionally does not account for quality of movement or ballet aesthetic, in terms of executed style.

1	Both the standing leg and the working leg are stretched throughout the exercise.	N
2	Turnout is maintained on both legs throughout the exercise.	C
3	Student articulates the foot, through the extension of the working leg, and when returning to the starting position.	P
4	The working leg returns to a first, third, or fifth position after each tendue.	P
5	Abdominals are engaged and lifted for the duration of the exercise.	C

This rubric could be scored with a "yes" or "no" at the end; a number, "1," "2," "3"; or other. Above I listed a letter (key below).

N—Needs improvement, skill not seen.
C—Competent, skill is present at a basic level.
P—Proficient, consistent mastery of the skill demonstrated.

How is this criteria less subjective to the instructor's personal aesthetic?

1. Student's quality of movement and personal aesthetic is not being evaluated.
2. Student's understanding of music is not being evaluated.
3. Students are given assessment tools in advance so that an assessment criterion is explicit and not structured around hidden rules or the instructor's aesthetic.

Another possibility is to create a rubric with students. This gets students invested in the evaluation and assessment process.

> *Students' ownership of their own learning is a wonderful lifelong value that you can instill and nurture.*

Conclusion

Diversifying any curriculum is a challenge, especially when it involves shifting historical information and ways of communicating information. Making content culturally relevant can be even more challenging, as it requires more specific attention to the cultures represented among students. Yet, just as all forms of dance relate to the human experience, if we as educators commit to the process, we can make any content culturally relevant to students. If we can change the way ballet is experienced in Dance Education, this could raise the glass ceiling in our society, in perception and experience.

Widening students' paradigm of who gets to perform ballet not only includes the many students who are otherwise excluded, it also expands possibilities to cross time-honored racial boundaries. When giving a lecture at a small private college in the Northeast on the scarcity of African American ballerinas, a student from Houston, Texas, treated my words with a great sense of curiosity. She listened to the stories of African American ballet dancers who had overcome racial barriers, but was perplexed by the idea. She had grown up visiting the Houston Ballet regularly. Lauren Anderson, the African American principal dancer there, had established a world of ballet that did not give reverence to racial margins. In this moment I saw the future. I saw what is possible when students are presented with a limitless construct of "who gets to dance." It is a gift with limitless possibilities. Educators cannot give students a world with no challenges, but we can certainly give them a classroom where they can flourish, with their culture acting as a bridge to success, instead of an obstacle to overcome. I challenge you to expand your students' possibilities in ballet through an approach that relates to their lives, cultures, and bodies.

Five

Culture, Music
and Composition Class

Dance composition speaks to the creative process integral to the art form. It is an expansive component of our national dance standards, most dance programs and departments in higher education. Just as culture informs all creativity and human understanding,[1] there are different cultural orientations to understand dance and choreography in different ways. For this reason it would be advantageous if dance composition courses explicitly identified the Western influences within which they were created, structured and taught. I advocate for a comprehensive framework of dance composition that explores compositional processes in multiple cultural contexts. However, when such explorations are outside the educational goals of the program, an honest acknowledgment of the Western compositional approach can carry great educational significance to students. Doing so recognizes that other approaches exist and are valid—that the way taught in this space is not the best or only way, it is simply one way.

Composition is part of long standing tradition in Dance Education. Alma Hawkins, Dance Education pioneer, was an advocate of dance as a creative practice. In Hawkin's 1964 book, *Creating Through Dance*, she describes the choreographic process, with particular focus on movement, and no mention of music. "Choreographing means more than assembling movements. The artist is concerned with what results from the organization of movement rather than with the mere arrangement. As a craftsman the dancer may construct a sequence of movements, but as an artist he creates an organic entity."[2]

Hawkins also established abstraction as an essential ingredient of dance composition.

Dance as a communicative art uses movement as its material, but the movement in dance is different from the everyday gesture in that it is distorted or removed from the natural and transformed into art. The creator strives to capture the essence of a particular sensory experience, and then, through a fresh and imaginative use of movement.... The experienced choreographer knows well that the magic of a highly abstracted work can be destroyed by the sudden appearance of a movement pattern that is closely associated with the everyday world.[3]

However, what Hawkins does not state is that values of abstraction and absence of music are culturally informed and not essential ingredients for creative artistry. It is simply one way to approach dance making. As we treasure the seminal work of foundational dance educators, I encourage an examination of the Western-centered approach in which the field of Dance Education has been entrenched. Dance educators need to recognize the possibility for multiple approaches, even within the context of a specific focus for a particular course.

CDP and Composition

My advocacy of critical dance pedagogy and culturally relevant teaching (CRT) in dance composition is not meant to be a call to overhaul curriculum of creative practice courses, but rather to inspire a pedagogical approach to bring students into the learning process. If students can relate course material to their culture and life, the learning experience will be more successful. CRT is not restrictive or limiting; it is *not* for teachers to say, "I can only teach my African American Students about African American dances." It is to help us be able to say, "No matter what content I am teaching, I will relate the content to my students." In learning situations where students have challenges relating to content, I draw attention to the differences, and ask students to enter into what may be a culturally contrasting learning experience. But I also acknowledge that what I am offering is different; not better, but rather simply another way to experience a dance making creative process.

I suggest that composition teachers should not only be sensitive to the personal nature of composition but also to the culturally-informed nature of the creative process. Consider the inscriptions of the body and how they interact within the context of a class where dance making is the objective. Inscriptions on the body cannot be denied. Lucia Matos, professor of music, explains: "It is through the body, with its specific cultural, physical, and historical marks, that identity is exposed and recognized (or not), and it is through this recognition that we perceive the limits distinguishing the subject, the world, and the other."[4]

The body is a descriptor. It reveals race, gender, age, culture, and class. The body can also expose one's addictions, vices, disabilities, and imperfections. People are aware of the social constructs perpetually in operation. Beyond body inscription, the moving body also has agency. The body may speak in ways that are outside its visible inscriptions. An acknowledgment of these descriptors is not an insult but rather a recognition of reality. With this understanding, I encourage teachers to shape composition courses through a lens that sees the body inclusive of its inscriptions as well as the story the moving body is telling.

The goal is student achievement, exploration, and growth. I advocate for critical examination of student objectives and culturally relevant teaching. This does not mean that students are not stretched or taken out of their comfort zone. It means that a safe place for learning is identified first and subsequently used as a launching pad for artistic discoveries.

Western-Based Structure of Composition Classes

My objective is to highlight the ways in which traditional composition classes are Western in structure, content, and values. With a critical dance pedagogy approach I begin with the title of the course, "Dance Composition." This title suggests a course that teaches how to make dances. The lack of specificity in the title, as to the approach, leaves questions. Is it a course that teaches how dances are made in all or many different cultures and contexts? If I have a composition student from China will her dance making approaches stemming from her culture be uplifted and validated? Will students from a competition dance culture feel affirmed in my composition course? Or is the course exclusively a "Western Dance Composition" course? If so, why not include "Western" in the title? A course that focuses on Asian or African culture will usually include that descriptive word in the title. Failure to include Western in the course title establishes a dominance of Western culture and suggests superiority. That is, Western, in essence, becomes the default, the standard. Why then is it not necessary within the context of a Western-influenced course?

No matter the name of the course, all dance composition courses are about creative practice. In fact, I often have been directed to the opportunities of self-expression for all through the improvisation and composition components of dance curricula when questioning the lack of diversity within dance curricula. It has been suggested to me that students are placed on a level playing field and offered genuine freedom of expression. Conversely, I have heard many dance students of color talk about how uncomfortable they are in improvisation and composition classes. There is a disconnect between the intent of these creative processes and how they are experienced. When students and teachers have different culturally informed ideas about movement and choreographic structures, the experience can create a clash of cultures. Typically in such cases the student is the one with the least power over the structure of the lessons and curriculum.

Creativity on Display—Vulnerability

A student's first composition course is a unique cultural experience in many ways. It is often the first time students have been asked to create and share a movement study and then receive public critique on their creative process. For many, publicly sharing the creative process is a foreign experience. The body, possibly the most personal aspect of the person (often an embodiment or expression of their ideas), is also on display in this new learning situation.

In studying the discipline of dance, students reveal their understanding of content in a personal, vulnerable way. The integration of physical and mental prowess and creative process is not displayed in any other art form or physical activity (i.e., sports). There tends to be a level of privacy when submitting a written paper, while struggles with the physical content (embodied or disembodied) particular to dance are open to public display. In composition, we "up the ante" from the traditional technique class where the body is the primary vehicle of cognitive expression. Students are asked to reveal their creative process which is to be evaluated on a standard designed by the instructor, often to take place with all students in the class aware and listening.

Music

This section focuses on how students relate to lyrics and the challenges students face when they do not have music to anchor their movement. Like other process-oriented courses, dance composition classes take many students out of their comfort zone. As a defined area of study these classes are designed to require more attention to the creative process than many students have previously encountered. For example, traditionally, composition classes are about problem solving. One of the first problems students encounter is to create with their body, and, at least temporarily, to sever ties to music. Often students resist not using music or using instrumental music. For many, this becomes a difficult obstacle to overcome. The challenge is even greater when considering that the educational process is not viewed as successful unless students' knowledge base has been expanded or reframed. Through such an assumption, student resistance in this area is seen as part of the learning process. However, for students who find creating movement in the absence of music or a rhythm to be a great challenge, recognition of this challenge, in a manner that affirms the knowledge students bring, can go a long way in putting them at ease.

Lyrics

Not surprisingly, the music most students relate to in their home or social lives is commercial music on the radio or accessed through the Internet. Whether it's pop, country, rap, or R&B there is usually one obvious commonality—lyrics. However, when students are inspired to delve into diverse forms of music they often find longer selections, complicated rhythmic scores, and diversity in phrasing within one piece of music. These aspects of non-commercial music can become a treasure to students once they are given the opportunity to explore and identify these attributes and how one might choreograph with them. Yet, in spite of these potential benefits, requests of separation from lyrics can be unsettling for students from cultures that embrace and find vitality in oral traditions of narration, storytelling, or an interdependent relationship between music and dance. For many, it is a conflicting paradigm and worldview to understand music and dance as separate.

Absence of Music

Of significance in understanding cultural relevance is the consideration of culturally informed relationships between dance and music. European art aesthetics are often experienced separately. Twenty-first century symphonies are presented in the absence of the dancing body, with the expectation that active listeners will refrain from explicit movement of the body. While dance within a contemporary Eurocentric context is often presented with music, music is not a requirement and its absence is transformative within the still practiced, post-modern genre. Many Eurocentric artistic contexts also feature distance (sometimes described as a fourth wall) between performers and audiences of music and dance.[5]

> *Consider that the relationship students have to music and dance is culturally informed and your requirement of augmenting this relationship may feel to students as a rejection their cultural orientation toward music and dance. In particular, if requirements to augment music are presented in a manner that suggests to students that the use of music or lyrics is sophomoric or unsophisticated (as this may be your culturally-informed perspective and aesthetic), it can be interpreted by students as a slight to their culture and their personal way of understanding music and dance.*

Kathak Informed Approach to Composition

For some cultures rhythm is integral to dance. It is an issue of cultural divide where movement invention and choreographic devices are concerned. Dances of the African diaspora are informed by rhythm produced by percussion. This stands in contrast to the widely accepted Western definition of dance that identifies time, space, and energy as the foundational elements of dance as an art form. Certainly there are many other definitions of dance, however, this one, referencing time, space, and energy, has been widely embraced by the field of concert dance in the United States. Within this framework, rhythm by way of percussion is not a required component of dance.

Similar to many African-derived dance forms, rhythm and storytelling are essential compositional components of Kathak, an Indian classical dance form popularized in the sixteenth century.[6] For the Kathak dancer there is no dancing without a rhythmic foundation. In an interview, Bagashree Vaze, a specialist in Kathak, noted that historically Kathak dancers were storytellers. The word Kathak comes from the word Katha, meaning "art of storytelling."[7] Today, this ancient cultural dance form is situated in the transcultural twenty-first century, global in nature due to the Internet and social media.[8] Still, when discussing choreographic devices, Vaze explained that Kathak dance is evaluated differently from Western or contemporary choreography.[9] Traditionally, trained Kathak dancers and musicians assess the relationship between the music and dance as non-negotiable. The dance stands on the music and the music speaks to the dance. In reference to assessment, she stated that "integrity of rhythmic composition is key in Kathak dance and execution of rhythm is essential."[10] However, she also recognized that in recent decades Kathak dance has been greatly influenced by Western contemporary dance forms as Western choreographic devices can be useful in Kathak, although criteria like "use of the stage," is not going to be purposeful without precision and accuracy (in terms of rhythm). In reflecting the choreographic processes of her teachers, Vaze recalled, "my teachers always began with music. Even if it began with an idea, like displacement, the first task would be to figure out the rhythmic language, then develop the movement from there."[11]

The choreographic process Vaze described centered upon storytelling and relationship to rhythmic accompaniment. While these components can be present in Western contemporary dance, they are not necessarily foundational essentials (i.e., the work of Merce Cunningham). In terms of criteria for successful artistic work, one can see where diverse and culturally informed ideas of quality work can develop contrasting evaluations of artistry. Vaze also explained that "even if people have really interesting ways of using the stage or different angles and that kind of thing in the choreography; its not going to mean anything if there's no precision and accuracy."[12] She also noted that production elements like costumes and lighting are great, but if the rhythmic execution is not precise, it is not valued within the form. Such culturally informed ideas of success in artistry pose a challenge not only to the creative process but also to assessment for dance educators, as discussed later in the chapter.

Africanist Informed Approach to Composition

Storytelling

Storytelling is used in many culturally-based dance forms. In African American artistic dance expression, it is a tenet, a cherished tradition that extends to music and dance. In many African traditional communities a "griot" storyteller and historian is a sacred and indispensable member of the community.[13] Stories that provide people with a voice gain cultural currency in communities where people are marginalized by the mainstream culture. Dance educators counter such marginalization when providing opportunities for students to nurture their unique cultural kinesthetic stories within their own choreographic processes. This can become an issue when following National Dance Standards or dance composition and choreography textbooks in regard to abstraction. At times, educators may choose to adjust and scaffold Dance Education objectives that focus on abstraction and allow space for students to create with the tools that reflect their identity.

In an interview, dance artist and scholar Kariamu Welsh identified storytelling as a choreographic device. She is drawn to create dance as a form of storytelling and artistic expression. For her, it is "not an option" to create in the abstract. She considers her work to be a voice of her people, community, and ancestry: "As an artist, I create in service to my community."[14] Her aesthetic often stands in contrast to her colleagues in academia, and has, at times, alienated her from her peers. Yet she is unable or unwilling to shed her culturally informed aesthetic. She saw that difference in aesthetic values between herself and her colleagues were often explored by proxy—through her students of color. Welsh noted times when she was called upon to explain or advocate for the composition work of students who would have otherwise been excluded by a Eurocentric aesthetic. She accepts the fact that to succeed in academia she has made many concessions. But conceding her artistic expression, which is intertwined with her cultural identity, was always a painful dilemma and motivated her advocacy on behalf of her students in similar positions.[15]

Interdependency of Music and Dance

Dance scholar Jacqui Malone has written about the function of music and dance in many traditional West and Central African countries as a lifeline and source of cultural vitality. She adamantly notes that "the close relationship between African musics and African dances is vital and cannot be overemphasized."[16] Many African Americans in the twenty-first century have retained these values. This knowledge contextualizes the hurdles some students face when separating music from dance or intertwining the two forms. This is not to suggest that educators should not expose students to a contrasting perspective of music and dance. Such differences can be used to teach students how to identify and appreciate the various characteristics and varieties. Nor should educators alter objectives to exclude developing new ways to approach creating dance—after all, what is learning about? Yet, in considering the magnitude of the challenge inherit in the task of creating dance to instrumental music, ambient sound, or silence, some educators may take these opportunities to encourage the artistic explorations of their students. Such educational endeavors can be pursued with a full understanding that students' culturally informed appreciation of lyrics, storytelling through movement, and interdependent relationships between music and dance are valid and substantive.

In a quest for cultural relevance for African American students, learning about Africanist approaches to dance composition is critical. Communities with ancestral ties to African culture have retained a number of African-derived dance traditions. By and large, within informal gatherings and events in the African American community, music is present and listened to with a physical response, be it small or large. This is in direct contrast to a European culturally informed formal structure where the audience is often expected to sit and listen without kinesthetic response. I compare an informal African American context to a formal European informed context because for students outside the dominant culture, this is often the context in which "high" Eurocentric and Western art is presented. For example, a common school experience is a field trip to the symphony.

> *There is a specific and culturally informed understanding of an inter-dependent relationship between music and dance.*

Within a composition framework, communities tied to African dance aesthetics demonstrate an affinity toward rhythmic frameworks in which to create dance. This does not mean that educators cannot teach students from such cultures to create to silence or ambient noise. Rather, when educators teach Western choreographic structures, it is possible to do so with the understanding that students may have other culturally informed strengths and preferences. Relevant pedagogical questions emerging from these ideas center upon how teachers can present compositional structures outside the cultural lens of students. The following suggestions offer several possibilities in sequential order:

1. Acknowledge students' artistic creativity as it is. Let them create in the way they want, with artistic freedom.
2. Affirm students' work, demonstrate to them the value in their work. Refrain from implicit or explicit messages that suggest or state choreographing to music is low level, low class, low art or sophomoric.
3. Find an aspect of students' work that you encourage them to carry over into the next assignment, which will utilize a Western choreographic structure.
4. Ask students to record the sounds in the neighborhood outside their house, at their church, or in their home, for one minute. Ask students to create a work to that soundscape. The accompaniment is inherently culturally relevant because students excavated the soundscape from their own environment.

There can be no question that dance and music within the African American community have a vital function. They are used as a lifeline that unites the community socially and spiritually. Dance is integrated into many general events within this community. As a result, many students from this cultural background, even outside formal dance training, experience a type of dance training within their community. These events range from block parties, weddings and graduations to informal evenings of card games. They are marked by the presence of music and dance and all present participate as a community. In addition, music and dance are also common components of African American churches (albeit some African America churches limit the dancing to a two-step). Unlike some cultures where the dancing body is deemed inappropriate in church, many African American churches delight in dance and view the body as a conduit to God.[17]

The African American cultural lens sees dance and music activities as a duel art form; music and dance go together. Separation is a more contemporary European construct of understanding music and dance. The differences between these two perspectives need to be understood if for no other reason than to ensure that the teaching of new perspectives does not value one over another.

Tongan Informed Approach to Composition

Adrienne Kaeppler's scholarship on dance ethnography, and in particular her work on culturally informed dance aesthetics, illuminates the nuanced creative practices maintained within a culture outside the dominant. Kaeppler's work is significantly pertinent to discussions of culturally relevant teaching in composition, as we are reminded that many people already possess a culturally informed system of creating and evaluating dance. She affirms that societies have "standards for production and performance of cultural forms."[18] Kaeppler writes about the qualifications of evaluations of cultural forms: "An individual cannot be said to understand the aesthetic principles of another society unless he or she can anticipate indigenous evaluations of artistic performances or products. To do this one must be aware of the essential criteria for forming judgments."[19] In addition, Kaeppler's scholarship can be a valuable resource for a dance educator seeking to diversify a composition course. Her work demonstrates how one can come to learn and understand the cultural aesthetics and criteria for artistic success within the context of another culture. Her research frames the problem encountered by students from outside the dominant culture when adhering to the aesthetic criterion of their native culture. Such students inherently need explicit education on the aesthetics and criteria for success within the dominant culture—if that is the system in which they will need to achieve in order to succeed in the educational setting where they are placed. Finally, Kaeppler's work can teach students that there are valid and functioning systems of assessment outside the dominant culture.

Kaeppler's research on Tongan dance includes an examination of this community's aesthetic criteria. She provides context for the movement and explains the evaluation system. Her discussion includes the structural form of Tongan dance as well as the language used to assess this art form. Reflecting how Kaeppler aligns movement context with assessment, consider the following:

1. What is the meaning and context for movement within this dance aesthetic?
2. Do students know which choreographic devices add value to this aesthetic, and how to use those devices?
3. How is this dance form impacted by using different choreographic devices and applying different values? For example, could a student who studied Flamenco dance succeed in a composition course that taught Western choreographic devices?
4. Might assessment criteria like "use of stage" de-center the rhythmic work of the performer?
5. Would success through a Western lens cause the work to fail if seen through the lens of the dance form's native culture?

While there are many possibilities of how the above questions can be answered, the dialogue is worth exploring. Reflections can help to widen student perspectives and prevent homogenized thoughts of choreographic values.

Culture Clash

Music is a significant cultural marker for many communities. Many people feel instantly culturally connected or alienated by the sound of a piece of music. Thus, music can be a significant factor in making classroom instruction more culturally relevant or less. The following are two instances of culture clash in the dance composition classroom.

While issues of cultural sensitivity can arise in any class, composition class is a common place of culture clash. The first incident is told through the perspective of an MFA student at Temple University who describes a discriminatory experience in a composition class. In most composition classes, each student's culturally informed aesthetic is displayed and evaluated. An international student from the Bahamas had this to say about an experience in composition class:

> To give my experience, in one of my classes that I had to choreograph for, I had a Jamaican artist, and she was speaking about poverty and fatherless sons and stuff like that. But, because they speak Patois (Jamaican dialect), the accent is really thick. So I got a lot of flack for that. But I feel like when people use Indian music or Spanish music or music that is not English there's no problem. They use music with chirping bird sounds and horse noises and it's no problem. So sometimes I feel like when ethnic music or music [by a person] of color is used, it poses a problem.[20]

The second incident is told through the lens of the instructor, a white, middle-class man. He describes an incident that occurred in a choreography course at a small private liberal arts college.

> I teach an introductory choreography course which is designed for non-dance majors and which treats dance as an art-making activity in the Euro–North American modern dance (concert dance) tradition. One semester, during the first week of classes, a young African American Muslim woman attended class with her body draped and wearing socks—choices that run counter to the tradition in which the course operates. In a private meeting I assured her that I had utmost respect for her to continue in the course in a way that was comfortable for her, but also suggested that the reason for taking college courses is to acquire new experience, some of which may run counter to our own habits and beliefs. I said that to submit to the authority of a discipline or even an individual teacher should be undertaken skeptically, but with a full commitment to a temporary suspension of the student's preferences and habits of mind. This was a relaxed amiable conversation, and the student continued in the class with her body and feet covered, but in a spirit of energetic engagement.
> Later in the semester, students were asked to perform a short solo movement study, which we viewed to the accompaniment of randomized and wildly varied sounds (including, among others the sound of power tools, an Alan Ginsburg poem, an Edith Piaf song, the sound of a thunderstorm, and a radio comedy sketch). We looked at each solo more than once and with different accompaniment, to see the potential for sound to over-determine meaning—to support or undermine choreographic intent—or reveal qualities not previously apparent. The student in question performed a lovely contemplative study, first to a drum score, and second to a 50s-era television commercial for Scott paper napkins. Soon after, I learned that the student was incensed and humiliated by performing her dance to the napkin ad, and particularly by my comment that the sound seemed to place her in a domestic setting and that her previously beautiful, rounded, abstract movements might now suggest household tasks. Of course, the point of the exercise was exactly to demonstrate how something beautiful might be trivialized, but she complained to me bitterly (in private) that my comments reflected a stereotype about Muslim women being suppressed, oppressed, and limited to domestic activity. I, on the other hand, thought I was teaching about the aesthetics of collage.

I know that there was good intent on the instructor's part to provide this student with an informative learning experience. Similarly, I am certain that this student was participating in this course with the desire to learn. Yet, in the midst of good intent, there was an injured party. Many dance educators whose purpose for teaching is altruistic are not sensitive to the ways in which students from outside the dominant culture experience traditional dance pedagogy. Within the context of a culturally relevant and responsive composition class, students and teachers would examine music and movement choices in a manner that would consider the Western lens through which they are looking. The incident calls attention to the need to have open dialogues about race, class, gender, and religion as a proactive as opposed to reactive practice. Educators can tell students, at the beginning of the course, that they understand that social constructs are operating in the space and provide students opportunities to process class experiences that may otherwise impede student learning.

Creative Expression and Responsibility

Kariamu Welsh notes the social responsibility she feels to create work that is socially relevant not only to herself but also to the African American community. The content of her creative expression must always speak to her community in some way.[21] This ethos is in line with a history of the arts in the black community. For instance, the 1960s Black Arts Movement was centered on the creation and expression of socially conscious African American art work. "The Black Arts Movement is radically opposed to any concept of the artist that alienates him from his community. Black Art is the aesthetic and spiritual sister of the Black Power concept. As such, it envisions an art that speaks directly to the needs and aspirations of Black America. In order to perform this task, the Black Arts Movement proposes a radical reordering of the Western cultural aesthetic."[22]

Providing students the opportunity to create socially relevant work can inspire their artistry and fulfill a social responsibility that instills pride. For communities with an aesthetic that embraces resistance, culturally relevant teaching is a necessity for academic success. However, this calls for both students and teachers to resist the dominant culture in some way or another. Educators teaching dance from a Western perspective and embracing a Western aesthetic should understand the implications of such a paradigm. If students are connected to a culture that is motivated by artistic expression that resists assimilation (i.e., Native Americans, African Americans, and

Latinos), it is crucial that great cultural sensitivity is used in the evaluation of student work as students' idea of creative success may differ from that of the instructor.

Improvisation

Improvisation, often a component of composition, is also a process-oriented component of dance studies that is, like most movement practices, culturally informed. Creating movement in the moment is a convention within many cultures, yet how this process is cultivated varies greatly from culture to culture. Within the African American community improvisation is entrenched and experienced as a retention of West African dance.[23] Within the Africanist aesthetic, improvisation most often is a physical interpretation or interplay with a rhythm or music. Music is an integral part of the improvisational process and in the case of live music kinesthetic inspiration guides an interdependent creation.

Within an Africanist context, improvisation is a communal experience wherein lines between performer and audience are explicitly blurred for the enjoyment of the community. Movement, even when being improvised, is shared and developed as an interactive device. This is in contrast to a Western approach to improvisation that focuses on the movement invention of an individual and encourages an introspective physical experience. Also of importance is the hierarchy of Eurocentric dance aesthetics, which extends to improvisation—usually given preference in a Dance Education context. This means students who improvise within a Eurocentric aesthetic, reflecting the dominant culture, tend to receive more praise and affirmation.

Prompts for Student/Teacher Discovery

Within the framework of culturally relevant and responsive teaching for dance, explore your students' culturally informed relationship to movement, music, and their body. Provide students with three prompts. Let students experience each prompt for several minutes. As they respond to the various prompts, take notice of their comfort and level of engagement with each.

1. "In silence, improvise around the room, feel your body moving through space." You may want to give students an image to work with, maybe they are a feather or water.

2. With a steady percussion background playing, ask students to "create movement that travels for 8 counts, then create stationary movement for 8 counts that can be repeated."

3. Ask students to "move around the room and connect to other students—connections can be visual (eye contact) or physical."

After students participate in all three prompts discuss or ask them to write a response to each experience.

Prompts to help them in their reflections could include: What did you experience? Explain a challenge you experienced? Describe a connection that you made. When did you feel most comfortable? When did you feel the least comfortable? Through this process you can learn about students' relationship to movement and rhythm—which by and large is culturally informed. You have information about students' comfort zones and stretch zones. This provides you with resources to develop future lessons and units.

Before students enter into a discussion on a movement assignment, request that students begin by explaining their position. Students can share their previous knowledge of the content being discussed and how and why they relate to the material or have little relationship to the material. This practice gets students in the habit of situating themselves in the context. They then have the opportunity to acknowledge biases and disparities in their own experiences as well as others and develop a better understanding of how peoples' ideas are informed.

Assessment—Shredding Teacher Affinities

With subconscious and conscious affinities and cultural informants at play in the classroom, how can teachers shed their personal "tastes" and assess students' work product? The stakes are high, when often synonymous with students' work are their personhood, bodies, and creative ideas. In dance composition classes, teachers must objectively assess that which is subjective—creativity and artistic expression. One composition teacher said to me, "How do I grade someone's soul?" in reference to the intimate work produced in class. I have found that the best assessment tool with which to give transparent and objective feedback is a rubric. Many educators agree that using rubrics can facilitate assessing students without factoring in the instructors' likes and dislikes. Rubrics come in countless formats. A sample 5-point rubric appears below.

(One point possible for each category.)

The work contained the following:	Yes	No
1) Beginning and end (thoughtful entry into and out of the choreographic study—not flat)	✓	
2) Use of stillness	✓	
3) Use of repetition	✓	
4) Gestural phrase	✓	
5) Use of space (utilized a minimum of three areas of the stage)	✓	
Total score for the study	5	

The choreographic devices listed in the sample rubric above pertain to structure. However, one can create a rubric for any skill you plan to assess. I encourage you to utilize the above sample as you like, feel free to adjust and augment criteria to meet your course objectives. Sometimes my rubrics include demonstration of variation in use of time, other times I focus on shapes (curved or angular). When teaching about space, I create five criteria related to space. For example, stationary movement, locomotive movement, levels, a floor pattern, and expanding and shrinking in the space.

The devices are culturally informed and may or may not align with a student's culture. I identify these devices as culturally informed because within some dance cultures they are identified as valuable components of choreography and in other cultures they are not—it depends on the aesthetic values of the culture. However, if students are given the rubric before the composition assignment they will not be knocked down by an assessment that is in any way obscure. Second, one can add or take out criteria based on the specific cultural needs of your students. For example, if I had Tongan students, or students from the Pacific Islands, I might want to include some culturally informed criteria such as use of poetry or presentation of the dance in a manner where meaning unfolds.[24] Third, I recognize that a gestural phrase from a hip hop dancer will look different than a gestural phrase from a contemporary dancer. Within this particular rubric assessment system, I will not assess the quality of the gestural phrase or in any way include my opinion of it. If a gestural phrase is present, regardless of the aesthetic in which it is crafted and performed, it will receive equal credit.

If students have an understanding of specific choreographic devices, and demonstrate knowledge of how to use these devices, a teacher can objectively assess their use without factoring one's own aesthetic preferences. Moreover, students are most successful when rubrics are shared with them early on in their learning experience. This way they can develop concrete objectives for the work from the beginning of the process.

Many dancers and dance makers learn how to give feedback and support other members of their dance community in their dance composition class. One approach is to use a feedback process protocol. Liz Lerman and John Borstel developed a protocol that is widely used for choreographic feedback that seeks to create space for formative feedback. It begins with statements of meaning, wherein readers of the text (composed dance study) state what was meaningful about what they have witnessed. Second, the artist is given space to ask questions to the audience about how their work was experienced. Third, responders are given an opportunity to ask neutral questions. For instance, instead of asking, "Why did you choose a red costume," which has an opinion embedded in the question, a responder might ask, "What led you to your choice of costume?" The protocol ends with "Opinion Time," a space offered to share opinions if and only if the choreographer wishes to hear an opinion. For example, "I have an opinion about _____, would you like to hear it?"[25] More information on the Liz Lerman Critical Response Process (CRP) can be found through her website or book *Critical Response Process*.[26]

Conclusion

Like culturally informed physical practices, people have culturally informed *creative* practices. Dance educators of dance composition courses where students develop dance studies as well as dance improvisation courses where students develop movement invention skills may want to consider cultural relevance in lesson plans. An exploration of culturally diverse approaches to dance composition can provide students with a wider range of compositional tools. In addition, students can develop a greater understanding for aesthetic values of other dance forms and a broader perspective from which to differentiate their own aesthetic—less homogenized ideas of dance.

Ultimately, I have experienced more success when I focus on course goals during the planning stage. I consider ways in which I might diversify course content to meet the needs of my students. This could mean that I will invite students to learn or consider a variety of ways to compose a dance. However, if I am teaching a Western dance composition course, my approach is different. I consider how I will relate course material to students in order to maximize student cognition and achievement. In these instances I may use cultural referents from the student's culture, while I maintain course objectives aligned with Western-informed choreographic tools. If the course is Western-based, I am careful to clarify this in the course title, description, and syllabus. Without such explicit statements, students may misinterpret my actions as a statement that the techniques I teach are the only ones of significance within an educational context.

Finally, I consider assessment processes that are designed to be as objective as possible. Often students appreciate an explicit acknowledgment that composition assessment, void of cultural or aesthetic bias, is challenging to provide. To be sure, dance composition is about creative activity. Focus on the learning objectives. Student potential can be maximized when students are able to utilize their cultural knowledge as a springboard for learning and creating.

Additional Suggestions for the Composition Teacher

Educators can scaffold beginning compositional experiences and support students through the learning process. To do so, Western compositional devices should be presented as tools to be explored rather than standards to which *all* dance is measured.

Below are several pedagogical points I use to facilitate my teaching:
1. *Encourage students to investigate multiple definitions of dance. Do not limit the definition of dance to only that which comprises Western dance aesthetics.*
2. *Challenge students to find ways to tell stories with their bodies without musical support.*
3. *Give examples of the kind of work you want to see students produce (i.e., abstract or without music) ideally, with a dance artist with whom students can identify.*
4. *Be aware that student resistance to this dance aesthetic is not simply stubbornness.*
5. *Be open to the idea that the student's way into movement may be through music and they may need not only to be open but also to approach movement with a new orientation.*
6. *If your course will focus solely on Western-based choreographic devices, state that upfront in the course title and syllabus.*

Six

Critical Dance Pedagogy for Repertory

Two Case Studies

BY SELENE CARTER
AND NYAMA MCCARTHY-BROWN

This chapter is coauthored by Selene Carter and Nyama McCarthy-Brown, the instructors of record for the two repertory courses at Indiana University wherein this research was conducted. The research, presented as case studies, is designed to support dance educators with resources to approach repertory coursework through critical dance pedagogy (CDP). This process can provide teachers exploring socio-political or socially sensitive issues through dance. Data was extrapolated from instructor methodologies and reflections, interviews with students, and audience responses.[1]

We created two distinct socially conscious choreographic works designed to widen acceptance for both spectators and performers in our communities who are otherwise often excluded or marginalized. The completed works were performed in the annual faculty spring dance concert in 2015. This chapter is divided into two parts, as McCarthy-Brown presents her research and process in creating *Wanted* and Carter shares research from her creative work *Tektonika Ondine*.[2]

Critical dance pedagogy asks questions about power structures and our personal biases. CDP seeks to find out who is disempowered within a space and seeks to understand their lived experience, with the belief that all people can grow from understanding the experiences of those marginalized. "Critical Pedagogy gives us the courage to say what we have lived ...

(and) challenges us to question our long-held assumptions."[3] This chapter provides teachers with insight on how controversial and socially charged issues within the dance classroom can be approached.

First, as co-authors, we will be transparent in saying that these dialogues are not easy to begin. Each time we enter the classroom with topics of race, class, gender, or physical difference in the lesson plan, we feel nervous, concerned, and full of hope that the work we are entering will succeed in contributing to students' educational process. Fear and hesitation are present because we know that students may not want to engage in challenging dialogue. In claiming these emotions, we understand why many educators do not engage in this dialogic space. We share our findings in hopes that teachers will be motivated by our experiences and engage dance students through critical dance pedagogy.

We come to critical dance pedagogy with similar ideas about politics in education. We are women, dancers, artists, dance educators, and mothers interested in politics on the most basic terms—who gets what resources, when, why, and how? We recognize that true political dialogue (and true human understanding) cannot take place without considerations of race, class, gender, and physical abilities. In the past, we believed that it was the responsibility of educators to keep the classroom as free of politics as possible so that the focus of learning is not muddled or interrupted by politics. Yet we saw politics at play in our classrooms on a daily basis as extensions of our larger society. Over time we realized that by not addressing the politics of our society, communities, schools, and classrooms, we were making a political decision to protect and uphold these politics. In different locations and times in our careers as educators, we were introduced to the work of critical pedagogy and feminist theorists.[4] Among these theorists are Lisa Scherff and Karen Spector, who wrote, "Educators who claim to be neutral by avoiding controversial topics or simply transmitting objective information do, in fact, support the status quo and legitimize the tacit assumptions of dominant society."[5] As we engaged more with Paulo Freire's *Pedagogy of the Oppressed* and critical pedagogy theory we came to understand that all education (dance included) is political whether we are talking about it or not.

Context of Students and Setting

The demographics of the students was relevant, especially in light of the subjects we were entering. For McCarthy-Brown working in the subject of race, of note is that the universities she created the work in were majority white, with 4 percent people of color. For Carter questioning difference and ability, it is significant to highlight that in her college dance program historically, the repertory and guest artist works featured students with European dance training and normative bodies and abilities.

Case Study for *Wanted*, Choreographed by Nyama McCarthy-Brown

My impetus for creating *Wanted* is multifaceted and has a great deal to do with who I am. I began taking dance lessons at the age of six. In college, I studied political science, and I joined a two-year teacher's corps immediately after graduation. I have found that my interest in social justice and the dancing body are intertwined in ways that I have been unable and unwilling to detangle.

Before I entered the creative process with my students at IU, I had to overcome my fears of being stereotyped. I was concerned about bringing up the issue of race. As an African American woman, I did not want to be perceived as the "angry black woman" or the "race lady" making everything about race—I did not want to be "read." I served predominately white students. I did not want to make them feel persecuted in their learning space, I did not want them to feel bad or guilty about white privilege or the hegemonic white supremacy infrastructure of our nation and discipline. However, I realized that I had to be who I am, and I am a person who questions power structures and relationships. I had to trust that my students would simply see me, an authentic person.

My black *and* white students deserve an unapologetic model of a black person leading a class. Students, within the context of a critical dance pedagogical approach, have to make sense of institutions of racism and white privilege and how they will relate to those structures. I believe that we all should live in acknowledgment of the social constructs and systems that have large implications on our experiences in the world. Oppressive systems cannot be dismantled if they cannot be seen (one reason I disagree with colorblind pedagogies). With this understanding, I made the choice to address the social issues that we all experience, whether in the conscious or unconscious realm, in all of my dance classrooms.

The dance I created with students, *Wanted*, reflects our American culture. There are countless ways to look at American culture and an abundance of sub-cultures in the United States. I acknowledge that the work is one reflection of our culture in a world of multiple truths. *Wanted* focuses a light on issues of race in the United States with an emphasis on the stereotype of black men as being criminal, aggressive, and threatening.

During my early discussions with students, it was imperative to acknowledge existent stereotypes; accept a diverse range of experiences and personal realities; and create awareness of other people's truths. The dance told the story of a segment of our population that is often marginalized and vilified. It was not the personal story of everyone in the class. Most of the students in the class knew very little about the topic of race. We entered into each discussion as a sharing of viewpoints and experiences and with a willingness to accept the experiences of others, even when such experiences did not seem possible.

Choreographic Process

Classes began in the fall of 2014. This was shortly after Michael Brown was killed in Ferguson, Missouri, and Erick Garner in Staten Island, New York—there was a mix of students familiar and unfamiliar with these events. On the first day of rehearsal, students sat in a circle on the floor of the dance studio and I explained to them that we would develop a piece focused on race relations and black men being seen as threatening figures in society. All the students nodded and leaned in with interest. No one displayed signs of disapproval or discontent. I opened a dialogue about race. I required students to go find evidence of the status of racism in the United States today. This was a critical first assignment. I wanted to present the topic to students, but I did not want to dictate how they would relate to the topic. I was open to shifting the work to reflect their ideas. I said, "If you believe we live in a post-race society, go find evidence to support that argument. If you believe we live in a racist society, go find evidence to support that argument. If you believe we, as a society, fall somewhere in between, go find evidence to support that argument." I wanted to give students the opportunity to present what *they* deemed important, and I wanted to provide space for students' ideas that were not shaped by my experiences and research. Questions were encouraged as students sought to develop their own understanding of the data presented. I gave the students permission to change their minds and to be uncertain.

During our initial conversation, many students said there was no racism in their community or they never thought about race. Some students shared that they had seen instances of racism once or twice and felt that racism was bad. Discomfort was apparent at times, with long pauses, sometimes silence, and the numerous predictable, politically correct responses.

Statements like "Racism is wrong" seemed to be the standard position that all participants felt safe to vocalize throughout the dialogue.

In order to ground the piece in a discourse, we had numerous early discussions on race relations in the United States. For the next two weeks, we began or ended each rehearsal with a dialogue, presentation of student research, or videos about race, often with the focus of black male stereotypes. I let students know that how they felt about race relations was not as important to me as the fact that they were actively listening to other perspectives, sharing their own, and focusing on the development of their own feelings and ideas. Understanding social constructs is an ongoing, multi-faceted process which is informed largely by personal experiences that vary greatly from person to person. In addition, our understanding is evolving with the times and our personal growth. My goal for students was not that everyone reach the same destination, but that everyone find their place on a path to deeper understanding. With each source presented students were asked to consider the vantage point of all of the subjects including the author/videographer.

The use of video as a research tool was of concern for me. I did not want to use valuable rehearsal time to watch videos. However, I knew that it was essential for students to engage with visual research data on race in the United States. So I shared the documentary *The Hunted and the Hated: An Inside Look at NYPDs Stop-and-Frisk Policy* during the first week of rehearsals, after which students were able to discuss and process the information together. I tabled additional videos until later in the rehearsal process. Some of the other videos I wanted students to watch and consider were graphic and I did not want to force students to watch. So I emailed video links and encouraged students to watch on their own. I let them know the videos were graphic and gave them the option to watch the videos in private or not watch at all. As the choreography developed, we danced more and discussed less. This occurred with the hope that the class had done the foundational research and processing to carry them through the rehearsal process.

During the rehearsal process students were given compositional prompts to develop movement aligned with the theme. I gave the students opportunities to embody their research and interpret the research material they chose. Here are some examples:

- Create a short phase around an image or idea of fight.
- Create a short phrase around an image or idea of flight.
- Create a short phrase around an image or idea of fear.
- Create a short phrase around an image or idea of escape.

Here are some sample scores.

- Pull
- Under
- Go through
- Push
- Fall
- Roll
- Jump
- Stand
- Rebound
- Twist
- Grab
- Arrest
- Jump
- Kick
- Stand
- Grab

A good number of the movement phrases that students created through this process were included in the final work. The research students conducted and conversations they had in class were integral to the development and performance of the phrase work. In addition, it was one way in which students stayed connected to CDP and questions of power.

Qualitative Data Student Responses

In the spring of 2015, five students from Bowdoin College, site of the original performance, and nine students from Indiana University were interviewed. Because I utilized similar choreographic processes with both casts, I interviewed students from both schools. The demographics from the sample were as follows: three African American men, three African American women, two Asian women, and six white women. After analysis of the data two themes emerged: initial responses, comfort and discomfort; and the choreographic process, relevance and awareness. I also present data that relates to my concerns that the material would be emotionally upsetting for students.

Initial Response to the Concept—Comfort/Discomfort

When I asked cast members what their first impressions were when they learned that they would be performing in a socio-political work about race relations in the United States, there was a mixed response. All of the African American women and one African American man responded that they were glad to see this type of work being done in school. One said, "I was excited to be in the piece, because its not everyday you do a piece that is so specifically relevant to what's going on currently in the world.... I was just tired of doing nice pretty safe dances. So it was nice to do something that actually meant something." Another stated, "I thought it [the piece] was a good step forward for the program." One of the African American men stated he thought it was positive, but was concerned that the lead faculty in the department would not find it acceptable. "I wondered what [name of director of the program] would think? Are they going to let her [McCarthy-Brown] do a piece about what's going on within the black community?"

The concerns of this young black male relate to the scholarship of sociologist Charles Mills in "The Racial Contract." Mills argues that African Americans are hyper aware of the implicit rules and guidelines set up to suppress and oppress them.[6] This student's response highlights the marginalized and silenced experience of African American men placed on stage to dance out the stories of others. Thus, clear messages have been communicated that his story is not valued or to be acknowledged within this performance space or his educational setting. His reference to "they" ("are *they* going to let...") demonstrates full understanding of the power structure and his position within it. There is agency in whose stories are told and whose work is presented on the stage. This student went on to state, "I thought it's a good idea to bring to the university, so that people would be aware of like, 'What's going on.'" This student's response goes to the heart of this piece. Through this CDP approach, students questioned power structures in education and sought to destabilize all the forms of cultural domination—including telling the story of students who are otherwise invisible.

One student interviewed stated that he was not initially excited about the work. He was an African American male who intentionally did not engage politically, as a coping mechanism, in navigating his space in a predominately white institution.

> I think in the beginning because it was so recent [referring to Trayvon Martin] I thought this will be emotional for me, especially as a black male. I did still want to do it. But, there was a part of me said, I don't know if this is a good role for me. Because, I usually try to steer away from being too political, I don't want to be on one side of a controversial issue. Some people just can't understand where the other person is coming from, because people aren't even listening—sometimes. It seems like sometimes people take positions on things and no one gets anywhere. So for me it was like, oh,

I'm in this class, so ... I guess I'm taking a stand on this. I didn't want to take a stand at first. But, after the fact, I was glad I did.

The two Asian students interviewed said they were initially interested in and excited about the work. Four of the six white women mentioned being "nervous" or "uncomfortable." Some of their responses are as follows:

I was a little uncomfortable, just by the nature of being a white person learning what it was about. I questioned whether I had validity to perform, just because I had never experienced, even remotely, anything like what we were talking about. I thought, it was a racially mixed class, but I am one of those white people who were just kind of there, so I definitely at the beginning of the process questioned my validity in performing it.

I was really unsure in the beginning, I was really nervous. I was worried mostly because it was a delicate issue and there were students of another race in the piece and they might think that I was speaking about something that I didn't actually know about. There were moments when I thought, "who am I to be dancing this piece and making a statement about this stuff when like I've never experienced racial issues?"

The concerns of these students were soon dampened by the energy of the African American students. Two African American students shared how important having a racially diverse cast was. One stated: "It was important that the cast was mixed. It was important that everyone was fighting this issue together, instead of we're fighting this issue by ourselves. Everyone was included in this problem, its not just a black problem." The other two white women interviewed shared positive initial impressions of being a part of this piece. Three dancers noted having an interest in learning how to convey a political message through dance. Two dancers appreciated an opportunity to learn more about what was going on in current events that they had neglected to stay connected to the world in the midst of their consuming college experience.

Response to the Choreographic Process—Relevance and Awareness

This section presents the data collected around how the socio-political context was presented and handled throughout the choreographic process.

All cast members said that they had a positive experience engaging in research and discussions throughout the choreographic experience. Twelve out of fourteen students stated that they wished that we had had more ongoing conversations. They noted that once the cast got immersed in movement phrases, the intent of the piece became distant. Respondents identified video viewing, articles, guest speakers (sharing firsthand experiences, particularly beneficial for non–African American cast members), and class discussions as valuable sources of information. Most students noted that the most valuable component to them was hearing other students' perspectives and experiences. Students also appreciated the opportunity to conduct independent research. One student stated:

> We had to bring stuff in, we had to know something about the topic in order to continue, and to know what we were dancing about. I thought this was important. Bringing things in made it open to what *we* found and what caught *our* eye. I don't think [the choreographer] giving it to us would have been beneficial. I like that we had to research and we chose what our experience was for ourselves.

While all students shared that the discussions were valuable, the African American students shared that the topic was something they were well aware of, and did not feel they gained new information from it. They were, however, glad that their experiences were being included in the course content and CDP process. I believe this is significant since students outside the dominant culture spend a great deal of time immersed in educational content focused on the dominant culture. All of the non–African American students shared that they learned during this process, some more than others. One student said:

> It was interesting because we would have discussions about Indiana being considered a racist state. I've lived in Indiana my whole life. And I grew up in Marion, Indiana, where the last lynching was. But I have never felt like I lived in a place where there was racism. And I don't know if that's because of the way that I was raised, or the communities I've been in, or how I've always had friends of multiple races and never really thought of them as any different. That's just me as a person, being oblivious to people who are not like me.
>
> It was shocking, it was unexpected. I didn't think that people still thought that way. Not having been affected by it, made me, like, "Wait, aren't we in 2014?" I was like confused.

This student felt that she gained an understanding of other experiences within her community.

Most students also noted that video viewing done on their own was not as effective as when done in-class.

> I think it would have been better to watch the videos as a class. So that that class could immediately react with each other, I think that might have been a nice bonding kind of thing. Because if someone had some kind of dissenting opinion right then and there, I think it could have been a cool forum to share. And, at that point in the process it wasn't like we were going to shun the person who didn't agree with us. I think we were already in this process together.
>
> I liked watching things as a unit better, because then we could have discussion after instead of like watching it on my own and then like having to recall feedback later. I had difficulties with that. Because I would watch a video, and be really affected and

then like two days later I no longer had the feelings or words to talk about it when we talked in class.

I asked students if the work was relevant to their lives. I expected the African American males to say yes. But I was interested in the response of other students. To my surprise, all students said yes. Many students felt distance between their reality and the stereotypical black male experience. However, all students felt that as members of society, the stereotypes that permeate our culture were relevant to them as citizens. One student said, "Yes, I'm an American too." Other responses included the following.

> I don't think it [race in the U.S.] could not be relevant to me in any way. The moment it hit home was when you gave Bryan [the lead] the black Bowdoin sweatshirt to wear for the final stanzas of the piece and related it directly to our community, as opposed to just America. Because branding something like that brought it to myself as my own self. I try to be as conscientious as possible, and the way I came out of it was that I need to be more conscientious about the dynamics that happen at Bowdoin and in the least be more aware of them. And going forward maybe try and do something constructive to make sure that micro-aggressions or weird dynamics that happen because of race don't happen or at least promoting conscientiousness among my classmates.

> Actually since being in the piece and throughout the process of the piece I've kind of been a lot more aware of the issues because I did feel a personal connection. I now feel some sort of mental pull toward these issues because I did participate in a piece that was about this for a semester. But, beforehand I would have said, "No," not really [issues of race were not relevant to me before].

Finally, one student said,

> I'm an African American woman, and race politics in the United States are important to me. But, when we talked about Trayvon Martin and his family it was far from my reality. It also signaled to me my privilege and I appreciated being able to acknowledge that.

Through this process, students were able to understand their identity and experience in the world better as they contrasted it to individuals researched in their projects. They also gained an understanding of their connection to others and their own participation in societal structures.

Emotional Drain?

I asked students if the rehearsal process or act of performing was ever emotionally draining or upsetting. The almost unanimous response was that it was not. Two students noted being emotional during the performance once they saw all the theatrical elements pulled together and heard audience responses; the work spoke to them. The most common emotion reported by students was pride.

Students were asked to describe the experience with one word. I heard "shocking, important"; "awareness, society, 'tossed salad'"; "challenging, eye-opening, exciting, depressing, hopeful"; "emotional, intense, focused, communal"; "knowledgeable, effective"; "change, issues, black lives matter"; "aware"; "fun and difficult."

I brought students into a space to create a work about an issue that some of them were being faced with daily and some of them had no awareness of. When I entered into these two dance communities, I entered with hesitation, nervousness, and a visceral knowledge that I would not dance around the pain in my heart for the group of young men in our society being marginalized. I did not know if the work would be well-received, but I knew I needed to try. In the end, my concerns that students would not feel comfortable in their own space or would be burdened with white guilt were unfounded. As one dancer mentioned, she was uncomfortable in the beginning, but she is usually uncomfortable in the beginning of a process with a new instructor. Ultimately, it was I who was often emotionally drained through this process. I had an investment in the work and cared deeply about creating a positive experience through which students understanding of humanity could be widened.

Finally, the openness that I was met with when I brought forth this concept speaks to the willingness of college students to examine our progress, in terms of race, as a society. However, one note of significance in working with these students was their uneasiness with direct language about race. I have been noticing this issue among students in higher education for the past five years, and subsequently I took notice when interviewing students. Students got uncomfortable when they needed to express an idea about race. Whenever possible, they would omit words like "race," "black people," "white people," and "African American." Four out of the six white students never used any of these words in their interviews, and compared to only one of the eight students of color. They would instead say things like "I'm originally from the D.C. area, and where I'm from, like, it's so diverse, but there's still, like, tension between the neighborhoods … this piece helped me to be more aware and a citizen in this society." Overall, students of color appeared to be more familiar with the issues explored in the piece and able to use race vocabulary with ease.

The data here supports arguments that younger generations have adopted a colorblind paradigm of race. Within this paradigm, discussions of race are limited or nonexistent within educational settings, in particular K–12 education.[7] By the time many students reach higher educational settings, they have embraced a colorblind ideology of race that does not acknowledge its existence. Without the acknowledgment of race there

Wanted, 2015 (photograph by Jeremy Hogan, courtesy Indiana University Department of Theatre, Drama, and Contemporary Dance).

is no prejudice to fight against, and we can uphold racial social constructs. Within this ideology, white people do not speak of race and claim that all is equitable. People of color understand that their issues are not to be discussed in mainstream settings and are further silenced and marginalized. Sociologist Eduardo Bonilla-Silva has contributed a body of research on this phenomenon, explored in his recent text, *Racism Without racists: Color-Blind Racism and the Persistence of Racism in America.*[8]

Responses to *Wanted*

Audiences said: "*Wanted* is moving in its celebration of African-American cultural contributions, paired with its inquiry into whose lives matter"; "I particularly applaud McCarthy-Brown for doing this work at this moment in history"; and "It is, I believe, the duty of dance faculty, who study bodies in motion, to speak about the devaluing of some bodies versus others."

Student dancers said: "I was floored by the overwhelming response. It made me realize what an impact dance can have in that kind of setting"; "I was worried about what people would think about the piece. But, after doing the show it was so nice that not only did my friends understand the work, but they agreed that it was an issue in our community of stereotyping black men"; and

> I felt the piece came together better than I thought it would. I wasn't sure about the research process and what we were bringing in. But, after I heard the feedback from the audience and how the audience got it, I felt so much better. Because I cared about the work, and the message, and to know that it was understood and well received was really important.

Similar to most works presented on a university campus, it was apparent from student responses, that students were very tied to the responses of their peers. Responses exceeded expectations and affirmed the work of students.

CASE STUDY FOR *Tektonika Ondine,* CHOREOGRAPHED BY SELENE CARTER

For the dance *Tektonika Ondine* I featured a guest performer I knew locally who was born with Cerebral Palsy. Nick had approached me some years earlier to train in dance and somatic practices, feeling that his lifelong experiences with physical therapy were plagued by omission of his creative and imaginative self. He had done some dance training in Chicago and noticed a marked improvement in his strength and coordination. I included him in my dance for students because I wanted to disrupt and challenge notions within the dance program about normative bodies and training. In essence, I wanted to ask, "Who is beautiful?" I began the process of making the dance by asking "How are we (both in our specific undergraduate dance program, and in the greater dance world) defining beauty and training that results in beauty?" "Is athletic physique and technical prowess the paramount aspect of contemporary dance to showcase in performances?" "Who has value, and based on what criteria?"

I was familiar with and had limited exposure to two artists who work with differently abled dancers: Danceability[9] and Joint Forces Dance Company, founded by Alito Alessi and Karen Nelson in 1987 using the dance principles of contact improvisation, and Liz Lerman,[10] whose work with the Dance Exchange and beyond for several decades involving mixed abilities and multi-age casts. Lerman asks: "*Who gets to dance? Where is the dance happening? What is it about? Why does it matter?*" I began the process with a gnawing fear that I would fail at integrating Nick into the piece and instead be left with a dance that exploited his status as a disabled dancer and patronized people with physical disabilities. I was afraid the work would result in a statement that I didn't want to make: "Look how cool and inclusive we are; we accept people with disabilities and include them in doing concert dance, even though their bodies don't fit the ideal we value or can do the styles of training we teach."

Initial Assumptions

I began the process by asking the dancers, "What do you want to do that you think you cannot, or seems physically impossible?" I wanted to prepare them for thinking about what Nick faces on a daily basis when his body cannot do things ably, in contrast to their own daily prowess. They mostly take for granted their own abilities and physical agency. Nick did not attend this initial meeting with the dancers. In retrospect, I see that this points directly at my own erroneous assumptions about physical difference. I assumed Nick had an awareness of what he was missing in his physical ability. I assumed he had an understanding and appreciation of concert dance. I assumed he wanted to move like us and felt lacking and incomplete. What I learned from the process was that he did not miss what he could not and had never perceived. This misunderstanding I held is something I am still grappling with as an artist and educator. It gets to the heart of my query about difference and experience and points directly to the need for CDP to open dialogue and understanding for students to engage in dismantling implicit cultural biases. As the leader of this process I uncovered my biases about how physical difference is perceived. To Nick, in his own body he was absolutely whole and functioning as he had known and learned to be his whole life. I was projecting lack, inability and deficiency onto his experience. As we worked on the piece my personal process was one of continuing to confront this in my own attitudes and dismantle them step by step as we went along.

Creating Community Through Cultural Mapping

During the first rehearsal with all of the students and Nick, I employed a community mapping process.[11] Using the cardinal directions and the physical objects in the room, a world map is established and agreed upon generally. The group members are asked to go to the spot on the map they most identify with and create an accumulated repeating sequence of movements or gestures that occur on the map and relate to the prompt. Here are some examples.

- Go to the place on the map where you live currently...
- Go on the map where you were raised ... where you were born...
- Go where your mother is, create a movement for *mother*
- Go to the place on the map where the ancestors of your mother immigrated from ... create a movement
- Where your father is from ... create a movement

With each map location a gesture or movement is chosen that represents this personal and geographic identifier. The query and re-locating continues as the facilitator offers more prompts. If the question is not geographically based, such as political voting behavior or color preference, simple spatial directions are deployed. For example, "Here is the color spectrum; the mirror is red and the *barres* are violet, place yourself at the location of your favorite color. Do a movement for this color" or "Line up by age from right to left. Line up by height from left to right." As the process unfolds each group member reveals aspects of themselves that would not be expressed or discovered from taking a traditional technique dance class. As participants accumulate points on the map and own and express their cultural and personal history the facilitator may ask, "Where are you?" so that participants can share and clarify their choices. For example, "I am moving towards the center and keeping my facing towards the left because my parents vote Republican but I might want to vote differently than them." Mapping builds a diverse community where difference is revealed, contrasted, and considered. Conflicts and tensions do arise. For example, a person who is adopted and has no knowledge of their biological parents is left in limbo. In the mapping I did with the undergraduate students for this work. it was revealed that most of them are non-voting and a-political, do not identify with a religion or chosen spiritual practice and do not read or enjoy books. The experience changes with the group gathered and with who is the leader. In the mapping I have been led through I have been the oldest person in the room, or the only one in the group with a child. At a different time I was the only person in the room who was not a person of color. Doing the mapping with Nick and the students cast for this piece set up a structure of understanding that there was much more about who each person was than their physical abilities.

Choreographic Process

I engage a choreographic process centering on movement generation by students and as a means to engage critical thinking. In my works with students I employ improvisational scores to create form and content and often retain the improvised scores embedded within the structure of the dance. My choreographic methods ask the dancers to generate phrase material based on their physical and personal responses to prompts and cues. There is no prescriptive binary about if the movement is right or wrong. This process invites the dancers to hone their choreographic sensibilities when they are outside of the frame of movement generation on their own bodies.

It was apparent that Nick had a keen choreographic eye. His choices were fresh and dynamic, spurring the dancers to new interactions and configurations that their own, more traditional training in dance making had not led them to. Giving the dancers the power to assert their choreographic eye made them more aware of the creative hierarchy structure. They could discern when it was democratic or collective and when it was empirical.

Nick's World: Falling and Mermaids

Nick lost his balance and fell often. Going from the floor to standing was challenging for him and involved levering himself up at acute angles in contrast to more central spiraling in and out of gravity that dancers and people with fully mobile spines can achieve. I took cues from the way he interacted with gravity to prompt the dancers to make phrase material. Falling by extreme shifting and reaching through unexpected pathways in the body were explored and utilized to make movement sequences.

Nick shared that as a child he had identified with Disney's *The Little Mermaid*. He wanted to be, as the title song states, "a part of their world," the world of people who moved on land. The image and metaphor of the mermaid was seeded into the piece. Rolling, dragging, and crawling became ways of locomoting in our process. The mermaid became a talisman image for us as we built the dance. She has exclusive agency in water and at the same time is disabled and excluded on land.

Contact Improvisation

I am influenced by the study and practice of contact improvisation (CI) and some of its core founders and teachers.[12] CI is done by any body as it does not rely on bipedal movement exclusively. If a person senses their weight in relationship to gravity, and senses touch they can participate in the CI regardless of physical ability. There is no wrong way to sense touch and weight. I utilized CI scores based on sensing and responding to weight and touch to create material among groups of dancers. We generated a quartet out of a CI score of reaching and extending through the core, out the distal ends of the body, and meeting the push and reach of the mover/ faller Each member was sometimes supporting and meeting the faller/ mover, and each had a turn at being the supported, faller/mover. It was a dance of mutuality, interdependence, surrendering to support, asking for what you needed, and accepting what was offered in any given moment. The integrity of the quartet was lost if any member lost connection, rushed through it or did not commit to the full sensation of support and surrender of their weight. For Nick, this experience was a watershed moment. He felt he had fully arrived at being an equal core member of the ensemble.

Task Based Interactions and Material Installation

Towards the end of the process I brought in multiple rolls of newsprint from the newspaper press. The paper was a concrete element that everyone in the dance had to manage. It created shared and continuous tasks that had to be attended to in relationship to each other. The paper visually showed the relationships and boundaries created in space and left a physical trace of the many human interactions. The paper was a barrier to the dancers regardless of physical ability. Including the paper added a shared neutralizing element between Nick and the others.

Supporting Experiences

Midway through the rehearsal process I held interview sessions that were recorded. I interviewed Nick about his experience of being in the piece so far, and the cast had conversations about what they were experiencing together. I was not present for the group conversations. A lot of ground was covered during these talks. It was an important mid-point to the process. Also, close to the end of rehearsals I made dinner and brought it in for the cast. We ate together around a big table before our final rehearsal in the studio. "Breaking bread" together was an effective way to reflect on our experience before we entered the challenging process of getting the dance ready for the stage and audience.

Student Dancer Responses

Out of the eighteen dancers cast, there were three men (one of the men, Nick, has a physical difference and was a community guest artist) and sixteen women (two women who might have been identified as nonnormative in terms of body size for a dancer). There was one student whose first language was not English and there were no students of color in the cast. Three of the students had worked with the Dance for PD[13] (Parkinson's

Disease) local program. Sixteen of the eighteen students had never worked with or interacted with a person who was physically different.

Four themes that emerged from the data analysis are pre- and post-responses to working with a disabled person; audience feedback; process based choreography; and questioning normativity in context of community. I include data that speaks to the construct of dance training styles and aesthetics perceived as exclusive or limiting since that was my initial query when I began making the piece.

The following student statement is summative of the ethos of the piece. She speaks to what was arrived at once we performed *Tektonika Ondine* and how the process of creating the work and including Nick led to its overall impact and message.

> The process was about discovering our individual abilities. The paper cast shadows and the piece cast shadows. There is the dancing that is only allowed in the shadows, not to be seen, and the dancing in the light is what is acceptable or expected, and the paper cast the shadows on different aspects of that. The paper switched it around. There were no correct positions, and we didn't showcase stereotypical dance. There was always a foreground and a background, asking about insider versus outsider status. Who is outside, who is in? Our common ground was that we were making something.

Pre-, Mid- and Post-Process Responses About Working with a Physically Different Person

Because a central part of my own learning process is confronting my assumptions about how people with physical disabilities perceived dancers with full physical abilities, I asked the students what their own assumptions had been, and if they entered the process with reservations or fears about working with Nick. Here are varying statements from five students about the proposed process before we began: "I was curious to see what it would be like for him to be in a room full of able bodied dancers, doing movement that he couldn't necessarily do…. How are we going to be making movement with him … how much would we be working **around** him?"; "I wasn't sure how it was going to happen, I didn't know how he would take it"; "I had never done anything like that, and I didn't know what was OK or not. It took time to get to know him"; and "I was skeptical. I didn't know how it was going to work. I thought, 'Uh, what are you doing, Selene?'" These responses demonstrate some of the angst students feel about working and interacting with people with disabilities.

As the students got to know Nick, they learned about how he is constantly approached by strangers who offer pity and concern on a daily basis. His struggle with this constant intrusion shapes how he relates with people. One student said, "He [Nick] has to have a lot more interaction with strangers, he can't just walk home without someone stopping him and asking if he needs help. There is a fine line, he can't just be normal and left alone." Another added:

> I learned about pity, when it comes up and how to handle it. I struggled with when to help and when to stand by. My instinct was to help him if he fell. I learned a lot about human nature and when it is right to help someone and when you need to stand back. Everybody has their flaws and insecurities … it's not out of pity. If you fell down I want to help you up! If anybody fell I'd want to help them up…. He has been dealing with this issue his whole life, it's a privilege we have that we don't have to think about. It was weird to navigate that and come to an understanding with each other.

As we began working together the students became aware that one of Nick's biggest challenges was joining their dancer culture as an outsider. His status as a person who was differently abled physically was an aspect to his otherness, yet his status as a "non-dancer" was as much a part of his difference as his disability.

> He had to break down a lot of walls. Coming into a group of people already established. He didn't know what direction it would go, he showed up every rehearsal. Each time he had rehearsal he had to subject himself to something new, he had to make a hard decision to show up, each time I think we proved to him that we wanted to be sensitive and celebrate him.

Another said,

> I've never really had to interact with someone with a disability like that. I learned how to interact in a way that he would feel the most welcomed and accepted. In the talks we had as a group it was clear that he was learning how to interact with us as dancers.

One of the dancers who was initially skeptical said,

> I had a duet with him and I had to actually work with and communicate with him one on one to make it seem effortless. It was like, "Oh you're like a normal person." I mean there is something wrong, but I'm not going to judge you on that. I just tried to connect with him as much as possible. He was a really cool kid and I didn't treat him any different than any other person.

Other students said, "He didn't want to be treated any differently and he made that very clear to us which is why I think we established this really great connection with him"; "I see them [people with physical disabilities] as us [people without physical disabilities]. They're just like us. It's upsetting when people don't acknowledge them as people"; and "I learned not to exclude any one and not to judge anyone based on body appearance."

Questioning Assumptions and Bias of Normativity

Through the process of making the dance the students became aware of the dichotomy of abled versus disabled dancers. They began to see how their own abilities were privileges that were aesthetically biased with preferential status within the concert dance culture. One said,

> I think the movement was so different, we are so used to dance-y dancing, and how he moved was so different. When he falls it's just a typical thing for him, and we would all jump back and react. His choreographic suggestions were so unique, he just sees thing differently than we would with our dancer brains.

They began to see the ways that their training as dancers was a culturally biased construct that had creative constraints and hidden rules. Students said, "In a situation like this you can't deny that someone is different. It was hard to find a way to not exploit it, but he doesn't walk like the rest of us. You don't want to hide that either, because its part of him" and "We were having an honest conversation about inclusion, and normality, we are all normal. We are all moving in different ways and that's what dance is."

Nick said this about his experience of making and performing the piece:

> I think my biggest challenge was realizing how much work the dance would actually be for me. I often don't realize my own limitations until I'm put in a situation where they become unavoidable, this was definitely one of those situations. But as time went on I saw what I could bring to the dance and what my body could do. I began to trust my body in ways I never had before. In talking about it with people, both those who have seen the performance and with others who haven't, I would always down play my involvement in it as I know it might sound foolish and unbelievable that I a person with a disability was in a modern dance concert. In the end though I had to stop feeling foolish and accept that I did enjoy what I was doing and that I had become a dancer in a lot of ways. I was the one most stuck on the idea of being disabled not the other dancers or Selene. I hadn't realized how much work I had put in and how confident in my own body and life I had become 'til the actual performances.

Nick and participating students were able to find a space where inclusion was more than an idea or politically correct sound bite in the abstract. Within this work, inclusion became normalized.

Process Based Choreography

One student remarked that the mapping process helped her to broaden her understanding of dance: "The mapping process. That was my favorite rehearsal. Technically we didn't dance." The students became aware of the culture of ability they were allowed to operate within. They realized that stepping beyond those assumed invisible boundaries was creatively liberating and opened up many new choreographic possibilities. As they confronted and shed cultural biases about physical difference, this process was mirrored in choreographic possibilities that opened up as they moved beyond preconceived concert dance biases:

Learning how to work with people who aren't in the dance environment. We are so used to working with people who understand bodies and are comfortable with each other. It opened up a different perspective on how to work with different people and to see how dance can really bring joy to people who don't do it every day.

When he would fall it got my gears turning. There are so many different ways to fall. How to fall without hurting himself? We are trained to fall gracefully and exploring how he falls opened up all of these new pathways and possibilities for movement.

Another commented,

It was hard at the beginning to define what would be exploiting someone who is clearly physically different. It felt like I learned how to successfully not exploit, but invite someone into a space and unify all of us, but also celebrate all of us as individuals. That was what I learned. That it was possible to create a dance that wasn't "Nick the disabled dancer, and we are the able dancers."

The students with more experience in varied approaches to choreography (and who were beginning to make their own dances) discerned that the way I was creating the movement and structuring the dance was the key to including Nick without exploiting or overtly commenting on his physical difference:

You didn't let him off the hook in creating movement…. You asked each of us to do what we could within our abilities. You didn't let any of us out of working. Everything was new for everybody all of the time. You knew when to push and ask for him to try again and when to move on if something wasn't working. But I don't think that is a disability thing, it's a dance movement thing…. A different person with a different ability, their process growing up with their childhood, just like anybody's childhood shapes us. Any kind of process working with someone new would get at this. I think the nature of the movement we created, it was about exploring ideas, abstract ideas, rather than about creating shapes or lines. It ended up that in the final product you are seeing shapes and lines, but the process wasn't "create this silhouette." "Dipped in blue" was one of the phrases that you used, how do you explore that in your body? Its not about creating a shape that looks like that, its about an internal experience. The fact that we were creating movement that had nothing to do with how our bodies looked. It was about the mental, internal experience.

Throughout this process students were asked to move beyond their ideas of their bodies, and to explore their physicality initiated from within, instead of traditional desired aesthetics of dance.

Audience Feedback

The students heard from several audience members that many of them didn't realize that Nick was physically different. They thought he was moving distinctively as part of the choreography. Responses included "They felt that he wasn't the star, he blended in with us, he was part of us, instead

Tektonika Ondine, 2015 (photograph by Jeremy Hogan, courtesy Indiana University Department of Theatre, Drama, and Contemporary Dance).

of it being him and then us"; "People asked me if he was a dance major and just faking it, if that (his way of moving) was choreographed? They didn't realize that he was a disabled person until the bow"; and "The audience didn't notice Nick as disabled. Lots of people didn't know why he was getting applause at the end [he was a featured guest in the bow because he was not an enrolled student]."

In closing the data portion of my section the following student statement speaks to the profound efficacy and impact of creating dance repertory with students that is politically challenging and questions norms, "Art has the ability to heal. It's a good and useful way to break down boundaries. It wasn't a statement piece, but for me I've never worked with a differently abled body. It teaches you patience, and understanding and compassion in all these different ways that you couldn't learn from reading a book."

Conclusion

As dance educators, artists, and citizens, we (Carter and McCarthy-Brown) wanted to create work that envisioned space for those marginalized.

We also wanted to participate in a communal creative process that would see those all too often unseen. bell hooks, cultural activist and critical pedagogue, wrote, "[as] a classroom community, our capacity to generate excitement is deeply affected by our interest in one another, in hearing one another's voices, in recognizing one another's presence[14] ... where everyone feels a responsibility to contribute."[15] Thus cultivating community within the choreographic process was invaluable to the learning experience.

CDP is most effective when it is experiential, and customized to the students in the space. We worked to cultivate mutuality, letting students know that making and performing a dance is always an act of will and choice. To begin the work, we first exposed and examined the constructs that we convened under as a group and identified our roles. As choreographers and teachers, we revealed processes of making and choosing. In that process we modeled meta-cognition and critical thinking. As the facilitators, we shared our own assumptions and biases in efforts to be transparent and mutable to the students. We shared our learning from them and their process. Students were empowered to make their own choices creatively based on instructive guidelines. By responding personally from a place of safety, self-reflection, and authentic experience our students negotiated challenging and socio-politically charged themes and ideas. We cannot emphasize enough that student choice was paramount to the success of our process. Whether in the independent student research as described in McCarthy-Brown's section or the improvisational movement explored in Carter's section, giving the students space and time to creatively negotiate these issues is what makes the work significant educationally. Social issues were always experiences first. It is important to bring students into experiences that construct and express relationship.

In *Teaching to Transgress*, hooks describes how her teaching philosophy developed. As a student, she was able to experience and learn from professors who supported and opposed student-centered learning.

> I entered the classroom with the conviction that it was crucial for me and every other student to be an active participant, not passive consumer. Education as the practice of freedom was continually undermined by professors who were actively hostile to the notion of student participation. Freire's work affirmed that education can only be liberatory when everyone claims knowledge as a field in which we all labor.[16]

Those in the field of dance know that dance is transformative, in the mind, body and spirit—dance has a healing property. Similarly, education is transformative. The research here presents two case studies, of college repertory works, where students experienced an integration of performance, education, civil activity, and humanity. As the field of Dance Education seeks to find innovative ways to reach students of the twenty-first century, and prepare them for a diverse world of ever-changing challenges, we have found and shared one approach. Through the co-creation with students of an artistic work, teachers can transcend a traditional teacher-centered model. We utilized a critical dance pedagogy approach to question normative practices, and examined structural and personal biases. Students transcended their place in a repertory dance work, by being invested creative artists. We found that relinquishing creative control was not a loss of power but an opportunity to empower students.

Suggestions for Creating and Staging Repertory Work with a Critical Dance Pedagogy Approach

1. Establish ground rules for discussions and rehearsals on day one.
2. Introduce the topic with neutral information, not propaganda.
3. Share a topic and ask what students know about the topic.
4. Create an open space where students are welcome to hold whatever views they choose.
5. Communicate to students that multiple truths can and do exist in this space, no one's beliefs are "wrong." Affirm all points of view shared.
6. Ask students to do research on the topic. They may find information on the subject in general, or they may choose to research evidence to support their personal position or ideas on the topic.
7. If sharing video materials, watch videos as a class, and process through discussion as a class.
8. Continue the dialog on the topic, or motivation of the work, on a regular basis.
9. Include ways for students to interact with one another that happen outside of the dance studio.
10. Give them opportunities to reflect on and process experiences together that you do not always hear or listen to.
11. After any public performance of the work you create together make sure to do a *post-mortem* meeting or celebration to hear and share how the students felt about the work in performance (as opposed to process) and glean any feedback they got from the audience.

PART III. CRITICAL DANCE PEDAGOGY
AND DIVERSIFYING CONTENT
AND APPROACHES TO DANCE EDUCATION

Seven

Reshaping Dance History
by Deconstructing Whiteness

BY JULIE KERR-BERRY

As I begin another semester of teaching Dance History to a room full
of junior and senior dance majors at a mid-size, upper Midwestern university, I am reminded of the complex task of teaching a course on the historical development of western concert dance. From the time that dance
became a part of the academic landscape in the previous century, concert
dance history was, and still is, commonly taught from a Eurocentric perspective. Over the years, my teaching challenge has been to consistently
integrate source material that fills in the missing pieces of such history by
incorporating an Africanist perspective—to deconstruct Whiteness from
a curricular position. To interrogate the western concert dance paradigm
means to depict both the richness *and* racist composition of our nation's
dance history. Paradoxically, this history is both a brilliant testament of
artistic invention and one fraught with practices that obstructed Black
dancers' access to the concert stage. Stark omissions still persist from the
pages of dance history. Such absence silenced and obscured how Blacks
dramatically altered the course of this history.

For several years, I have been revising my curriculum to include the
work of diverse dance scholars whose work plumbs the depths of the
Africanist movement and aesthetic principles, and their impact on concert
dance. Some selected notable scholars include the work of Thomas
DeFrantz,[1] Brenda Dixon Gottschild,[2,3,4] Susan Manning,[5] John Perperner,[6]
and Peggy Schwartz.[7] I have benefited from the plethora of such scholar-

ship that emerged over the past three decades. Their rigorous work was constantly woven into the fabric of my course. Drawing from so many diverse sources that strove to tell the whole story of concert dance history revealed the forces and figures that dramatically altered the development of modern dance and ballet in the United States.

At the turn of the last century when modernism was finding its foothold in American concert dance, it is important to note that while Native American and Asian American dancers influenced this history they did not have the initial and sustained impact that Black dancers did. Native American and Asian American influences occurred less through actual representation, namely as choreographers and dancers, and more through appropriation by White choreographers and dancers such as Ruth St. Denis and Ted Shawn. José Limón, who was Mexican, is one exception. Japanese American Yuriko Kikuchi is another exception who danced with the Martha Graham Dance Company throughout the early to mid-twentieth century.

In regard to Native dancers, there were five Native American ballerinas from Oklahoma—the "Five Moons." They are particularly relevant to this discussion because of how race factored into their success when compared to a Black ballerina dancing at the same time. The Five Moons achieved international success, though not all in the United States. Maria Tallchief was among them and most notably became a prima ballerina with the New York City Ballet.[8] Yet, because skin color is such a racial marker in the United States, it is worth factoring in Black skin color and hair texture as a more racially distinguishable trait than Native attributes. Consider for example the fate of Black ballerina Raven Wilkinson who danced with the Ballet Russe de Monte Carlo. Wilkinson eventually had to leave the company when she could not longer pass for White, particularly when she toured in the southern United States.[9] In contrast, four of the Five Moons danced with the Ballet Russe de Monte Carlo; none were asked to leave, but rather went on to join or form other companies.[10] The focus of this chapter is on the impact of Black dancers and choreographers on concert dance. Though less representative, Native and Asian Americans encountered racism as dancers.

Critical Dance Pedagogy and Whiteness

This chapter employs a critical dance pedagogic approach. Paulo Freire's seminal text, *Pedagogy of the Oppressed*, sought to disrupt authoritarian teaching methods. To many, he developed critical pedagogy. His approach was through an "anti-banking" method of teaching.[11] In essence, Freire problematized the authoritarian model and the notion that students were empty vessels into which knowledge from a teacher must flow. He felt that students brought knowledge to the classroom that should be acknowledged and built upon—very much like a constructivist approach in which students build knowledge based on what they already know.

While Freire's approach did not specifically examine race, it can be applied because of his focus on the oppression of others.[12] However, it is important to consider that without integrating the dimension of race into this approach, deconstructing Whiteness does not necessarily occur. By factoring in race, critical pedagogy can interrogate Whiteness by toppling the authoritarian/White model of teaching so endemic in college or university settings—both in content and through methodology. The "banking system" positions the instructor, often a White male, as the single authority of his discipline. The dominance of White, upper-middle class males continues to reproduce Whiteness pedagogically in higher education.[13] Integrating issues of race into critical pedagogy debases the authoritarian model and White, dominant teaching practices; values the diversity of student's knowledge; integrates their backgrounds into the teaching process; and develops content and experiences in which all students recognize themselves in what they are learning.

Other models were later derived based on aspects of critical pedagogy, which also inform this chapter. From a feminist pedagogic perspective, Lynne Webb et al. distilled six principles of feminist pedagogy through a "comprehensive review of multidisciplinary literature."[14] The six principles clearly parallel critical pedagogy. They are "reformation of the relationship between professor and student, empowerment, building community, privileging voice, respecting diversity of personal experience, and challenging traditional pedagogical notions."[15]

Closely aligning with feminist pedagogy is another model referred to as culturally relevant teaching. Some notable scholars in this area are Lisa Delpit,[16] Geneva Gay,[17] and Gloria Ladson-Billings.[18] Essentially this model considers the learner's lived experience in the development of curriculum and teaching methodology. This approach considers factors like the student's race, cultural orientation, and class.

Finally, there is critical race theory (CRT). CRT was initiated among a numbers of lawyers and activists in the 1970s. In effect, CRT seeks to study and transform "the relationship among race, racism, and power."[19] In recent years it has been applied to the area of education, for example, regarding "controversies over curriculum and history."[20, 21]

Collectively, these approaches to teaching provide inroads to toppling Whiteness. As such, they develop a sense of community in the classroom, honor student narratives—including those most impacted by racial identity. Such narratives are rife with meaning and significant to teaching and student learning. Critical dance pedagogy draws from these roots, combining and applying them, in this case, to teaching Dance History.

More About Whiteness

In the past, my instructional focus has centered on "the what" of teaching and less on "the how" of teaching.[22] This chapter will take a somewhat similar approach, but will drill down deeper as to how content and methodology deconstructs Whiteness by providing specific learning strategies. As Jean Charbeneau notes, the very act of teaching can be "enactments of whiteness," which she identified in the pedagogic practices of White faculty in university classrooms.[23] Whiteness also extends beyond skin color and is normalized in academia affecting content selected and modes of delivery. Essentially, Whiteness functions as a default to Whiteness.[24] In other words, it is systemically engrained in our American psyche and in our institutions as the standard against which all Others are measured.

Further, Frances Maher and Mary Kay Thompson Tetreault described the classroom environment and the ways in which Whiteness is constructed and maintained:

> Perceiving how the assumption of Whiteness shapes the construction of classroom knowledge is understanding its centrality to academy's practices of intellectual domination, namely, the imposition of certain ways of constructing the world through lenses of traditional disciplines. Such domination is often couched in the language of detachment and universality, wherein class, race, and gender of the "knower" is ignored or presumed irrelevant.[25]

Whiteness manifests itself in practice through instructor demeanor, which, in turn, affects classroom dynamics and overall tenor of the learning environment. Likewise, an instructor can select content that defaults to Whiteness to maintain a curriculum that is a universalized standard—further perpetuating the Anglo-Saxon norm.

In dance, this occurs when Black and Brown dancing bodies are left out, either through omission or by relegating them to separate chapters in dance history. When operating from this norm, content becomes an endorsement to dismiss certain ideas, positions, or groups because they do not fit into dominant approaches to teaching dance history. Such are entrenched in a Eurocentric paradigm—whitewashing content and teaching methodology in the process.

In the United States, racism marked Black and Brown bodies as inferior, and White bodies as superior. Educational leadership specialists Glenn Singleton and Curtis Linton trace this origins to a racial binary that began "with the arrival of Northern and Western European settlers in the 1600s, a period marked by the extermination of indigenous peoples and enslavement of Africans. Each of these occurrences establishes in this country the racial hierarchy of Whites over people of color, or the American racial binary of White to Black."[26] Dancing bodies were no different. They too were a product of a racial binary, deemed inferior, subjected to racism, and removed altogether, or minimized in American dance history.

Further Ruth Frankenberg examines Whiteness as a race. She contends that "in a social context where white people have too often viewed themselves as nonracial or racially neutral, it is crucial to look at the 'racialness' of white experience."[27] She continues with, "To look at the social construction of whiteness, then, is to look head on at a site of dominance," or essentially at White privilege.[28] Pedagogically, an examination of racial hierarchies in dance history can reveal how Whiteness is racially normalized and neutralized. From this perspective, White bodies become more recognizable as sites of dominance in dance.

When Whiteness is problematized and Black and Brown dancing bodies are fully integrated, White privilege becomes more visible. Making the invisible "more visible" required some class members to confront their racial bias and prompted a defense of their White privilege. From my experience, some students are challenged when they fail to see themselves as dominant in this historical landscape. In essence, when their histories are not the prevailing norm they may feel slighted. Their defense of Whiteness prompts them to make statements like "There is an overemphasis on Black content in the course."

Selected Critical Dance Pedagogic Strategies

Through a critical lens, my focus is on a revisionist approach to Dance History pedagogy. Specific strategies are offered that debunk Whiteness in order tell a more comprehensive story about the evolution of American concert dance. To this end, what follows is an in-depth description of such strategies, in which Black and White dance histories intersect.

Dance History Walk: Choreographic Narratives

As was previously discussed, critical dance pedagogy disrupts an authoritarian model of teaching and deconstructs Whiteness by valuing all student voices. It is important to recognize that knowing the learner is not only meaningful to the instructor, but it is also important that students know one another, helping to build a sense of a respect and diversity within the community. For example, on the first day of my Dance History course, one technique I use as an icebreaker was adapted from an improvisation I learned from Liz Lerman.[29] I termed it a "Dance History Walk."

This exercise demonstrates how students are different from one another. As experience has taught me over the years, conflict and resistance can arise in students over how they are *different* from one another, rather than their similarities. Deconstructing Whiteness in concert dance history exposed such differences to students as follows: (1) from the Dance History they thought they knew and (2) from themselves as a class of predominantly White students by integrating the Other or Black dancing bodies into course content.

Dance History Walk was developed as an improvisation; students were instructed to move around the room, preferably a studio space. Once they make eye contact with one of their peers, they ask her/him: "What is your dance history?" The student asking records the response on a notecard then steps away to create a short gesture or phrase based on what she/he heard. The process continued for two to four more students. Then, the student's peer's movement is added to her/his own gesture or phrase. Next, each student assembles the dance histories they record and create movement for a longer phrase. Students perform the phrases for the class by first identifying the students they represent and then by dancing the phrase.

As students perform their phrases, the diversity of their dance histories is evident through the array of movement/gestures they develop for each of their fellow classmates. Results could be hip-hop moves, a *ginga* reflecting capoeira, inversions reminiscent of breakdancing, and *pirouettes*. Among many reasons for developing this exercise, one was so students understood themselves as having a dance history, which introduced them to the relevancy of a Dance History course. They recognize themselves as part of it. However, most importantly, they experience how different one another's histories are by recording, embodying, and performing it to the class. The reason students record what they heard on the notecards is for a short paper in which they document each of their peers' histories, analyze what they heard, and find a conclusion.

PowerPoint and Discussion:
The Paradox of Our Past

Within the first couple weeks of class, I present a brief historical snapshot, which establishes the origins of Western theatrical dance and its link to ancient Greek ritual. While not a novel approach, it establishes the ritual basis of dance. This approach helps students consider the link between ancient dance ritual and contemporary dance theatre.

Further, by moving into the second millenium and drawing from the work of Afrocentrist scholar Molefi Kete Asante, I historically establish the vibrancy of ancient kingdoms that existed in West Africa.[30] Referencing Asante's work helped me to deconstruct the dominance of Whiteness in Dance History by presenting Ghana from a more historically accurate perspective. This fact is significant because it helps students re-examine their assumptions about West Africa.

By the late fifteenth and early sixteenth centuries, I then compare the artistic sophistication of a Benin ivory mask (1550) to Michelangelo's *La Pietà* (1449) (see pp. 134–135). I draw from visual art because there is a better record of it than dance, at least in West Africa. In fact, the mask was carved during the same time period that ballet was gaining its foothold in Renaissance Italy. I purposefully situated the two sculptures together in the same PowerPoint slide so that students can see them side-by-side and consider the fact that the ivory mask was carved by a Benin artist 51 years after *La Pietà*. I state that the Kingdom of Benin reached the pinnacle of its artistic grandeur in the fifteenth and sixteenth centuries, and that it continued to flourish until the late 1800s "when the palace was sacked by the English in reprisal for an ambush that had cost the British vice-consul his life." Under the slide, the caption from a website that focuses on ancient West African art reads: "When Europeans first saw Benin art, they supposed a non–African origin because they did not think Africans capable of such sophisticated work."[31]

Presenting early concert dance history to students by comparing the kingdoms of Benin and Italy provides an historical foundation and documents the level of artistic sophistication in both traditions. Further, it presents students with an understanding of each culture at a time when an intense collision and fusion was beginning between enslaved West Africans and White slave owners in the southern United States.

The final slide of the class session ends with the following summation so that students connected the historical pathway that led to our nation's vibrant, yet troubled, concert dance history.

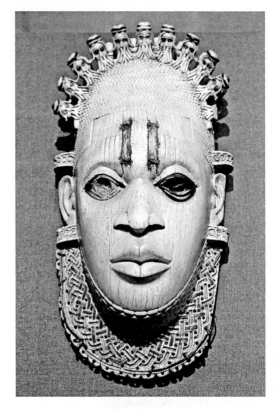

Benin mask (Wikimedia Commons).

1. Greece gave birth to theatrical performance, which flourished in Italy and France beginning in the 1500s.
2. What Greece was to European theatrical dance, Benin was to West African dance ritual.
3. The transatlantic slave trade (1500–1800s) meant the forced contact of West Africans with Europeans in the Americas. Benin is the ancestral home of many African Americans.
4. Later as we advance through the millennium, West African and Western European dance traditions fused in the Americas because of the transatlantic slave trade.
5. Despite the horrific crime of slavery, this history yielded a rich tradition of theatrical dance in the Western hemisphere—now a global form.

Museum Field Trip: A Journey from Modernism to Africanisms to Racism

Once the course progresses past the Romantic ballet era, focus shifts to the impact of modernism, primarily in Paris at the turn of the last

Michelangelo's *La Pietà* (Wikimedia Commons).

century. Beginning with the visual arts, students examined Pablo Picasso's impact on how the female body was deconstructed through paint on his canvases. Reflecting on a recent field trip to a large urban museum, students recall Picasso's work they viewed. Students also view the African collection at the museum, which contained several masks and sculptures from West Africa. For example, there was an *Egungun* mask from Nigeria.

When we reach this part of the semester, I ask students to discuss any correlation they observed between the African masks they viewed in the museum and Picasso's Cubist approach to the face. Students are shown a slide of Picasso's *Les Demoiselles d'Avignon* (1907). They are asked to focus on the faces of the women in the painting and to compare them to the masks they saw in the museum.

Through class discussion, students make connections between Picasso's work and his appropriation of Africanisms in the faces of the five women in the painting. I ask them to consider how Picasso's appropriation impacted modern art, and how Cubism, while considered European in origin, was actually the result of such fusion. Discussion helps students lessen the artistic divide between Africa and Europe and acknowledge the influence the former had on modern art. It also deconstructs Whiteness by problematizing the European basis of Picasso's work.

As discussion continues to unfold, I point out two important themes to students that will apply later in the class. Regarding the exchange between Blacks and Whites, I make the following statements:

1. Such appropriation by Picasso was commonplace; it was a one-way street in that Africans were never credited by the painter for their contribution to his work during the burgeoning growth of modernism in the Western art;
2. Such exchange would only intensify in the United States during slavery through the 21st century—reiterating again that such forced contact yielded a richly diverse, yet racist, and complex concert dance history.

Next, I introduce Serge Diaghilev's Ballets Russes in relationship to how modernism propelled the explosion of artistic innovation and collaboration in Paris and its subsequent impact on ballet. I also note Picasso's impact on the Ballets Russes through his sets and costumes.

In sum, I state that once modernist influences crossed the Atlantic, they began to affect American dance, resulting in modern dance. The new form considered itself a rebel and freed the dancing body as a vehicle of artistic expression. Isadora Duncan is often credited as one of its originators. When I present the birth of modernism in dance, first through Diaghilev and later through Duncan, students are introduced to the following traits that characterize modernism, and subsequently, modern dance artists because they:

1. pushed against artistic boundaries;
2. violated social norms;
3. inhabited the margins of society;
4. created new artistic ideas and approaches through experimentation; and
5. collaborated with other artists.

As the course progresses with a focus on the birth of modernism, I address how racism plagued Black dancers in the early 20th century in the

United States. Students read the first two chapters from Julia Foulkes' *Modern Bodies: Dance and American Modernism from Martha Graham to Alvin Ailey*.[32] In it, she points out that while these dance artists were marginalized, particularly because they were women and practiced an embodied art form, it did not make them more empathetic to the plight of Blacks who were barred from the concert stage. Racism persisted in this progressive and radical, yet racist period of dance-making. Foulkes states, "The easy ignorance among white Americans of racial discrimination was common in the 1920s, even though the mix of many different kinds of people was also increasingly common particularly in New York City."[33]

With regard to racial stereotyping, students read from dance historian John Perpener's *African-American Concert Dance: The Harlem Renaissance and Beyond*. Perperner notes, "Preconceptions about a group of people—whether they were African American, Jewish, Irish, or Native American—were based on their differences from the Anglo-Saxon *norm* and became accepted as *truth*."[34] I point out to students that Perpener's statement is significant because it is an example of how a default to Whiteness operated both in American society and in concert dance because of the persistence and dominance of this norm.

I ask students to consider that, on one hand, the early modern matriarch violated social norms and inhabited the margins of early American modern dance. On the other hand, they were no different than the rest of society as White privileged women when it came to their treatment of Black dancers; in other words, racism trumped art.

Students also examine the racist treatment of Edna Guy by Ruth St. Denis. They read about St. Denis' treatment in Foulkes text and view the first episode of the DVD *Free to Dance: What Do You Dance?*[35] Foulkes is featured in the DVD as well. In addition, students read the first chapter in Perpener's book, "Early Influences on Black Concert Dance," to provide the historical context between Black and White dancers.[36] They are asked to analyze the content of one of the letters that St. Denis sent Guy as follows: "Dear Girlie, Yes, I know you have this race problem with you constantly, and a big problem it is. But, you see, dear, you are a very ignorant little girl in relation to the conditions in this big city. Some things cannot be forced or hurried."[37] Students are instructed to examine this statement and the infantile and racist caricature that St. Denis paints of Guy.

However, in a subsequent class period, I point out that despite their treatment, Black concert dancers challenged social norms. Indeed, the first generation of White modern dancers were racist in practice. Advancing into the twentieth century, some of these dancers also appropriated both movement and subject matter like Helen Tamiris' *Negro Spirituals* (1928–1942) and *How Long Brethren* (1937). Nonetheless Black concert dance artists gravitated to modern dance because it offered them access to an artistic voice and embodied principles of modernism through which they:

1. pushed against artistic boundaries through their persistence to access the concert dance stage;
2. violated social norms of Whiteness and racial stereotypes;
3. inhabited the margins of society through the intersection of race and gender as Black, female dance artists;
4. created new artistic ideas and approaches through experimentation such as in the work of Katherine Dunham and Pearl Primus; and
5. cultivated opportunities to collaborate with other artists, specifically Black artists such as when Edna Guy and Alison Burroughs directed the *Negro Dance Evening* in 1937.

Comparative Analysis Table: Africanisms and Europeanisms

Prior to Dance History, dance majors complete a three-credit course called Worlds of Dance. In this course, they examine dance from around the globe in a way that does not privilege western concert dance over other forms. The course is also purposely titled to suggest an inclusive approach. When I developed the course, I referred to Susan Foster's *Worlding Dance: Studies in International Performance*, which reminds us that "the substitution of 'world' for 'ethnic' at UCLA in various labeling practices ... has worked euphemistically to gloss over the colonial legacy of racialized and class-based hierarchizations of the arts."[38]

The course is organized around a series of interlocking themes. One in particular is Dance as Cultural Fusion. As is reiterated later in my Dance History course, Worlds of Dance lays the initial foundation to the ways in which movement is appropriated by different cultures to create new forms. After students read and view several examples of such interchange, coupled with discussion and PowerPoints, they are asked to break into groups of two to complete the below table entitled "A Comparative Analysis of Africanist and Europeanist Dance/Movement/Design Characteristics in the 1600s."[39]

Comparative Analysis of Africanist and Europeanist
Dance/Movement/Design Characteristics in the 1600s

African-Based	European-Based
gender prescription: male to male; female with female	*gender prescription*: male and female; closed couple
physical contact: no touching	*physical contact:* touching
body shape: asymmetry (limbs to torso)	*body shape*: symmetrical
clothing: loose fitting clothing	*clothing*: corseted, wigs, etc.
feet: bare and relaxed; improvised step-based movement	*feet*: shod and pointed; set step-based patterns
position of feet: parallel	*position of feet*: moderate turn-out
center of weight: low (pelvis); "get-down" or going into the earth	*center of weight*: high (chest); escaping from the earth
rhythmic structure: polyrhythmic	*rhythmic structure*: mono-rhythmic
choreographic structure: improvised	*choreographic structure*: set, step patterns
transmission: oral tradition	*transmission*: notation & oral tradition
social organizational principle: sacred	*social organizational principle:* secularized
dance & religious experience: participant/possession	*dance & religious experience*: observer
performance content: outside in earthen spaces	*performance context*: inside, in ballrooms
use of spine & pelvis: full and supple with mobile pelvis	*use of spine & pelvis*: straight spine with stable pelvis
knees: bent	*knees*: relatively straight
participation: communal and highly participatory	*participation*: based on social hierarchy and highly selective

The purpose of the table is for students to compare the disparate movement vocabularies and ideologies between West African and European-based dance forms. At the risk of dissecting each tradition in order to make a point, I ask students to identify traits that characterize each.

The actual implementation of the table in Worlds of Dance unfolds in the following way. One portion of the class receives a table with only the left-hand column complete. While the other half receives a version with the right-hand column complete. With a partner, their task is to fill in the blank half of the table. With only one-half of the table filled in, students grapple with the markedly disparate characteristics of the dancing body in order to complete their side. Once tables are complete, responses are compared through discussion, during which, students are asked how they arrived at the decisions they did. It is worth noting that I disclose to students that the table is an over simplification of African-based traits, as well as European. Nonetheless, the exercise serves the purpose of recognizing the Africanist presence in concert dance forms. It also helps students identify the Europeanist presence in concert dance forms. Wrongly, I have made the assumption that they come to class with an understanding of latter, which was not always the case.

Later, when students advance to Dance History, they reflect on their knowledge of this table as a way to identify the Africanist presence in American modern dance and ballet. I consistently bring back the fact that dance in the United States was a product of cultural fusion, particular between Blacks and Whites. To reinforce this, students read American history professor Peter H. Wood's "Gimme' de Kneebone Bent: African Body Language and the Evolution of American Dance Forms."[40] However, before they read Wood's essay, students are asked to reflect again on the appropriation by Picasso of African masks. Then I ask them to consider Helen Tamiris' use of Black subject matter in her work. Wood's essay is significant because it reinforces an earlier concept about how Blacks and Whites appropriated one another's cultural sensibilities; in particular, it links Africanisms to American modern dance. I emphasize the following statement by Wood regarding the first half of the 20th century by placing it on a PowerPoint slide:

> Nor is it surprising that American modern dance, created largely in the urban North during this era of enormous social movement, owes more than it yet realizes to roots that are black and southern, and ultimately African. During the first half of the 20th century, pioneer American dancers found it both possible and exciting to work closer to the ground, to plant their feet and bend their knees, to thrust their hips and point their elbows. And when troubled critics explained that these "new" movements had been "discovered," because American dancers and audiences are a step removed from the balletic traditions of Europe, they were half right. They could have added, had they realized, that although America was still a segregated society during the first half of the 20th century, all of its inhabitants, black and white, were moving closer to the continent of Africa in body movement all the time.[41]

From this perspective, students are able to examine the work of Tamiris, or Graham, and are better able to recognize what makes it African, for example, through the use of weight or the contraction of the pelvis. While at the same time, students are also able to recognize what is European in Dunham or Primus' work, for example, through the use of ballet and presentation of work on a proscenium stage.

A specific strategy is to present photos of Pearl Primus' *Speak to Me of Rivers* (1944) and Martha Graham's *Lamentation* (1930) side-by-side. Together, they depict the use of a modernist aesthetic informed by an Africanist one. For example, the dancers embody asymmetry, bent knees and pointed elbows in these two works. The photos also illustrate how both Black and White modern dancers were drawing from the same well for inspiration. (See photos on this page.)

Approaching the Africanist and Europeanist complex in concert dance creates a critical lens through which students can discern how easy it is to "racialize culture" as Singleton and Linton note. They contend that culture "describes how we live on a daily basis in terms of our language, ancestry, religion."[42] Dance can easily be included as another marker of cultural heritage. Yet, when many Whites view Black dancers dancing, the tendency is to attribute how they move to their skin color, not to their cultural heritage, because, as Singleton and Linton also note, "race typically trumps ethnicity and nationality in our interactions."[43] To "racialize culture" assumes that Black dancers dance the way they do because they are Black, not because, they, like their White counterparts, had specific cultural experiences that shaped how they danced.

Top: (Rivers) Speak to Me— **Pearl Primus (UCLA). Bottom:** *Lamentation—***Martha Graham (in fabric) (UCLA).**

Similarly, Whites dance a certain way, not because they are White, but because they also had specific cultural experiences.

However, and at the risk of contradicting myself, because of how race was socially constructed in the United States, Black dancers were marked for their Blackness before their culture. Due to skin color, Blacks cultivated some of the dance/movement forms we have today because they were relegated to certain sectors of society. For example, tap and jazz are forms that Perpener describes as: "The artists who were closer to the folk roots of African-American culture were the thousands of singers, dancers, and musicians who peopled the clubs, cabarets, the vaudeville houses and minstrel shows, and the hundreds of theaters (black and white) across the country where popular entertainment thrived."[44]

Participation in such forms fed stereotypes of Black dancers solely as entertainers and incapable of creating works for the concert stage. Black skin operated to bar such dancers from the concert stage. They were not allowed to train due to segregated studios, or perform on stage, nor until fairly recently, perform in ballet companies—although their presence is still minimal. Here, skin color trumped culture, affecting how the dancing body of Black dancers differed from Whites. Again, as Singleton and Linton note, "as a result of our racialized culture, people's skin color tends to define much of their culture, as well as determine whether they should gain full access to the benefits of U.S. citizenship."[45]

Nonetheless, the aforementioned table helps students recognize African-derived dance characteristics in White dance, and European-derived characteristics in Black dance. Undeniably, this table does have its shortcomings because it is reductive, overly simplistic, and lumps cultural traditions altogether into two columns. However, at least momentarily, it can guide students to better distinguish the Africanist from Europeanist presence in American concert dance.

Analytic Teams: Critical Analysis of Pearl Primus' *Strange Fruit*

Over the years, I have problematized my own teaching and dismantled some of my previous practices. I no longer stand at the front of the classroom behind a media cabinet and project a series of PowerPoint slides. I no longer lecture. Rather, I move among students and often sit opposite them in an empty student desk when they respond to questions, or react to a multitude of readings or choreographic works they have just viewed. Questioning this pervasive teaching paradigm means replacing it with discussion-based strategies and collaborative learning techniques.[46]

Applying collaborative learning approaches help revise the dominant "talking head" paradigm. Collaborative learning techniques are inherently an anti-banking and approach to teaching because they de-position an instructor from a dominant position of power. When teaching and learning becomes a collaboration between teacher and students, both have agency.

Using the collaborative learning technique called "analytic teams," students discuss what they view and their reactions to it in small groups.[47] These teams allow them to address the subject of lynching and racism through the medium of dance in small groups. Students then share their findings to the entire class. Approaching *Strange Fruit* in this manner permitted students to examine the work in a multi-layered and complex manner as they search for how the dancing body makes meaning through this snapshot in early American modern dance history. In this learning strategy, students address the issue of racism through the subject of lynching. At the same time, students examine how Primus' work was not only an historical and artistic statement, but also a political one.

One collaborative learning technique I use is called "analytic teams."[48] I apply this approach to a unit called "Pioneers in Negro Concert Dance" and adapt it to prepare students to view Pearl Primus' significant work *Strange Fruit* (1943). I create two levels of analysis. For the Level I Analysis, students read Foulkes' chapter "Primitive Moderns."[49] They then take on roles as either (1) "proponent," listing points they agreed with, or (2) "critic," listing points they disagreed with, found unhelpful, or unclear. In addition, they prepare a list of examples of key points, a short summary, and questions they want to know more about or found confusing. Students submit a one-page paper, but before this, I ask them to share what they wrote.

Foulkes' chapter provides vital contextual information about the racist time that Primus was working. To prepare students for the Level II Analysis, I supplement this reading with a PowerPoint presentation that provides an historical snapshot of the lynching of Blacks in the U.S. I reference the book *Without Sanctuary: Photographs and Postcards of Lynching in America* by James Allen and John Littlefield.[50] Through the medium of photography, the book documents the magnitude of lynchings that occurred between 1882 and 1950. It helps lay the groundwork and provides a visceral context for Primus' work. It also helps students understand this atrocity in a more concrete way, as opposed to an abstract way by viewing some of the photographs.

Next, I provide the history behind Abel Meeropol's poem, *Strange Fruit*. Meeropol was a Jewish schoolteacher from New York City who saw a photograph of the Thomas Shipp and Abram Smith lynching that occurred in 1930. Students view a photograph of the actual lynching. The next slide is a text of the poem with an audio link to Billy Holiday singing *Strange Fruit*. Before students view Primus' choreographic interpretation, I include specific history on why she created it and the statement it made.

Students view a DVD of Philadanco dancer, Dawn Marie Watson, performing the solo from the *Dancing in the Light*.[51] Before students see *Strange Fruit*, they break into small groups. Each group is comprised of one analytic team. Each group member is assigned a role as they view the work. They are as follows:

1. movement analyst: comment on how the dancer's body is moving (e.g., quality, use of level changes, emphasis in the body, rhythm, breath, etc.);
2. text analyst: comment on the poem's text and its relationship to the dance;
3. character analyst: comment on what the dancer's role is in the work;
4. historical analyst: comment on what the work says about the time it was choreographed;
5. racial analyst: comment on what the work says about race and racism at this time in U.S. society;
6. gender analyst; comment on what the work says about women;
7. and, connector analyst (all): comment on how an aspect of Foulkes' chapter or the PowerPoint applies to the piece.

All students take on the role as "connect analyst" because it requires them to link Primus' work to Foulkes' chapter and to the PowerPoint. Students write as they view. After they view the work, in their teams, they compare responses and prepare a collaborative response to share with class.

Focused Listing: Revealing the Blackness in Balanchine

Cultural historian and dance scholar Brenda Dixon Gottschild's chapter "Stripping the Emperor" from her text *Digging the Africanist Presence in American Performance: Dance and Other Context* addresses the "black text"

Focused Listing Table: George Balanchine and Neoclassic Ballet			
Russia	Aesthetic	Dancing Body	New York City

in George Balanchine's neo-classical ballet aesthetic.[52] Students are assigned Dixon Gottschild's chapter. I reference her statement in a PowerPoint slide as follows: "In spite of our denials, opposites intermingle more than we admit. Cultures borrow from each other, and fusions abound."[53] Using the collaborative learning technique called "focused listing," her quote serves to anchor our investigation and discussion of the "black text" in Balanchine's ballet.[54]

Focused Listing is a collaborative learning technique. When I use the strategy it occurs over two class meetings. Day one is devoted to Balanchine and provides historical background on him and his work. Students read historical information and view excerpts of his ballets *Apollo* (1929) and *Stravinsky Violin Concerto* (1941). While reading about and viewing his work, they complete a "Focused Listing" table as indicated below.[55]

On their own, while they view the DVD, students jot down relevant associations with the concepts listed at the top of the table that are important to understanding the content. Once tables are complete, students break into groups of two. Within a set time limit of two to three minutes, they share the content of each other's table. Students come to consensus and report out their findings to the rest of the class.

This strategy focuses students' attention to specific aspects of Balanchine's history and aesthetic. It also supports the second class session that focuses on Dixon Gottschild's chapter. Particular emphasis on the dancing body equips students with a visual and analytical reference point to support discussion on "the black text in Balanchine's Americanization of ballet."[56]

Students analyze the dancing body in Balanchine's work. They reflect on their completed tables and describe how Balanchine deviated from the classical ballet aesthetic through the use of flexed feet and hands, a displaced pelvis, the use of parallel feet, angularity in the arms, bent knees, turned in legs, and the density and speed of his work, traits Dixon Gottschild references in her chapter. I also ask students to recall the "Comparative Analysis Chart" they complete in Worlds of Dance the semester prior, which compared Africanist and Europeanist dance characteristics in the 1600s. The table helps students identify distinct traits in the dancing body that are characteristic of West African forms. Such reflection enables them to recognize how they are infused in Balanchine's aesthetic.

During the second session, we discuss Dixon Gottschild's chapter in which she problematizes the still prevailing belief that ballet is White. I preface this session by reiterating her statement "In spite of our denials, opposites intermingle more than we admit. Cultures borrow from each other, and fusions abound."[57] In this context, the quote supports the concept that American ballet was the product of cultural fusion; at the same time, it dismantles the notion that the form is White. For students, referencing this quote helps them recognize that ballet also absorbed Africanisms at Balanchine's hand, as did others.

Next, students reflect on the movement traits present in Balanchine's choreography from the previous class period. I highlight certain points Dixon Gottschild makes in her chapter to focus class discussion. Some examples include the following:

1. the ethnicity of ballet (p. 61);
2. Balanchine's aesthetic (pp. 63, 64);
3. the black dancing body in ballet (p. 65);
4. Balanchine and Broadway (p. 69);
5. evidence of Africanisms in specific ballets (pp. 70–76); and
6. "Blue Note" (p. 78).

Through such discussion, we begin to problematize Balanchine's aesthetic and that it was only possible because he lived and worked in the United States where he could appropriate Africanisms. I am careful to acknowledge Balanchine's genius, but also challenge how his success was in part predicated upon his close contact with black dancers such as Katherine Dunham (Dixon Gottschild).

The topic of Balanchine's appropriation of Africanism continues with a PowerPoint that contains a photograph from Dixon Gottschild's book of him working with Arthur Mitchell in which Balanchine's hip is displaced to the left, mirroring Mitchell's. The photograph of Mitchell partnering a White dancer, Diana Adams, in Balanchine's *Agon* (1957) is also included. I point out to students how unprecedented it was to have a Black male partnering, or touching a White female body in this manner at this time. Further, students are asked to reflect on the larger historical context, because it was choreographed on the heels of the Civil Rights Movement and during a time when lynchings were still practiced in the south.

The final slide in a PowerPoint presents a quote by Dixon Gottschild: "At this point it will be silly to talk about Africanist presences as 'the Africanist contribution.' That is the outdated language of disenfranchisement, the mindset that implies that the European is something bigger or better into which the African—the Other—is subsumed. But there is no Other, *we are it.*"[58]

This statement helps trigger the final discussion about how Blackness and Whiteness are one in the American dancing body—despite how racist stereotypes and practices banned Blacks from the concert dance stage. It also helps my White students understand how Othering operated in a hierarchical manner to privilege one dance form over another—Whiteness over Blackness—normalizing Whiteness and making invisible the magnitude of Africanisms in American concert dance.

This course segment culminates with an essay test, which requires students to critically apply their knowledge of Balanchine to Alvin Ailey. Aimed at their critical thinking skills, the essay question began with a familiar quote to students as follows:

> Cultural historian Brenda Dixon Gottschild stated, "In spite of our denials, opposites intermingle more than we admit. Cultures borrow from each other, and fusions abound" [Dixon Gottschild, 1996, p. 60].
> How was the work of Alvin Ailey and George Balanchine examples of dance fusion?
> *Select one of their works and provide specific examples to support your response.*

This essay question required students to tease out how Ailey, who was Black, modern-based, and narrative driven, could be perceived as opposite to Balanchine, who was White, ballet-based, and abstractly driven in his approach to narrative. Further, that Ailey and Balanchine's opposites were not so opposite through appropriations of Blackness and Whiteness in their aesthetics. Ailey borrowed heavily from ballet, while Balanchine borrowed heavily from jazz/African-based movement sensibilities ubiquitous in American dance/movement culture.

Learning Logs: Assessing Student Engagement and Conflict

Learning logs are a pedagogic strategy that I adapted from an informal writing activity. Logs provide a vital way to assess student learning in course content and discussion.[59] The logs also reveal both students' increased awareness and conflicts they experience because of how Whiteness and Blackness are addressed in the course. Because the dialogue is a closed one between myself and individual students, students are more open to express how they are challenged, sometimes channeling it in ways that also challenge course content. As I previously stated, the fact that most students in my class are White has an impact on how students grapple with course content.

Entries are based on a series of prompts that students cannot repeat. Prompts are derived from John Bean's text on how to integrate writing, critical thinking, and active learning.[60] Logs are collected every three weeks. The prompts are as follows:

1. summarize a discussion;
2. explain why a reading was difficult to understand;
3. raise a question and discuss why;
4. apply some aspect of the class to personal experience;
5. make connections between different strands of the course;
6. express excitement in learning new ideas;
7. explain what confused you in a class;
8. express frustration about a point that was raised in class;
9. describe what effect this course is having on your personal beliefs, values, and previous understanding; and
10. relate this course to another course.[61]

Most of the students in my classes are open to examining dance history through a lens that deconstructs Whiteness. They acknowledge that they are unaware of the complex ways Black and White concert dance histories were so intricately interwoven. Others disclose that they are very naïve about the racism that Black dance artists encountered in early concert dance history. Most acknowledge how privileged they are as White dancers, as were White dancers from a century ago. Others discern that as dancers they are still privileged by their skin color even though they are marginalized as women. Students understand the impact racism had over the years in the United States and its impact on Black concert dancers.

In the early portion of the term, Foulkes' discussion of the relationship between Edna Guy and St. Denis, coupled with the first segment of the DVD *Free to Dance: What Do You Dance?*, were particularly helpful and resonate with students; they have to relfect on St. Denis' treatment of Guy. Others are able to problematize the inauthenticity and motivation of Ted Shawn's work through his appropriation or misappropriation of Native

American dance traditions in works like *Zuni Ghost Dance* (1931) or *Hopi Indian Eagle Dance* (1934). As well, some students are challenged by the course content.

Pushback and Privilege

As I previously stated, not all students are able to approach dance history in a manner that interrogates the western European concert dance paradigm. Some students do resist, exposing their racial bias as well as the ways in which they are unwilling to acknowledge how they benefited from their Whiteness. White privilege is problematized on two fronts in the course: (1) by developing the course in a way that White dancers, their history, their works, were not privileged over Blacks and (2) by exposing how such privilege operated in student's attitudes toward the course.

Since the Obama presidential era, anti-racist activist Tim Wise notes that, "evidence of white privilege has been even more ubiquitous than before."[62] White privilege, for many of us, means that we are unaware that we benefit from it and are less likely to relinquish it when it is threatened. My classroom is no different.

As I continue to teach this course, it has shed light on the ways in which students are challenged by my approach. For instance, a common concern that students express is that there is an overemphasis on Black content and that this equates to a disregard of White contributions. As demonstrated here, when race consciousness is integrated into course content, students may resist. Because Whiteness is normalized and dominates, blotting out other narratives. When it is problematized, a defense of Whiteness can arise. I suspect students would not respond that there was too much White content if I separated Black dance history to one chapter or segment of the course.

Another level of conflict arose in students when course material chronicled the plight of Black dancers trying to enter the arena of ballet. Some students contend that White dancers had to work just as hard and that Black dancers encountered only a slightly more difficult time—minimizing how racism permeated ballet studios and stages then and now. Students read Nyama McCarthy-Brown's article "Dancing in the Margins: Experiences of African American Ballerinas," which documented through oral histories what Black ballerinas face in the twenty-first century.[63] Nonetheless, it can be difficult for students to understand how systemic racism operated when Blacks auditioned for ballet companies as compared to their

White counterparts. Also present in their perspective was the inability to understand the corollary aspect of racism, which is White privilege.

Yet another indicator of student pushback was their perception that little attention is given to Native American contributions. I point out that with a few exceptions, Native Americans were not present in early concert dance. Further, because Native ancestry is harder to trace, it might not have been documented in American dancers. Arguably, there is no great body of Native American work that I exclude; it simply does not exist. As previously mentioned, I state that Native American influences occurred primarily through White appropriation in the work of modern choreographers such as Ted Shawn and Martha Graham. Student responses indicate that exposing the Blackness in concert dance can be difficult for them because of the perception that Native American contributions are not recognized. Problematizing the western concert dance paradigm by disclosing systemic racism in its practices is not easy for some students.

As previously stated, students are challenged by course content because of their perceived over emphasis on Black dance. The inability of students to discern the difference between presenting concert dance history in a manner that equally investigates the contributions of both Blacks and Whites, and their perception that there was too much Black content, indicates their racial bias. At other junctures in this course, student resistance manifests itself in responses like they have "Black friends." I suspect that they do so because they do not want to come-off sounding racist when their Whiteness needed to be defended.

Challenges and Opportunities

A Dance History course taught in a small classroom of twenty to twenty-five students in the early twenty-first century is still a microcosm of larger American society. This country, like my classroom, has a hard time talking about race because of an unwillingness to acknowledge how Whites have benefited from their skin color. We are founded on racism; it still permeates our culture. Academia is no different, nor my class. As Peggy McIntosh states in her seminal article "White Privilege: Unpacking the Invisible Knapsack," "Many, perhaps most, of our white students in the U.S. think that racism doesn't affect them because they are not people of color; they do not see 'whiteness as racial identity.'"[64]

Yet, despite the resistance I encounter from some students, such resistance can be channeled into opportunities for growth. Admittedly, I have been naïve in assuming that all students would willingly engage in dialogue that problematized concert dance history and the Anglo-Saxon norm that plagues the Black dancing body. Following Freire's anti-banking model that acknowledges students' backgrounds, even if they are racially biased ones, can be integrated into the teaching process. Content and learning strategies can be developed in such a way that students recognize themselves in what they are learning. Challenges can become teachable moments.

Based on some of the previous examples of student reaction to course content, here are some examples of how such challenges could become teaching and learning opportunities.

Present students with dance forms they have studied intensely like ballet. They recognize themselves in the dance form. Historically document how Black dancers were afflicted by racism. If students contend that Black dancers had only a slightly more difficult time succeeding than their White counterparts, I can problematize the student's own racial bias through a response to a journal entry. In this closed space, it is easier, perhaps safer, to suggest that a student consider focusing her final research paper on the subject matter to investigate the underrepresentation of Blacks in ballet. Encourage the student to include McCarthy-Brown's article "Dancing in the Margins" or Dixon Gottschild's book *Joan Myers Brown & the Audacious Hope of the Black Ballerina: A Biohistory of American Performance* in their references.[65] In addition, ask to them to read dance ethnologist Joann Keali-inohomoku's seminal article "An Anthropologist Looks at Ballet as an Ethnic Form of Dance."[66]

Present students with the complex and interwoven histories of Black and White concert dancers, including how racism was a part of this history. If students contend that there is too much emphasis on Black dancers, I can bring this forth in the form of a class discussion in which I ask students to grapple with this perspective. Presenting this issue in a public forum removes me as the target, refocuses it on the subject matter, and gets students discussing the issue from multiple viewpoints. This approach also reinforces Freire's anti-banking approach to teaching because it treats student understanding of complex subject matter as springboards for discussion.

Present students with various modern-based choreographic works in the early twentieth century by Black and White choreographers. If students state that Native Americans are underrepresented, implying again that there was too much emphasis on Black content, pose this as a take-home essay test. Develop the question in a way that students need to include examples of work, justify why it is an example of Native American modern dance, and who choreographed the work. Student responses, if accurately researched, will help them to find a historically accurate response—essentially that White dancers appropriated Native content, but that there was little choreographed or performed by the latter.

Conclusion

Racism, if left unchecked, will continue to divide this country. The institution of racism was so masterfully engineered from its inception that it still functions today. Yet the dancing body can offer one way to address this issue because it is rife with memory. Tracing this history requires that its contours are reshaped so that we can look at Black and White dancers and their works with new eyes—disrupting the western concert dance paradigm in the process. Approaching concert dance history in this way can help deconstruct the legacy and cultural dominance of Whiteness in dance and reveal the role racism played in shaping it.

The dancing body is a particularly powerful site because it is inscribed with both a rich and racist history. When students embark on a journey that seeks to dismantle privileging White concert dance over Black concert dance, it can also help them understand themselves and one another. In the classroom, this can occur when students discover what is new, different, similar, or challenging.

Moreover, students in the twenty-first century must be prepared to solve the challenges of our global society, which requires sophisticated, communicative, collaborative, and critical thinking skills; they need to know how to get along with one another. Often conflict erupts over differences between people, not their similarities. In this country, part of such discourse requires greater knowledge of how racism was built and is maintained, forming racial biases. My students are no different because they share the same history, as does the art form they study; they bring with them all the trappings of racism. Pedagogically, the key for me is an awareness of such thinking, its "contours," and the subsequent reshaping of such reasoning, even if this causes my students angst.

From a critical dance pedagogic perspective, students must recognize themselves in what they are learning. Their thoughts and opinions cannot be silenced, even if what they think is racially biased due to their own White privilege. Nevertheless, the classroom can become a place where students express such biases, and subsequently, as Frankenberg states, "look head-on at a site of dominance," even if that site is their own.[67] When students arrive at a place where they recognize the Blackness in their Whiteness—in their *own* dancing bodies—they then have reshaped their thinking. They understand the complex and interwoven history between Black and White dancing bodies in this country.

Eight

Native American Dance History and Powwow Styles

BY KELLY FAYARD

As an enrolled tribal member of the Poarch Band of Creek Indians, I have attended and participated in many tribal dances. These range from small, local tribal specific dances, like the stomp dance, to the largest pow-wow in the United States, the Gathering of Nations Powwow, held each year in Albuquerque, New Mexico. On most occasions I participate as a dancer, however, I have also been a tribal representative princess and a pow-wow committee member for the annual Poarch Band of Creek Indian pow-wow held each Thanksgiving. I served on the powwow committee for the first powwow at Duke University and for the Dance for Mother Earth Powwow in Ann Arbor, Michigan. The latter is a large student-run pow-wow that has been gaining momentum for decades. In this chapter, I share my personal experiences with powwow dances. However, because there are a myriad of powwows held across the United States, each with its own flavor and style, each person you talk with about powwows may have a different experience and reaction to teaching Native American dance styles.

I will first discuss the history of Native dance in the United States. Next, I will explain a few of the most popular dance styles with explanations of Native music and regalia that would be worn for these dances. Following this, I will discuss the cultural appropriation of Native culture and how to avoid that by using culturally sensitive teaching methods in your classroom. I will also include a discussion of teaching Native and non–Native students. The inclusion of Native dance in your course is a component of diversifying course curriculum and actively resists historic efforts to eradicate Native culture. Finally, I will provide a list of resources to consult as you explore Native culture and dance within your classroom.

When introducing Native American dance to students, there must be an acknowledgment and understanding of what kinds of activities and dances are appropriate for public consumption. Due to the fact that stereotypes and cultural appropriation of Native American culture, art, and spirituality happens regularly in the United States and internationally, we as educators must take care to make sure we do not present information in any way that reproduces or reinforces stereotypes, farces, or disrespectful representations of Native American issues and art forms.

Consider introducing Native American dance forms in your classroom by making contact and building partnerships with local Native American communities. The Bureau of Indian Affairs (BIA) keeps a list of federally recognized tribes, state recognized tribes, and tribes that are petitioning for federal recognition on their website. Get as close to the source of Native dances as you can. Make contact with the local Native community. Invite them into your classroom to present local traditions of dance. This is the most respectful way to bring Native American dance to your class.

A critical point to make when introducing Native American dance and culture into your classroom is diversity. According to the Bureau of Indian Affairs, there are over 566 recognized tribes in the United States (with new ones added periodically, most recently in summer 2015 the Pamunkey tribe of Virginia became federally recognized), and each of these tribes has a particular history, culture, and even dance that is particular to them. Not only does each of these tribes have a separate history and culture, but their experience with colonialism, racism, and ability to practice their culture is different. For example, many pueblos in the Southwest practiced their traditional dances since colonialism because of the resistance of pueblos to colonial cultures[1]; however, there are other tribes that no longer practice their traditions due to the forced assimilation of Native groups into the larger local American culture.[2] So the experience of each Native group is varied in its ability to practice traditions. Many tribes have, either in addition to or instead of their traditional dances and ceremonies, begun to practice the more Plains Indian tradition of a powwow since the early twentieth century. Powwow dancing is very popular in most parts of the United States by various Native nations.

A note about terminology. Many people question whether we should use American Indian or Native American. Many Canadian tribes use the term First Nations. The general rule of thumb for most Native people is that if you are talking about a particular tribe, you should use their name. For example, if you are talking about Creek stomp dancing, introduce it as Creek as opposed to Native American because it is particular to the Creek nation. If you are discussing a San Ildefonso pueblo antelope dance, describe it as San Ildefonso or Tewa. On the other hand, if you are discussing a dance where multiple tribes will participate, such as a powwow or other multi-nation event, then American Indian or Native American are both appropriate. As with many terms for identity markers, depending on who you ask, you will get a different answer about which is more appropriate. Other terms that may be used are indigenous, Native, aboriginal (usually only used in Canada), or Indian (many elders I know prefer the use of Indian). It helps to discuss this with students, as they are sometimes concerned about what terminology to use in their discussions of Natives.

A Short History of Native Dance

Discourse on the history of Native dance is deficient without addressing the attempt to wipe out Native people and culture from the landscape. The ways in which this process of ethnocide occurred had an emphasis on Native religion. Native religion is like many other religions found around the world, dance and other embodied expressions. It was these embodied expressions that missionaries and later government agents attempted to wipe out in an attempt to assimilate Natives into European/American culture. Whether English, French, or Spanish, missionary attempts to convert Natives began with their first contact. Jacqueline Shea Murphy, a dance educator at University of California–Riverside, writes in her book *The People Never Stopped Dancing: Native American Modern Dance Histories* that in many cases, from the perspective of explorers that encountered Natives and later Indian agents or government officials, Native people were considered heathens, with no souls, and were treated as bad as, or worse than, dogs or other domesticated animals.[3] As one Indian agent to the Hopi wrote in 1882:

> I have not yet attended any of their dances and cannot speak from personal knowledge; but, judging from reliable authority, the great evils in the way of their ultimate civilization lie in these dances. The dark superstitious and unhallowed rites of a heathenism as gross as that of India or Central African still infects them with its insidious poison, which, unless replaced by Christian civilization, must sap their very life blood.[4]

The prejudice and deep hatred of Native ways of being is apparent from this Indian agent's report; the agent's attitude towards Natives was common. Not only did most Indian agents and government officials look at Native people as having no souls, but government policies and procedures for how to deal with Natives came from this same sentiment. These sentiments—to wipe out Native culture—are inextricably linked with the mission to remove Native people from the land to allow it to be purchased and established by settlers. What must be emphasized here is that this was a systematic and institutionalized attempt on behalf of the United States and Canadian governments (as well as state governments) to dominate, and to make submissive, Native nations, inclusive of their cultural arts, across North America.

During the missionary period, before the United States was established, Catholic and Protestant missionaries alike worked to end Native religion. But since religion and culture are inextricably linked in Native communities, this meant that no part of Native culture was allowed to exist peacefully—every portion of Native culture and religion was constantly under attack. Once the United States was established, a more systematic genocide and ethnocide was introduced to Native communities. There were massacres meant to wipe out entire communities (see Wounded Knee Massacre and Sand Creek Massacre); there were removals of Native people to make more room for European settlers arriving in droves (see Trail of Tears that affected the Southeastern tribes, the Long Walk that affected the Navajo). In California, among other places, there were bounties offered for Native scalps.

Settlers were threatened by Native spirituality and religion. As Murphy explains, the fact that Native religion tended to be bodily—that praying involved "bodily movement through ritual practice rather than through sitting, reading, and believing, threatened colonizers' notions of how spirituality is manifested."[5] It was after colonizers began to see Native dances as solidifying the differences between whiteness and Indianness, allowing dancing to equate to Indianness, that anti-dance regulations began being passed by the government. This is the beginning of the movement by the government to "kill the Indian and save the man": by removing as many aspects of Native culture as possible and forcing Natives into white, patriarchal, Christian "civilization." This allowed the government to more clearly define who and what was Indian, and "having constructed Indianness via dancing, any shifts in the dancing could later be used to dismiss the Indianness of practitioners."[6]

In 1883, Indian agents from around the country were ordered by the secretary of the interior, Henry Teller, and the newly appointed Indian commissioner, Hiriam Price, to establish a "Court of Indian Offenses" in each of the Indian agent's territories. These courts were to be run by "civ-ilized" Indians who would be able to make judgments against Indian cul-tural institutions found to be problematic by the United States. The very first Indian offense called into question was dancing:

> 4. (a). Any Indian who shall engage in the sun dance, scalp dance, or war dance, or any similar feast, so called, shall be deemed guilty of an offense, and upon conviction thereof shall be punished for the first offense by the withholding of his rations for not exceeding ten days or imprisonment for not exceeding ten days; and for any subse-quent offense under this clause he shall be punished by withholding his rations for not less than ten nor more than thirty days, or imprisonment for not less than ten nor more than thirty days.[7]

Examples of other types of offenses that may have been charged against Native people were plural marriage, following the directions of medicine men, destroying other Indians' property, immorality (following a Christian based moral standard, this usually meant sex out of wedlock or same-sex relations), and intoxication.[8] The punishment for these offenses were the same as for the dancing—either taking away food or imprison-ment.

It was during the time period of the 1880s to the 1910s that dance shifted from being banned because it was seen as a prelude to war, such as the Ghost Dance, to "the more subtle threat to European dominion of bar-barism."[9] In 1904 regulations of Indian dances focused on the Sun Dance: "The 'sun-dance' and all other similar dances and so-called religious cer-emonies, shall be considered 'Indian offenses,' and any Indian found guilty of being a participant in any one or more of these 'offenses' shall, for the first offense committed, be punished by withholding from his rations."[10] Murphy continues, "In other words, the anti dance rhetoric shifted from a primary concern about Indian dancing as a prelude to warfare, with a focus on scalp and war dances, to a primary concern about Indian dancing as barbaric and immoral, with a focus on what officials called the Sun Dance."[11]

The effects of these governmental policies on Native dance practices cannot be underestimated. In fact, Andrew Brother Elk notes that "knowl-edge of federal governments' literal and spiritual genocide of Native Amer-icans—and the subsequent loss of Native dance practices—is still much too often dismissed or ignored in academia, from elementary school cur-riculum on."[12] The way in which Indian agents attempted to impose these laws and regulations was, in many cases, as violent as outright war against Native people. This is not to say that all Native dance culture was lost, quite the contrary; there was outright defiance from many Native people and communities to combat these policies. Many Indian agents noted "insubordination" by the tribal leaders in the communities where they worked. "This 'insubordination,' or refusal to participate in the prohibitions—to follow them or aid in enforcing them—formed part of the way in which Native dancers actively rejected the worldview government officials attempted to enforce on them."[13]

Another way, beyond outwardly defying the regulations, was to hide the dances and take them underground. In some cases, people told church officials and government agents that the dances were for United States Independence Day or to commemorate their patron saint. Native people became very creative in the ways in which they continued to dance and practice their religion. As one Santee wrote in protest of the Department of Indian Affairs:

> The Indians have dances for pleasure and help each other to put in their crops, and we saw a notice at the agent's office door to stop these dances; if they don't stop we will stop scouts' pay. The scouts want to dance till July 4, because Cleveland was elected. Have they a right to stop us if we disturb nobody?[14]

Native people persisted to perform their dances. In 1934, John Collier, who was the Commissioner of Indian Affairs at the time, repealed the anti-dance restriction, but the wording of the repeal suggested that torture (what many considered the Sun Dance to be) was still illegal until about 1952. Clyde Ellis, in his book on powwows, notes that by the time Collier overturned the dance bans,

> Southern Plains Indian people had already won much of the battle to maintain such practices. In the end, dance was more resilient than reformers, agents, and policymakers realized…. "These are still our traditional ways," says Ralph Kotay, a Kiowa. "Our people have been doing this all our lives."[15]

What is ironic is that even during times when the government outlawed these dances, white Americans lusted to see Native dances as they were historic. For many Americans, this is when Native people become a part of a vanishing past—no longer were Native people seen as contemporary to white society. Rather, Native people were seen only as a relic of the past (See Deloria and Ellis for further discussions on Wild West Shows and Indian dancing).

Styles of Powwow Dance

A powwow is a Native American celebration of song and dance that began on the Northern Plains but now stretches from its origin communities across the United States and Canada. I focus on powwow dances in particular because generally powwows are open to the public. Although some of the dances are for particular tribes, or groups, usually there are intertribal dances that invite anyone to join in.

I cannot emphasize enough the diversity and various types of dance among communities in Native North America. In addition, in many Native communities, there are sacred dances only performed secretly. Unlike in Western culture where there is a tendency to think that all knowledge should be knowable, or at least accessible, by everyone, that is not the case here. In some cases, only members of a community initiated into a particular society are able to know particular dances. It is for this reason that I choose to only describe dances that can be seen in public, mainly in powwow celebrations. Check out your local Native communities—chances are you will find some within driving distance of your institution, making it easy to visit with your classes.

Cultural Appropriation of Native Americans

Given the above described history of Native dancing in the United States, I hope that you can understand why cultural appropriation of Native American stereotypes, regalia, designs, dance, and other art forms are severely frowned upon by Native communities. Adrienne Keene, blogger and founder of Native Appropriations, said in a keynote at the University of California–Berkeley's conference "Perspectives on Native Representations": "There is no representation of us, without us."[16] Therefore, it is important when teaching Native dance to be sensitive to this issue. Including Native people—whether in a class or a demonstration—is the most important way to make sure you are being respectful. Multiple Native people involved in your class would be even better! If you have Native students, do not assume that they know these dances. Some tribes do not participate in powwows.

Many students may not understand the power of stereotypes surrounding Native Americans. Have them think about how their idea of Native dance developed. Is it from Peter Pan? Pocahontas? Discuss with your students why these images are stereotypes, and why it is important to get an accurate representation of Native dance in your classroom. Beyond these cartoons caricatures familiar to many of our students is a new trend of "hipster headdresses" coming in from fashion shows such as Coachella and Urban Outfitters, among others. Another place many students will have learned about Native Americans is through Native mascots such as the football team from Washington, D.C., or the Atlanta Braves baseball team. It is extremely important to recognize this as a stereotype and confront expectations before you begin talking about this in your class. These types of representations and assumptions are harmful and hurtful to Native people.

What's a Powwow?

A powwow is a celebration of culture, music, language, and dancing, with the main focus on dancing and music. Additionally there are vendors selling Native American art, jewelry, and other crafts. Typically there is at least one food stand selling Native food, such as corn soup or frybread. People are mostly in attendance to have fellowship and fun with other Natives.

Dancing is the main event. There are usually contests—people compete in different categories to be the best dancer in that event. The categories are usually divided by age (tiny tots, juniors, adults, seniors) and by gender (men have different dance styles than women). There are usually some "specials" at the powwow as well. This is when an individual or family sponsors a special contest for a particular group with an additional prize for the winner. For example, at the 2015 Gathering of Nations powwow held at the University of New Mexico basketball arena, the head man (the lead man dancer for the powwow) sponsored a "best traditional man" special. The winner received a chair, a jacket, and one thousand dollars. Some families celebrate graduations, birthdays, the birth of a child, marriages, or such life events. Some use the opportunity to honor the memory of a family member they recently lost. In any case, these specials are sponsored by families, as opposed to the powwow committee.

The structure of a powwow is generally the same. The dancing starts with a grand entry. This is where every dancer who will be competing comes into the arena at the same time. Typically, the grand entry is led by the American flag, any Native flags for tribes hosting or nearby, and an eagle staff, which is a staff with eagle feathers attached to it. U.S. military veterans bring these flags into the arena. Next, the head man and head woman dancers enter as well as any royalty (tribal princesses who have usually competed in a contest in their home communities). Then, various types of dancers are brought in, usually by dance category. There is an arena director who makes sure that everyone is where he or she is supposed to be. A master of ceremonies explains what is happening to everyone throughout the event, and makes jokes when things move along too slowly. There is also a head judge who organizes the judges for all of the contest dances.

The music played is provided by drum groups. Drum groups have a wide range of members. A small group usually has three to five drummers; I saw one large group with fifteen drummers crowded around one drum. While women usually do not play the drum, they are often part of the singing. There are two types of drum groups: northern and southern. Southern groups tend to have a deeper sound, and women's voices really highlight the songs; Northern groups sing at a higher pitch and women's voices compliment the songs in a more harmonic way. You can find examples of both styles on YouTube.

The songs themselves can be traditional, and therefore passed down through the generations, or they can be newly composed. Usually powwow songs are made up of a combination of traditional language and vocables, which sound like words but are not. Some powwow songs are in English as well! The songs usually have four "pushups" or verses. In each pushup, there are honor beats. This is where at least one member of the drum group beats the drum incredibly harder than others in the group. Usually dancers do something distinctive during the honor beats in order to mark the sound. For example, jingle dancers raise their feather fan to the sky in order to mark the honor beats. Drum groups also, in some cases, try to trick the dancers. They may end a song suddenly, or begin again suddenly. There is a real play between the music and the dancing at powwows.

Dance Styles

In the descriptions below, I am giving a general definition of each of the types of dance, but please understand that there is a large variety found across the North American continent. Within each category, there may be a number of alternate ways to perform the dance. Also, note that the regalia (powwow attire is referred to as "regalia, " as use of the word "costume" is seen as offensive and implies there is no real meaning behind it) that men and women wear at powwows is usually hand made. The beadwork is exquisite. The time and energy it takes to fringe a shawl or attach feathers to a bustle is intense and amazing. Powwows are also a time to feature the extensive beadwork of the culture, and many in attendance proudly display their cherished regalia and admire that of others.

Men's Dances

Grass Dance

The men's grass dance is considered to be a traditional form of dance. Men who are grass dancers wear regalia usually that is covered on the edges with ribbon or yarn. The other characteristic grass dance piece is the roach— a headpiece with a tall feather that includes tufts of hair on both sides, almost like a mohawk haircut. The story goes that grass dancers were the first dancers usually out onto the plains where tall grass grew. It was the job of the grass dancers to "dance down" this tall grass so that other dancers would have an easier time of dancing. Pieces of grass were tied to their outfits (this eventually became the yarn or ribbon). When looking at a grass dancer, one notices their graceful movements and wide steps—imagine a grass dancer in a sea of tall grass. When he brings his foot out wide and sweeps the floor, imagine that he is bending the tall grass so that others can dance more freely.

Northern Traditional

Men who dance traditional style will wear a bustle, attached to their back with feathers in a U-shape, along with a fan they carry in their hand. They will usually have a breastplate made from bone on their chest. They may also wear a roach headpiece like the grass dancers do. These men dance with grace and dignity. In some cases they are described as dancing like a chicken. In other cases, they have been described as looking as if they are tracking an enemy or tracking large game. Alternatives for this dance are the Crow Hop or Sneak Up dance (my personal favorite).

Southern Straight

This men's dance is similar to the Northern Traditional. Southern Straight dancers wear a ribbon shirt, usually made of calico (floral) material in the style of that first traded between settlers and Native people. There is usually no feather bustle, but a lot of beautiful and coordinated beadwork. Men usually carry a dancing stick or fan in their hand, or, if they do not have a stick, they might carry a mirror board. The dance style for Southern Straight is very regal, and looks as if the dancer is tracking something or someone. This style of dance is believed to have originated with the Ponca tribe in Oklahoma.

Fancy

The fancy dances, for both men and women, are considered the most exciting at the powwow. This is not a traditional dance. It was created in

Oklahoma in the mid 1900s. Visitors to their first powwow will notice the bright colors and the amount of feathers on the fancy dancers' regalia. This style of dance involves a regular dance step, with intricate fancy footwork featured as the trademark. These dancers really compete with the drum, with the drumbeat in some cases becoming increasingly faster in tempo until it abruptly stops. This is a very fun dance to watch.

Chicken

This dance, originally from the Blackfoot tribe, involves wearing a head roach, a small bustle on the back, and usually a string of bells that go on each leg from a belt to the moccasins of the dancer. This dance style more intricately imitates chickens dancing.

Women's Dances

Jingle

This dance originated around the Great Lakes region with the Ojibwe people. It is also referred to as the healing dance. Traditionally, dancers wore a dress covered in deer hooves that jingled as she danced. Eventually snuff can lids were rolled up to enhance the sound of the jingle. Today these jingles can be bought commercially but every now and then the more traditional materials are used. The dancers hop on their toes the entire dance, and raise their feather fan when the honor beats occur.

Traditional Southern Cloth

Dance regalia for traditional southern cloth is made from the same calico print material as many ribbon shirts. There is usually ribbon work attached to the dresses. In many cases there is an apron (with a pocket) worn over the dress. Dancers carry a shawl over one arm, and usually a fan or basket purse in the other hand. Imagine that dancers do not move their upper body, and their feet always remain close to the ground. The shawl's movement come from the bounce that the women do, not from swaying the upper body. The idea here is that the shawl is to massage Mother Earth as the dancer makes her way around the arena. When the honor beat occurs, she dips her head and changes directions from her path.

Traditional Buckskin

This is similar style to Southern cloth. Long buckskin fringe hangs from the dancer's regalia. This buckskin is also meant to massage Mother Earth as she dances. In many cases, a dancer may stay in one place the entire time she dances. Similar to some of the other dances, honor beats are acknowledged by lifting a fan to the sky. In the same style as the Southern cloth, women bounce or side step around the arena without moving their upper bodies.

Fancy Shawl

The fancy shawl dance was created in the mid–1900s as a response to the men's fancy feather dance. The movement of this dance is said to mimic a butterfly, and the quickness and lightness of the dancers' feet are important. Women wear a shawl across their backs, usually decorated with bead or applique work and dance on their toes the entire song. It almost seems like they barely touch the ground as they dance their way across the arena.

Other Dances

Hoop Dance

The hoop dance is a beautiful and intricate dance done usually by one person at a time at a powwow. This is based on the fact that the hoop represents the circle of life. As many as fifty and as few as four hoops may be used in a hoop dance, with each dancer deciding for him or herself how to interpret the dance. Usually it involves using the hoops to make intricate shapes and figures such as a bird, a sphere, or a butterfly. Dancers may also use the hoops to do quick and agile movements such as jumping through the hoop like a jump rope. Hoop dancers tend to be men but there are more women and girls picking up this dance style. A hoop dancers' outfit is relatively sparse as they need to be able to move through the hoops at various times.

Round Dance

A round dance is a community dance in which everyone participates. It can be very simple (a side step) or a bit more intricate, but it is a time when the community bands together to dance. In some cases, leaders can take round dances into a circle, or lead it into spirals or other formations.

Two-Step

The two-step is a type of couples' dance. In most cases, it is a women's choice dance with repercussions for a man who turns her down. Usually the head man and head lady of the powwow lead this dance. There are a few different forms of this dance from around the continent, but usually one can pick it up just by watching the person in front of you. In some cases, the men and women separate and go in opposite directions as they dance, but eventually they do come back together. Spins, comedic miming, and interesting turns are all a part of the two-step.

Conclusion

Native culture lives and thrives through its cultural dance forms. The dances discussed herein are expressed, with variety, throughout the United States and Canada. While each tribe has a variety of traditions and religious practices that are practiced individually, powwows are important because they bring together different tribes for one goal: to dance, compete with one another, have fun, and keep important powwow traditions alive for future generations. There is unity through the diversity of tribes to come together for these events. Given the government's attempts (in the United States and Canada) to wipe out these dances through ethnocide, it becomes even more vital to ensure these traditions and ways of life are preserved.

In dance classes where I have been invited to share these styles of dance, the instructors and the students have found the dance styles accessible and enjoyable, with an overwhelmingly positive response from both. According to colleagues, students remembered these sessions in particular, because they knew so little about Native culture before, and were appreciative, I think, of having some exposure to Native culture and dance. For instance, students found the *round dance* easy to follow, a unifying dance that is done at many a Native gathering. Through this embodied experience students were able to understand how many groups achieve unity through diversity.

Although this chapter is a short introduction to Native American powwow dancing, it can serve as a resource to encourage understanding Native culture and sharing with students in a respectful manner. It is significant to note that this type of community cultural event was illegal for a long time in the United States. Only through the resilience and determination of Native people are these dances and traditions kept alive today. Given the great strides taken by government laws and agents to try to stifle all Native dance and culture, it is worth noting that the dedication that Native people have to keeping culture alive despite all odds is what enabled many of these traditions to continue.

Resources for the Classroom

Blogs and News Sources

Native Appropriations
Beyond Buckskin
Indian Country Today
Indianz.com
Powwows.com

YouTube Videos

Grass dance
Jingle dress dance
Women's traditional
Men's traditional
Men's straight
Women's fancy
Men's fancy
Gathering of Nations Powwow
Denver March Powwow

Books

Playing Indian by Phil Deloria
The People Have Never Stopped Dancing by Jacqueline Shea Murphy
The Heartbeat of the People by Tara Browner
A Dancing People by Clyde Ellis

Movies

Reel Injun (general stereotypes about Native Americans)
The Ways (www.theways.org; there is a specific short film about a
    young college student who powwows on the weekend called
    "Powwow Trail")

Local Native groups

http://www.ncai.org/tribal-directory
Bureau of Indian Affairs (BIA) website

Considerations

- Try to make contact with the local Native American community. Invite them to your classroom. It is preferable not to teach any Native dance without consulting with a Native community before hand.
- When talking about a particular tribe, encourage students to use that name! Discuss terminology with students, as they are sometimes unsure what language they should use to discuss Native people.
- Discuss stereotypes of Native dance and Native images that your students might hold.
- Ask students what they know about powwow dances, as a class discussion. This way if you have Native students that do not know about or feel uncomfortable sharing this aspect of their culture, they are not put on the spot.
- Do not refer to Native regalia as "costumes."

Native women in regalia. From left: Ashton Megli, Choctaw Nation of Oklahoma, Choctaw dress and apron; Rose Bear Don't Walk, Bitterroot Salish, traditional wingdress; Katie McCleary, Little Shell Chippewa and Crow, Apsaalooké Elk Tooth Dress; Charelle Brown, Santo Domingo Pueblo, Santo Domingo Pueblo traditional black manta and dress; Kelly Fayard, Poarch Band of Creek Indians, traditional Southern cloth/Creek dress; and Alanna Pyke, Saint Regis Mohawk Tribe, traditional Salish wingdress.

Nine

World Dance

Retire the Term

In 1992, professor of Dance Education Sarah Hilsendager shared the below sentiments to a group of dance educators at a conference. It is problematic that more than twenty years later the same statement can be made of Dance Education in colleges and universities throughout the United States. "The majority of university dance programs emphasize ballet and modern genres, 'which are Eurocentric in both content and teaching approach.' Dance forms with origins other than in Europe are often slighted, causing future teachers to be unprepared for working with diverse student populations."[1]

Within the context of a critical dance pedagogy (CDP) approach, the question of language often comes to the forefront. In an examination of Dance Education nomenclature, one should consider how language supports and informs institutional racism. Language has been utilized to support Eurocentric infrastructures that permeate the field of Dance Education.

Through a CDP lens, this chapter asks what "World Dance" means. In the United States, many intuit the meaning of the term. The implied definition is as much confusing as subtle for those experiencing life through a filter whereby race and class are markers. World Dance has come to be applied to the dances of disenfranchised people, almost impossible to define without referencing the privileged position held by non-included dance forms in the description. Although the term might very well have come to be created with the intent of respecting diverse cultures, its usage has come to communicate pervasive social constructs of race and class in the U.S. Today, the term has come to divide and marginalize, no longer serving the purpose of years past. More pointedly, Clinical Professor of Dance Pegge Vissicaro speaks to these issues in *Studying Dance Cultures Around the World: An Introduction to Multicultural Dance Education*.[2] She asserts that in educational institutions the term perpetuates cultural, ethnic, national and racial stereotypes, and that it reinforces a Eurocentric hierarchy of dance. Such stereotypes lead to this chapter's examination of terms that have been strategically used to contribute to the hegemonic power of European and U.S. based art forms.

The work of dancer, scholar, and historian John Perpener III confronts the issue of cultural dominance of Western dance forms. He writes: "The central authority imposes its concepts of art and culture upon the subordinate people. Under these circumstances, the cultural and artistic expressions of those who are ruled may continue to exist, but they are labeled with new referents by those who rule."[3] Perpener bases his work on the work of philosopher Francis Sparshott who identified classifications such as Ethnic Dance as masques used to downgrade subordinate groups and solidify cultural dominance. Perpener moves further to assert that such tactics are utilized to "insure the cultural hegemony of European and American art."[4] He also notes the historical effort to label black artists performing Western dance forms as black dance. The idea that dance created by black dance artists is inherently black dance, even when the technique the dances are expressed and presented through is modern/Western-based, is racist. Moreover, the need to categorize such dances as black dance is born out of an elitist need to create divisions and subjugate those with less agency. However, there is something to be said for identifying a dance that relates, describes, and speaks to the black experience. This is a valued practice, and many artists, like myself, take great pride in creating black dance. Yet would one categorize all dances created by white people as white dance? Blanket categorization enacts a double standard and is dangerous in its ability to oversimplify and overlook individual artistic expression.

Dance scholar Drid Williams writes, "The dance world is not immune to ethnocentric ways of thinking. A taxonomic distinction that is widely used among dancers, teachers, choreographers, critics, and dance historians is that of "ethnic" dancing, which simply distinguishes *their* dancing from *ours*.... The "ethnic dance" category is particularly damaging, for it creates a false picture of the activity and of the people who dance."[5] She also notes the dominance of the Western perspective of dance and Western dance forms throughout text resources on dance. Privileging Western dance in this manner contributes to the *their dance* versus *our dance* mentality that permeates the field of dance.

Dance scholar Brenda Dixon Gottschild writes of ballet's ethnicity in *Digging the Africanist Presence in American Performance.*[6] She explains that to describe ballet as an Ethnic Dance form is to acknowledge a democratic dance community void of hierarchies. In addition, such an act would nullify ballet's high art and elitist position. Ballet has been and continues to be isolated and placed "above other world art forms."[7] Thus, one can see the way racially tinged dance terminology and language supports divisions within the dance community.

This chapter explores the history of the term World Dance, how it is used in higher education, and offers alternatives. Suggestions of alternatives are intended to honor the heritages of the people to whom these dances belong. Although a number of possibilities are given, ultimately, I advocate for specific recognition of dance forms, and, optimally, for the term World Dance to be eradicated.

Methods

I used language as a theoretical frame of symbolic power to examine the term "World Dance." Recognizing the impact of the Internet, I also explored how globality and new systems to transmit culture and dance influence our understanding of dance forms. A historical lens was employed in order to examine how the meaning and usage evolved over time and its functions within the field of dance today. Historical documents such as dance reviews, encyclopedias, books, and programs were examined for this part of the research. Finally, through a content analysis, I studied concert dance programs and websites of various metropolitan performance venues to examine how non–Western dance was presented.

Primary focus for this research were programs and dance departments offering bachelor's degrees. *Dance Magazine's College Guide 2012–2013* was used to locate more than thirty dance programs that offered World Dance courses in the United States.[8] I added two international institutions for comparison. Once identified, I examined each dance program's curriculum design, course offerings, and mission statements. Germane to this research, it is important to note that *Dance Magazine* identified schools offering World Dance only if courses had words such as World Dance or Dances of the World in their course names. *Dance Magazine's* roster also included schools that offered dance forms other than ballet and modern such as African or Irish dancing.

This study was an outgrowth of my dissertation research completed in 2010. In that research, case studies of cultural diversity in the curricula of three dance departments were made. In instances in this chapter, where the name of an institution is omitted, it is because the data was extrapolated from this initial research. In the previous study, departments participated contingent upon anonymity because I conducted observations and surveys in addition to a content analysis of curriculum. I have synthesized some of this data to enhance the research present herein.

Language and Categories as Tools of Subjugation

Many people recognize the power, agency, and, indeed, privilege communicated by and wielded through language. Sociologist Pierre Bourdieu has written extensively on the symbolic power of language.[9] Language is a system of communication used to establish a shared understanding of symbols—words. Use of words can be industry or institution-driven; individuals using the word may be compelled to do so by their institutional structures. A word, as an extension of language, is an agreed upon symbol to all parties communicating through a given dialect. However, there are instances when an individual uses a particular word for lack of a better term or because of its recognized meaning. For example, I have used the term World Dance in classroom discussions in recognition of the nomenclature currently in use.

Bourdieu wrote that language is a socializing agent, used to communicate laws, educational instruction, and appropriate etiquette, among other constructs.[10] It is in this way that "World Dance" communicates a socializing message about its status as usage places ballet and modern, the excluded genres, in a position of dominance. Use of the term by dance departments in institutions of higher education and performance promoters gives legitimacy for World Dance. Yet, at the same time, the way the term is used, racism and classism are also exposed. Even though the word "world" is very inclusive, it is exclusive when used in conjunction with another inclusive word, "dance." The result is a term that excludes Eurocentric dance forms that have been historically privileged in funding and curriculum.

In *Identities and Inequalities*, professor of sociology David Newman examines the use of language to conceal variation. "While linguistic terminology—whether imposed from without or embraced from within—marks groups as different, it can also be used to gloss over relevant internal variation, thereby lumping together disparate groups different with different languages, cultures, religious beliefs, and histories."[11] World Dance is an excellent example of a linguistic term that lumps different groups and identifies the larger group with a term imposed from outside. In *Worlding Dance*, professor of dance Marta Savigliano notes that the term World Dance was imposed by those outside the cultures in which each dance form originated. To support this notion is the reality that few dancers identify themselves as World Dancers. One may identify as a practitioner of a World Dance form or as an applicant for a World Dance position.[12] But these instances are limited and often used for the purpose of validation within the Western world of dance or to gather the appropriate applicant pool. In *The Dance Catalog*, a number of Ethnic Dance companies are identified. For instance, Ballet Hispanico, Chiang Ching Dance Company, Aman Folk Ensemble, Maria Alba Spanish Company, and Chuck Davis Dance Company are listed.[13] It is interesting that none of these dance companies self-identify as an Ethnic Dance company, unlike ballet companies, i.e., San Francisco Ballet Company. Those companies categorized under terms such as World Dance, or, in the past, Ethnic Dance, have not been given the opportunity to consent to or contest these labels.

Issues of power, agency, racism, and classism cannot be separated from the discourse of language or usage of a term, giving significance to the symbolic power of language. Savigliano addresses this issue by posing the following questions concerning the polarizing, subjugation, and privilege that is inherently tied to the term.

> Who keeps the World Dance collections? Who finances World Dance in globalization? Who owns the modes of production of World Dances? Who gets to decide which dances and dancers qualify as worldly? Who gets to present World Dances, where, and for the spectatorial pleasure of whom? Who provides the dancing labor? Who migrates with little more than world dancing labor to sell for his/her subsistence in the World Dance metropolis of the world? Who has no choice but to dance their way into the world and who World Dances for the heck of it?[14]

These questions highlight the deficit of power held by World Dance practitioners and disenfranchised groups that have developed various dance forms. The term World Dance has helped to categorize these dance forms for easy commodification.

Bourdieu asserts that language can be used as a "structuring instrument of communication ... which [helps] to ensure that one class dominates another."[15] He explains that as the dominant culture establishes the structure, it also decides on what grounds the culture will be divided and unified. To look at World Dance through this lens, one must consider who decides how dances are categorized, who benefits from the categories, and who is suppressed. Categories are created to organize understanding of a given content. But what seems missing from this dialogue is the recognition that a single dance form is already a category. The question then becomes "What is communicated in holding one space for ballet and modern and another space for other forms?" Ballet is one category just as hip-hop is another, and Bharatanatyam yet another—all with numerous sub-categories. Moreover, World Dance distorts understanding of individual cultures in establishing a category with a collective identity.

To better discuss Western dance techniques, I created the term Western and historically privileged technique. It is a bit cumbersome, but Western needed a qualifier because it failed to include all Western dance techniques.[16] For example, hip-hop originated in the United States, but it is not considered a Western dance form in the traditional sense, like modern dance that also has origins in the United States and Germany. The African-based dance characteristics that hip-hop demonstrates deem this dance form be identified as non–Western. Moreover, the term "Western dance" refers to more than location of development, but rather a Eurocentric ideal of the West. With this understanding, World Dance provides a category for many dance forms outside the "Western and historically privileged" dance frameworks of modern and ballet.

Presenters of professional dance companies currently use the term World Dance to categorize themselves for funding and publicity purposes. Savigliano explains that World Dance represents others' "fascinat[ion] with difference as they elicit culturally progressive cosmopolitan values."[17] She adds that World Dance engages a specific market for the consumption of a particular kind of dance—dances of "the other." It is the othering of these dances that makes them a commodity. "Scholars, critics, professional artists, and presenters work transnationally as 'cultural intermediaries,' selecting and shaping the kinds of dancers and dancings that constitute World Dance."[18] As Savigliano highlights, the work of scholars and presenters serves not only to enhance World Dance as a commodity but also to shift the context and content in which the dance was created—chipping away at the authenticity of the form.[19] It is unfortunate that the good intentions to present multicultural perspectives in the dance classroom, in the literature, and on the stage have created additional locales of dance imperialism.

Globalizing World Dance

Today we have access to dances from all over the world. People are connected through the Internet, cell phones, Skype, iPads, conferencing software, gaming systems, and new devices that are constantly entering the market. Such access can be better understood through the term globality, defined as "tight global economic, political, cultural, and environmental interconnections and flows that make most of the currently existing borders and boundaries irrelevant."[20] Building on this definition to better contextualize this discussion, I refer to this phenomenon as cultural globality.[21] As cultures distant from us become more accessible, they also become threatened. There are no controls on how specific cultural dances may be appropriated, altered, misinterpreted, exploited, and redistributed.

Cultural globality can be seen in the appropriation of the Harlem Shake. The Harlem Shake is an African American vernacular dance that was created in Harlem more than thirty years ago.[22] It focuses on articulate and rhythmic isolations of various parts of the body. A poor imitation of the Harlem Shake that wiggles, shakes and flops the body about indiscriminately has developed, representing a co-opted version by people erroneously interpreting the movement. In February 2013, participants in this appropriated dance posted a video online and it went viral. Video posts identified the dance as the Harlem Shake. Due to such mass social media forms, the altered and proliferated versions gained more popularity than the original Harlem Shake. In essence, participants of the new dance craze were claiming a dance form that was rooted in the experiences of African American urban culture, where it had begun decades ago.[23] Williams wrote, "Attaching the wrong nomenclature to moves in someone else's body language game connotes lack of respect for them and what they are doing."[24] This is especially disconcerting because Harlem and the entire African American community has been the victim of cultural appropriation, without acknowledgment of the community in which the art was created, since at least the late nineteenth century.[25] What happened to the Harlem Shake represents just one of the challenges continually being faced through the globalization of dance.

The relationship between risk and reward must be acknowledged and considered in understanding the impact of globality on dance. With the rapid globalization of the world, categories of world and global dance become less descriptive and increasingly more insufficient.[26] Although further discussion of cultural globality and appropriation are beyond the scope of this chapter, within the framework of mass communication, cultural identity and artwork are vulnerable. This is especially true in regard to under-resourced groups that hold little agency beyond the boundaries of their locale. The importance of respecting the cultural identities of dances must begin with the nomenclature in the field itself.

Global Dance and Beyond

The term Global Dance came into existence in the last decade as a remediation of the term World Dance. However, Global Dance carries the same misunderstandings and has never gained wide acceptance. Because of an expanded sense of dance throughout the world, finding one term that includes all the multiple and diverse artistic and cultural achievements within dance becomes more challenging. The dilemma, ongoing for now almost a century, has brought forth numerous options. In fact, World Dance is the revision for the previously used term "Ethnic Dance." However, with each remediation, the problem remains: what dance form is not in the world? All dances possess qualities of ethnicity and are thus world dances of one kind or another or a fusion of dance forms. In the following section, I provide a brief history on the origins of these terms.

Origins and Use of Ethnic Dance

When examining the term World Dance in context with its lineage, reasons to retire the term become pronounced. Historically, dance forms derived from ethnic groups and sub-cultures were categorized with descriptors that today would be politically incorrect, e.g., heathen, pagan, savage, folk, and tribal. These became categories which were regularly used in dance critiques, dance encyclopedias, and books on dance at the time.[27] These terms consistently contributed to a culture of white supremacy, as they were assigned to disenfranchised people, denigrating them as having an inferior status. At the same time these terms gained significance during the 1930s, dance in higher education was in its infancy.[28] Thus, terms that preceded the use of Ethnic Dance (i.e., primitive dance, see page 178) were not part of the academy.

The dances of Ruth St. Denis, included in the category of Ethnic Dance, were also categorized as "exotic" dances. She built her repertory focusing on dances that, at the time, were considered "Oriental dances."[29] Because of the extensive critical analysis given to "Orientalism" in dance, the topic deserves further discussion.[30]

In *Sweating Saris*, dance scholar Priya Srinvasan explains how for many in the United States, the expectations of Oriental bodies were not satisfied by the modestly dressed Indian dancers with their skilled artistry who came to the United States in the late 1800s. Instead, white women, like Ruth St. Denis, were the ones able to satisfy the thirst for bodies from the Orient. With their ability to reinforce the stereotype, white women in "brownface" would embody, promote, and proliferate the exotic ideals held about Indian people. As Srivasan describes, "temple and court dancers, swathed in jewels and rich silks, doing sexy erotic dances to tantalize men. Women of color (particularly Asian women) were hypersexualized within the discourse of both orientalism and U.S. racialization."[31] Further, the historical context of this term of Orientalism and others like it began a paradigm of understanding, whereby dance forms outside the dominant culture were named and understood on the terms of the dominant culture. It perpetuates a history of othering people outside the U.S. mainstream. It is time to seek identifying labels and understanding of dance forms from the originators and practitioners of the form, rather than the dominant culture.

Professor of anthropology and women's and gender studies, Jane Desmond connected the work of St. Denis in the piece *Radha* to the philosophic frameworks of Edward Said and Sigmund Freud in "Dancing Out the Difference: Cultural Imperialism and Ruth St. Denis's *Radha* of 1906." Desmond describes how *Radha*, viewed through the lens of Orientalism and defined by Said,[32] communicates that "the mute colonized female represents the sensuality of both the 'female' and the Orient."[33] Said used the following words to describe the West's view of the East, "childlike, irrational, sensual, and sexual," adding that the East had been framed in a manner to be well-served by the voice of the West for interpretation. Desmond builds upon this idea, noting that women are often also described in the same manner, creating a duel lens of subjectivity for persons female and of Asian descent.[34] Desmond brings forth the work of Freud to support her claim: "Freud's description of women's sexuality as the dark continent reminds us of the intimate relationship among orientalism, gender, and the third register of otherness: race … like female sexuality and imaginative geography of the colonialism, the 'dark races' were represented as objects to be illuminated, mapped and controlled."[35]

As one examines the othering of women and Asians, a double bind of sexual and racial subjectivity becomes apparent. It is worth noting that white women proliferated this stereotype early in the twentieth century, and, today, it is being perpetuated through the U.S. mainstream, in relation to the growth, practice, and presentation of belly dancing.[36] In recognizing these historical and insidious forms of misrepresentation and irreverent appropriation, one must consider the terms in which we participate, teach, and perform World Dance forms today in relation to forms such as Oriental or exotic dance of previous centuries.

The term Primitive Dance was used as a descriptive term as early as the 1930s[37] and most often connected to black dancers. John Martin, dance critic for the *New York Times* from the 1930s to the 1960s, encouraged the "primitive ritual dances" of Negroes.[38] In the 1940s the term "primitive dance" was often associated with modern dance pioneer Pearl Primus. Her discussions of Primitive African dance and its influences on churches of the South are part of dance historian Anatole Chujoy's seminal work *The Dance Encyclopedia* published in 1949. Primus described the importance of religious, social, and political practices reflected in African dance and the relationship between the dancer and the drummer. She also acknowledges the commonalities between Primitive African dance and movements seen in black churches of the South.[39]

The term Ethnic Dance, coming into use a decade later, was coined by La Meri (Russell Meriwether Hughes), self-described Ethnic Dancer. In *Total Education in Ethnic Dance*, La Meri explains that she introduced the term in the 1940s.[40] La Meri defined the term Ethnic Dance in a way that separated Ethnic Dance from ballet, a reflection of the time in which it was written:

> The term "ethnic dance" designates all those indigenous dance arts which have grown from popular or typical dance expressions of a particular race.... In the larger sense the term "ethnic" is so all-embracing that it is easier to define it by saying what it isn't than what it is. The ballet is not an ethnic dance because it is the product of the social customs and artistic reflections of several widely-differing national cultures.[41]

Le Meri's definition fails to take into account that many dance forms that would fall into the category of World Dance (formerly Ethnic Dance), like ballet, are "artistic reflections of several widely-differing national cultures"[42] such as Afro-modern, Bollywood, salsa, and West African Dance (often a mixture of dances from several countries in the Western region of Africa).

The term Ethnic Dance has inspired controversy for decades. This is largely because Ethnic Dance (World Dance) became a catch-all term for dance forms outside ballet or modern. Early challengers argued that ballet and modern dance also reflect a culture from a specific part of the "world," and can, therefore, be identified as Ethnic Dance forms. One could also interpret these definitions as a justification for a system of covert racism since dance forms excluded from the term are Western and historically privileged. Because all dance forms reflect cultural traditions, or a cultural ideology embodied and valued by practitioners, it is not logical that some dance forms are Ethnic Dance and others are not. All dance is culturally informed.[43]

Anthropologist Joann Kealiinohomoku questioned the term "Ethnic

Dance" in her seminal 1970 article "An Anthropologist Looks at Ballet as a Form of Ethnic Dance" which outlined the reasons why ballet is not considered an Ethnic Dance form. She also acknowledged the negative connotations associated with the term Ethnic Dance, stating that "all dance forms reflect the cultural traditions within which they were developed."[44] Kealiinohomoku claimed that ballet was not included in the category of Ethnic Dance because Western dance scholars only assigned this category to dance forms held in lower esteem than ballet. To further assert her viewpoint, she noted how Western scholars historically would not apply terms such as folk and primitive to ballet. Use of the words primitive and ethnic diminished greatly in the 1970s. For example, in her text about Zimbabwean dance, professor of dance Kariamu Welsh decided to exclude the term "primitive" due to the word's stigma and inaccurate interpretations.[45] A number of scholars, like Kealiinohomoku previously, have written about the challenges of terms such as "primitive and ethnic."

In the 1979 edition of *The Dance Catalog*, dancer and choreographer Matteo contributed a section on Ethnic Dance. He noted the complexities of the term and its problems as a category, even in the late 1970s. Matteo described Ethnic Dance as folk dances and explained that the cultural context and geography of the region where the dance originates informs the movement, purpose, clothing and footwear worn in the dance. He wrote that Ethnic Dance stands in contrast to ballet, modern, jazz, and tap. Spanish, Indian, and black dance were identified as Ethnic dance forms—each maintaining dance forms within the sub-category (i.e., Spanish dance was a category for Spanish classical, Spanish regional, Flamenco, and Spanish neo-classic-contemporary).[46] The inclusion of black dance as an Ethnic Dance form is especially interesting because black dance presented in the U.S. during this period was largely presented as concert dance.[47] Thus I argue that the term Ethnic Dance was not needed to separate concert dance forms from indigenous dance forms, but was used to separate white dance forms from black dance forms.

Although Matteo separated jazz from Ethnic Dance, choreographer and author Frank Rey wrote of jazz being America's Ethnic Dance in 1971. In his essay "Jazz: America's Ethnic Dance," Harlem and New Orleans are identified as the place that holds the roots of jazz.[48] Yet the African American community that provided the foundational movement vocabulary[49] is not mentioned in his essay, nor is any other ethnic group. He states, "As in other ethnic forms, jazz has evolved from folk dance." But he does not identify to what ethnic group these folks belong. While Rey describes jazz as an American Ethnic Dance, he connects the dance form to several white men, Luigi, Gus Giordano, Jack Cole, Peter Gennaro, and Matt Mattox.[50] Thus, Rey perpetuates a long- time practice of not crediting the African American community for its artistry.[51] Rey's contribution to the literature is interesting because, just several years later, Matteo identifies jazz as a mainstream staple, in contrast to Ethnic Dance.

I have seen jazz taught as an African American dance form described as "vintage jazz." This style of jazz included African American vernacular movement vocabulary such as truckin', pickin' cherries, and the boogie woogie. In contrast, I have seen jazz taught within the context of Western dance forms, using ballet terms such as tendue and plié. In this context European dance aesthetics of an upward orientation with the upper body are embraced along with an Africanist aesthetic and grounded orientation with the lower body. Here one can see the challenges with categorization and classification as both are subjective. Similar to the way Matteo described Spanish dance, there is great variety within the genre of jazz. This could explain why today jazz is widely accepted as a category of its own and usually not included in the category of World Dance.

An accurate history of these terms must acknowledge their racial and class connotations. The racism insinuated through use of and society's interpretation of the terms brought about changes in the twentieth century terminology. These issues of race and class underpin the terms Ethnic Dance, World Dance, and Western Dance. Consequently, few dance artists want to be placed in these categories.

In 1973, anthropologist Judith Lynne Hanna wrote "Ethnic Dance Research Guide: Relevant Data Categories." The guide provided criteria to document an Ethnic Dance form that presumably would be outside the traditional research format of a "*non*–Ethnic Dance." Researchers collected data on specific categories such as the dancers' "clan, tribe" and "clothing (ordinary, different from ordinary)."[52] The term "Ethnic Dance" came to suggest more than one's ethnic group. There were implications of a static repertory of dances representative of a people, but not necessarily having artistic or classical merit; in other words, non–Western dance forms. For numerous reasons, the term was problematic. Later in the decade, Hanna redefined Ethnic Dance in *To Dance Is Human.* This definition focused on group commonalities: "Dance is ethnic when it is explicitly linked to an ethnic group's sociocultural traditions; an ethnic group has common cultural tradition and a sense of identity based upon origins; its members constitute a subunit within a larger society."[53]

While this definition can be considered more culturally sensitive, it fails to embrace the globality of dance in the twenty-first century. Globality today allows dances to be practiced through personal choice as opposed to cultural affinity or tradition. In many instances, ethnic heritage is not a criterion for dance practitioners. The result is these dance forms are danced by people who are not directly related to the ethnic group or culture. For instance, Bharatanatyam is not exclusive to dancers of Indian heritage. Some forms such as ballet, modern, and contact improvisation are practiced by people who are connected through sociocultural traditions as opposed to ethic affinity or professional performing context. For example, in Portland, Maine, Marita Kennedy-Castro, a white woman, leads the West African dance community and most participants are white. Globality allows for this shift in locale, for the form to change, adapt, and be practiced and celebrated in new places. Today dance forms from all over the world are being exported and cultural background is no longer a criteria for practitioners.

Cultural sensitivity around language has heightened in recent decades. Many are cognizant of the power of words and select their usage of words wisely. For this reason, I find this following definition in dance historian Selma Jeanne Cohen's *The International Encyclopedia of Dance* describing Ethnic Dance to be regressive:

> [It is] viewed as a leftover category—dance that is not from a classical tradition such as ballet, or the classical dance of India, not theatrical, not social, and not popular. Terms used to designate this troublesome category in the past include primitive, tribal, peasant, and folk. These terms apply to societies that have been considered either non–Western or non-industrialized.[54]

Although I appreciate the honesty of Cohen in calling the term a "leftover category," the term still seems to describe the dances of disenfranchised groups. It is interesting that the 2005 encyclopedia exempted Indian classical dance along with ballet, unlike the 1967 edition's definition. No examples are presented for Ethnic Dance, merely a list of what is not included, such as not theatrical, not social, not popular non–Western, non-industrialized—and yet what is included remains unidentified. The field of dance has struggled for decades with issues of terminology and how to describe that which is outside the mainstream. The transient nature of these terms demonstrates the problems found with the terms in each incarnation. Unfortunately, the challenges of finding an appropriate term still exist today.

World Dance in Higher Education

In higher education, the term Ethnic Dance was discarded in favor of World Dance, yet the difference between the two remains unclear.[55]

Although Ethnic Dance was identified by the American Alliance for Health, Physical Education and Recreation's *Dance Directory* in the 1990s[56] and became an entry in the 2005 edition of *The Dance Encyclopedia*, today the term is rarely used, seemingly replaced by the term World Dance. In dance departments across the U.S., both terms have been used to title courses, describe curricular areas, distinguish degree requirements, and, in particular, to identify dance forms outside the genres of ballet and modern. Students are required to take ballet or modern every semester and World Dance once or twice over the course of four years. The paucity of required credit hours of forms outside of ballet and modern communicates to and imposes upon the students a Western preference. Although further discussion of degree requirements falls outside the scope of this chapter, the position of World Dance courses in higher education indicates an attitude within the academy and larger society toward dance forms outside of ballet and modern.

Dance education pioneer Margaret H'Doubler is recognized for establishing the first dance major in the United States in 1927. Although H'Doubler made great strides, social change in the area of race was slow to shift within the new field of dance in higher education. Dance scholar Janice Ross brought this issue forward in *Moving Lessons: Margaret H'Doubler and the Beginning of Dance in Higher Education* when comparing H'Doubler's context of dance in higher education in the United States to that of Isadora Duncan. H'Doubler, like Duncan, "had an implicit vision of America as Caucasian, Europeanized, and without significant social, racial, or economic diversity."[57] Ross also notes that black music and dance were excluded from H'Doubler's teaching repertory[58] as a result of her belief that jazz dance lacked "any artistic sense."[59] Because of H'Doubler's significance and status, such mono-cultural values became entrenched in the roots of dance in higher education. Although dance in U.S. higher education has changed immensely since then, its foundation still reflects a historically embedded social hierarchy. The remnants of this foundation remain in the language and thinking.

In 1965, professor of dance education Alma Hawkins delivered a keynote address to the Dance Division of the American Association for Health, Physical Education and Recreation, whereby she advocated for the study of creative/modern dance and Ethnic Dance forms.[60] The Ethnic Dance forms were to be taught through "a series of performance courses taught by experts." An upper level course, Dance Cultures of the World, was also proposed, wherein "different cultures and their dance" would be studied in depth.[61] The curricular format is still utilized and has become an ethos that focuses primary studio studies on modern and supplemented by the study of other dance forms. While considered to be a model of inclusion in the 1960s, this format fails to offer proficient study of dance forms outside of modern. Dances from other cultures are often presented "à la carte" from the Ethnic or World Dance category with any dance form within the category being able to satisfy the student's World Dance elective requirement.

A similar attitude about World Dance, as a term, can be found in higher education institutions outside the U.S. The University of Surrey identifies areas of study under their "Programme Structure" on the department's website. In year one, the module "Dance Technique and Performance (African People's Dance, Ballet, Contemporary and Kathak)" is listed in which dance forms are identified by name. In year three, another module listed is "National Forms/Global Forms." Although labeled with a different name, the issue of the leftover category is present with the term "global forms." However, the department foregoes blanket descriptions through its identification of specific dance forms on its website.

In describing its curriculum, the University of Cape Town (UCT) also specifically identifies three dance tracks. Each track includes history courses as well as dance practice (courses include Western Dance History, African Dance History, African Dance Practice, Contemporary Dance Practice, and Classical Ballet). Moreover, a full curriculum of study for each technique is available through offering multiple levels.[62] That the UCT curriculum offers only three dance techniques is a relevant point. It is manageable because Cape Town and its surrounding community have the needed instructors available to support these course offerings. A wide range of dance courses can easily become a staffing issue, especially when in remote or homogenous locations, due to limited instructor access. It is significant that the UCT program has ensured, without privileging one technique over another, extended course levels. The University of Cape Town School of Dance has developed in spite of a program history entrenched in a Eurocentric model with an emphasis on classical ballet. When I visited the School of Dance in 2002, I saw African dance classes and professors and students of African descent. Although I felt a privileging of ballet in the atmosphere and challenges in developing a more integrated program were expressed to me then as well as in more recent years (2015), overall progress was apparent.

At the New Worlds School of the Arts (NWSA), the "Progressive Program" reads as follows:

> Dance majors participate in a progressive program of intense technical training which is grounded in classical ballet and modern dance techniques and leads to jazz and ethnic

dance studies as well as exposure to newer dance forms. Supporting these technical studies are courses in dance composition, music, dance history, anatomy and kinesiology, movement analysis, dance criticism and dance production. Performance is integrated into the training process at all levels and students are encouraged to participate in the student choreography workshops, concerts of works by faculty and guest choreographers, and the many other performances presented by the Division.[63]

The dated use of the term "Ethnic Dance" is surprising. Within the NWSA curriculum, there is no World Dance requirement. There is, however, an optional one semester residency in World Dance offered each year. Limited offerings outside of ballet and modern are typical of a conservatory-based program like that of NWSA. Usage of the term World Dance can be found in many programs. For example, Pomona College lists courses as "Traditions of World Dance" and "History of Dance in Western Culture."[64]

Other problems with these terms can be found in issues of equality and equity. The University of California at Irvine offers five levels of ballet, four levels of modern, four levels of jazz, and three levels of tap. One level of the following is offered: Spanish, selected World Dance Forms, and repertory (ballet and modern). Within this framework it is evident that the dances within the category of World Dance are not valued enough to be identified by name, nor is more than one level of study necessary. Moreover, to earn a degree, students need to give considerably less time to the study of World Dance forms.[65]

The University of Georgia offers a traditional BFA program. As is the case with many programs, students may elect to take a World Dance Forms course as an elective. In addition to requirements of three levels of ballet and contemporary, students must take a two-credit course in Classical Ballet Forms and a three-credit course of World Dance History. Interestingly, the World Dance History course includes topics from "Primitive Dance" to "Early 20th Century Ballet in Europe and in America."[66] One could argue that since ballet in Europe and America are included in the World Dance History course, the course in Classical Ballet Forms is not necessary. A curricular possibility that would dismantle the hierarchy would be to consolidate the course into a year-long course of World Dance History and include dances from all over the world—including classical ballet.

The University of Hawaii at Manoa consciously works to diversify Dance Studies. On the Department of Theatre and Dance Website, "Program Overview," the program is described as being "unique for its offerings in Pacific and Asian dance." In this program, BA students are required to take three credits of modern, three credits of ballet, and three credits of Pacific or Asian dance forms. Although this structure highlights an equitable curriculum structure, it should be noted that BFA students are required to take two credit hours of Asian and Pacific dance with the remaining technique requirements limited to six credits of ballet or modern.[67]

There are a few departments in the United States where students can study dance forms outside ballet and modern to a level of proficiency that would enable them to obtain a degree. These programs feature culturally relevant teaching in dance as they were designed for students who have an affinity for dance forms other than ballet and modern. The University of New Mexico offers a track of study in Flamenco dance. Driven by students' interests expressed through enrollment, Arizona State University offers a dance degree with an emphasis on Urban Movement Practices.[68] Columbia College in Chicago has restructured its dance major under the direction of Onye Ozuzu. The program requires the same number of ballet courses as West African courses and allows students to concentrate on the genre of their choice. Offerings include an African-based contemporary track with hip-hop as an option.[69] Similarly, Denison University offers the opportunity for students to focus on African-based dance aesthetics or Modern/Postmodern.[70] These institutions are exceptional and illustrate that programs with a degree focus outside of ballet or modern are very limited in the United States. CDP and CRT can be a catalyst for educators and administrators to raise awareness, re-examine, and remediate curriculum.

The disproportionate focus on ballet and modern is common within higher education. The infrastructure of dance departments is rooted in societal constructs of racism and classism. Without examination, status quo practices serve to perpetuate the privileged position of ballet and modern dance. This racism and classism are exhibited in use of terms like Ethnic[71] and World Dance, and, as discussed, move beyond language into curriculum, which reveal issues of acculturation and assimilation. Questions about appropriateness are complex and cannot be easily addressed in the midst of negotiating space for "other" dance forms to enter the curriculum.

Twenty-First Century Terminology

Worlding Dance, a collection edited by professor of dance Susan L. Foster, takes the term World Dance to task through eight essays. Each author investigates the interworkings of World Dance in various contexts and perspectives. In the introduction, Foster questions if dances from disenfranchised people are commodified as an expression of artistry or for purposes of a globalized curriculum.[72] Foster discusses the hierarchies of dance and the implicit imperialism that lives within the dance lexicon and culture in regard to ballet, modern, and World Dance. The text underscores the discontent connected to the term World Dance as a category and the exploitation of forms within that category. Discourse for change has been opened and reform within the lexicon is feasible.

In discussion of dance forms often identified as World Dance, I propose an articulation for each dance form that brings it full dignity. For example, Javanese dance is a stand-alone description. It does not need to be identified as World Dance in order for people to understand what it is. To be sure, the individual title of the dance form is far more descriptive than the term World Dance.

In recent years, the term "movement practices" has emerged. This offers an alternative to the term "technique" which exclusively refers to selected dance classes involving body practices (commonly ballet and modern). This new term succeeds in giving all dance forms equal status as a movement practice. Although the term does not address spiritual, social, and healing forms, it does leave space to include such domains. The important point is that identifying all genres as movement practice removes the stigma of labeling some genres as techniques and others as a dance class or elective.

Dance departments at Princeton University, Texas Women's University, and Arizona State University have chosen to use the term movement practices for all dance forms. Within such an umbrella, each dance form can be specifically identified. The benefit of movement practices is that it includes all dance forms. A similar option to this term is "dance techniques," acknowledging all dance forms as techniques. Although these terms have yet to achieve wide acceptance, they could be useful in addressing the nomenclature of higher education.

Unfortunately, the term movement practices does not solve the complex issues of terminology. This is especially true for dance presenters as the term does not provide the same salacious appeal of exotic othering that the term World Dance provides. That is, the term movement practices is more viable in a "practice" context as opposed to a "performance" context. The latter would require consumers to read descriptions, a marketing challenge in the twenty-first century.

A shift in focus and thinking about performance and process must occur in order for other dance forms to be included in equitable ways. An example of such a shift is hip-hop. Even though originated in the West, it has been excluded from the category of Western dance through its inclusion as a World Dance form. This suggests that it is not a matter of location of origin but rather of race and class that leads to identification. Without noting divisions of class, one could legitimately place hip-hop in the category of Western dance, but to do so would negate hip-hop's second-class status within the hierarchy of dance in higher education and mainstream ideals of high art. The term Western dance techniques typically refers to techniques that were predominantly developed, performed, and supported in Western countries such as ballet (largely developed in France, England, Russia, and Italy) and modern dance techniques (originating in the U.S. and Germany).

The term Western dance technique typically excludes a number of dance forms that lack the agency of ballet and modern. As a result, the term signifies Western and historically privileged dance forms of ballet and modern when the need to use the term arises. Moreover, the term holds currency within the U.S. in regard to funding, media attention, training facilities, and infrastructures for training.[73] Conservatories of these techniques include dance departments in higher education as well as professional dance schools (e.g., the School of American Ballet, the Ailey School, the San Francisco Ballet School, and the Martha Graham Center for Contemporary Dance). Historically these techniques were limited to middle- and upper-class individuals with resources and access to training. Although some people of color have had access, few have experienced professional mainstream success or been included in the dance history canon. Just as limited are the places where economically disadvantaged students or students of color have access to training through special programs, arts high schools, and so forth, the reality is that by and large people of color are under-represented in Western and historically privileged dance forms on concert stages in the mainstream United States, giving support to the notion that these dance forms are elitist.

Currently, there is growing discussion in the field of dance that expresses a need for alternative terms. Another option I would like to offer is the term dance forms. It includes all technique forms and is specific enough to dance to not include movement practices outside the field of dance (i.e., soccer or swimming). Other options are being generated through dialogue with professors charged with teaching "World Dance" in institutions of higher education. For example, Charlotte Griffin, assistant professor of dance at the University of California at Irvine, offered the terms Movement Traditions, Body Techniques, Neuro-Kinesthetic Practices, and Corporeal Lineages. These options show promise as they highlight, that with more thought, possibilities for a more appropriate term exist. More alternative terms could very well emerge if the infrastructure of dance in higher education were to be disrupted and reshaped. Without addressing the underpinnings of the institutional foundation, only superficial change will occur. An overhaul of the curriculum is needed to eliminate the bias that lies beneath the surface that, unintentionally or not, obstructs agendas for diversity and inclusion. Nonetheless, growing discomfort with the term is inspiring dialogues in the academy. Progressive change is eminent.

Conclusion

Categorization and classification can be useful in Dance Studies and Dance Education.[74] Comparison and contrast help us form a better understanding of dance forms. The term World Dance does not meet this need since it has no defining criteria other than what it is not. It is an umbrella term that communicates little more than the second-class status of dance forms outside the Western mainstream. The term World Dance has become synonymous with division and marginalization and so can no longer be considered appropriate.

World Dance as a category has grown immensely since the days of primitive, pagan, and Ethnic Dance.[75] The field of World Dance is abundant with new dance forms being welcomed into the fold regularly.[76] If practitioners interested in sharing a new dance form are willing to remain relegated to the category of World Dance, seemingly many "other" dance forms can find entry. Although "other" dance forms are no longer seen as primitive, they have yet to attain a status equal to ballet or modern. Such status is critical to issues of funding for companies and course approval for dance departments. As long as dance forms outside the dominant culture are perceived as inferior or low art, it is unlikely they can attain the agency to be fully actualized in the mainstream. While the argument can be made that the U.S. systems of education and funding sources should focus on U.S. art forms, such an argument does not address the lower status of U.S. dance forms such as jazz, tap, and hip-hop. As U.S. society has developed and become more diverse, so too should curriculum requirements. The call to dismantle dance hierarchies must be made. It must begin with the communicative power of language as a recognized symbol of power as it is the language used that stratifies dance.

The lineage of the term World Dance illustrates that lexicons are in a continuous state of evolution. The struggle to find an appropriate and non-discriminatory description for dance forms is not a call to establish yet one more catch-all "other" category. Each dance form can be acknowledged according to the origin of the dance, not by lumping it into a category. We can honor the heritage and identity of Bharatanatyam and South African Gumboot dances by calling them those exact and specific names. Terms like Indian dance and African dance are overly large umbrella categories that hold many dance forms. Senegalese dance could be included in the vast category of West African dance. However, it could also be its own category, as there are countless Senegalese dances. There are numerous dances that are connected to different tribes of Senegal, and still more dances connected to various life events such as marriage, chief installments, rite of passage, etc. Where catch-all categories devalue the variety of dance in the world, more specific categories highlight the diversity of dance within a region.

I argue that terms such as African dance and Indian dance can be seen as their own categories, just as modern dance and ballet are understood to be. A class may be listed as "ballet" even though the course could be more specifically described as Vaganova or Cecchetti technique. Similarly, a course in Horton or Graham technique is listed under the umbrella term "modern." Instead of placing Bharatanatyam under the category World Dance, locate it within Indian dance, leaving space for Kathak, Odissi, and other dances of India. Such a framework could extend to Argentine dance, Pacific Island dance, Asian dance, etc. This frame would maintain a system of categories, respect diversity, and communicate an understanding that there is diversity within all categories of dance.

The categories created in the past served the purpose of compartmentalization. This need no longer exists. We are now able to maintain relationships with people around the world, something that was not possible just several decades ago. Today, people from lands far away reside in the United States, bringing their language, culture, and indeed their dances with them. Dance forms deserve respect and should not be relegated to a category for art forms outside the privileged status "Western." I argue for the identification of each dance form by its individual name; if not possible, I then urge the usage of more defining categories. CDP offers a framework to enter discussions about the power of language in dance. As members of the dance field we own the nomenclature and we hold the power to change it.

Ten

From Conservatory Training to Teaching Dance in Public Schools

A Cultural Shift

BY CORRINE NAGATA WITH LIZA KROESCHELL

Acknowledgment: Corrine Nagata is grateful for the editorial assistance of Liza D. Kroeschell.

"You are two feet tall and you dance like it. Don't waste your parents' hard-earned money trying to study dance, especially if you plan on letting your stomach hang out like that and dancing shorter than your already short self."

So began my first class with Reginald Ray Savage. For the several months that followed, my dance uniform included a belt wrapped around my stomach so tightly that my ribs spilled over its taut leather edge. It hurt. Only when holding in my stomach and dancing tall did I experience relief from the belt's clench and the red skin craters it left behind. Today, Mr. Savage's belt strategy would amount to cruelty to teenagers, or at least an inappropriate teaching method. But the pain of the thick strap as it probed my skin was effective incentive, and I learned—quickly—to lift up and support my stomach. Yes, Mr. Savage's approach was questionable. He often delivered honesty in confrontational, and harsh ways. However, his truthful, consistent, passionate teaching certainly produced results. His class was originally intended as a punishment to my high school ballet class for disrespecting our regular teacher, but, after that one class, we liked him and his brutal honesty so much that we requested he teach us regularly. Mr. Savage cared, more than any teacher I knew, that his students absorbed his lessons and our improvement reflected that care.

As a pre-professional and professional dancer, my favorite teachers, including Mr. Savage, valued communicating the lesson over making sure I had fun or felt good about myself. So, when I started teaching dance, I copied their result-oriented approaches (minus the questionable belt strategy!), and, with a natural authority developed from years of bossing my younger sister around and taking classes with Mr. Savage, I was good at it. My students remembered the choreography, danced with strength, and performed in unison. Since teaching my first dance class over twenty years ago, though, the way I go about fostering the success of my students has evolved dramatically. I have learned that the conservatory training model is not a "fit" for all learning communities.

Make It Fun

After graduating from North Carolina School of the Arts, where I majored in dance, I moved to New York City to continue my dance training, perform, and, like many young dancers, support myself by teaching. My first year in the city, I acquired a job teaching for former New York City Ballet dancer and dance teacher Jacques d'Amboise's National Dance Institute (NDI). This organization offers dance classes for grades four through eight, predominantly in New York City's public schools. I taught NDI's Saturday Celebration Team, a scholarship program that still brings students together from a variety of schools throughout the city. The distinct NDI teaching method developed by d'Amboise has been proven to increase student confidence, academic aptitude, and parental involvement in schools. NDI's belief that the arts inspire excellence in unique ways inspired my own teaching for the nine years I lived in New York City and continues to influence my organization, Nagata Dance, which I founded there and now operate in San Francisco.

On my fourth day as an NDI teacher, my mentor and the artistic director of NDI, Ellen Weinstein, observed my class. I was pleased with the students' progress and my teaching; by the end of the hour, formations that once were blobs were lines and pyramids, and popcorn arm movements had transformed into clear, unison gestures. I smiled and congratulated the dancers on their hard work before dismissing them. Ellen applauded. Then, as the last student trailed out the door, and I packed away my teaching notes, she turned to me and said, "Corrine, the students still have to like dance and want to move, not be forced or scared into dancing."

My neck stiffened and a series of defenses swirled through my head: Was the dancing not significantly better? Were the students not quiet and respectful? For the entire hour, I had not witnessed one collision in a group of over 50 dancers! My teachers never seemed to care that I was enjoying myself. Was this not a class? Were we not learning? Who ever said learning had to be fun?

In retrospect, the class Ellen watched me teach was probably full of tedious and inflexible robot commands:

- You dance. I will watch.
- Again. Again, with tall backs. Again, with tall backs, plus high jumps. Again until I'm satisfied.
- Start from the top. Start from the top again. Start from the top again again.

Traditional methods that I learned from Mr. Savage and the rest of my favorite dance instructors produced results, and my teaching also needed to lead to results for my students. The outcomes I now desire, however, have become more specific to the students I teach since I began my teaching career. The Bachelors of Fine Arts Students I teach in the Alonzo Kings Lines B.F.A. Program at Dominican University of California in San Francisco, for instance, have already fallen in love with dance. As one of their technique teachers, my responsibility is not to inspire them to want to dance, but rather to support the passion for dance that they already have by helping them develop strength, expression, and flexibility, and providing information that will keep them dancing injury-free for as long as possible. But these elementary school children I was teaching with Weinstein didn't necessarily want to become professional dancers. They just needed to have fun and release their energy and feel good about themselves, and my teaching approach needed to change to support those unique needs.

To start, I employed my most effective strategy for sparking my growth as a teacher: observing classes led by master teachers I admired. In efforts to learn how to engage pre-professional dancers, I took classes with Milton Myers, director of the modern program at Jacob's Pillow Dance Festival, and a highly-valued Horton instructor at the Juilliard School and the Ailey/Fordam B.F.A program, and Kazuko Hirabayashi, a Graham teacher and Graduate Program Director at SUNY Purchase College also on faculty at the Juilliard School who has directed of The Martha Graham Ensemble. Taking classes with these gifted instructors revealed ways to keep a class active and flowing. Similarly, when I took Weinstein's advice to find ways to make dance class more fun for my young students, I was amazed by Ellen and Jacques' mastery: their students smiled, sprang off their bottoms to demonstrate steps, and practically sang the words and counts without the teacher ever demanding, "Dance with enthusiasm!"

Though I admired the excitement in Jacques and Ellen's classes, inserting fun and play was not natural to me. For example, when I invited the students to create their own choreography, my classroom erupted in noise and chaos. Before I knew it, students were drawing on the walls with their fingernails, somersaulting into each other, and saying,

"I don't want to learn her move."

"He kicked me!"

"Are you coming over to my house after school?"

Finally, after all of the time I spent managing that commotion, we produced, at most, eight counts of choreography. I scrapped that activity.

Play Games

As I watched more classes with master teachers, I noticed that, in addition to creative prompts, games energize and incentivize students. But games suggest winners and losers, and I like dance because, as an art, it has nothing to do with winning or losing. I promised myself that, if I played games in my dance class, I would not use words like winner, loser, best, or worst.

I still play one of the first games that I developed to incorporate fun while maintaining classroom safety and avoiding competitive language, called Group-by-Group. To play, I divide the class into two groups that take turns demonstrating and watching. After one group performs a step big and beautiful, the next group tries the step with the challenge to dance even bigger.

When I started playing Group-by-Group in my Nagata Dance classes in New York City's public elementary schools, I immediately noticed improvement in my students' stamina. Maybe because sitting and watching allowed them to rest, or because seeing the dancers move with energy inspired the watchers, or maybe the idea of competition ("Good luck, second group. The first group just danced with really big arms.") encouraged the dancers to test just how big they could move those arms. Whatever the case, without me explicitly asking them to work hard, they maintained energy throughout the class.

Asking one group to dance bigger or smoother than the other group generates competitiveness, but I always prepare the students for success by making my expectations explicit ("I am looking for spaghetti noodle legs and open hands after the jump") and I never identify a winner. In fact, Group-by-Group actually leads to greater support among students. When the dancing group finishes, I tell the watchers, "Raise your hand and name one dancer who jumped really high." Sitting and watching while searching for a big dancer allows the children to actively rest while silently cheering on the dancing group. It's also a great opportunity for me, the teacher, to sit close to the students and say great, positive things about what they are viewing: "Oh, wow, look how big Ariana is dancing. Her hair is flying all over the place!" Best of all, when it is time to switch, the second group is inspired, energized, and excited to try their best. Group-by-Group had such a positive impact on my Nagata Dance classes in New York City schools, that I brought it to my more technique-based dance classes at The Ailey School and Dance Theatre of Harlem School. Whether my students were learning the mechanics of pirouettes or just releasing energy after school, Group-by-Group was an effective way to establish high expectations in an environment where learning was fun and the students looked forward to dance class.

As I noted earlier, I avoid competitive language when designing and playing games like Group-by-Group. I value dance as a way to celebrate the unique expression and interpretation of each dancer in pursuit of a communal aspiration and prefer to curb the urge to compare. That said, not all of the fun activities I play in class are as balanced as Group-by-Group. In fact, a teacher I helped train, who is sensitive to student equality, kindly has reservations about a game titled Elimination that animates my dance classes. This is an activity in which dancers strive to complete an entire phrase of choreography without making a mistake.

* * *

"Alright dancers," I say. "Two more practices before Elimination."

Every spine in the room straightens. I hear a "Yesss" from the giggling girls in the front who suddenly give me their full attention. The five-year-olds suck in their breath, stretch their eyebrows up to their foreheads, and lift strong arms to the front, ready at any moment for the first "Elbow." "Other arm, Benji!" I remind one of them. Everyone is ready. "Five, six, say-the-words-and—"

I hear a chorus of "Elbow Elbow Splash Down," as the students dance while saying the words that correspond with the choreography. When I teach dance to children, I use words more often than counts, because a child is more likely to remember the moves that go with "Elbow Elbow Splash Down" than "1 2 3 4," and performing steps that match words is a fun way to help young students and second language learners expand their vocabularies.

"Last practice! Ready, Go!"

"Elbow Elbow Splash Down!" The younger dancers watch older dancers and make fewer mistakes. When they've finished the steps, nervous chatter catches and swells like fire:

"Gah! I forgot 'Down!'"

"I almost tripped!"

"I need another practice!"

I clap to regain attention. "Okay, dancers. This time, we're playing Elimination. Make sure the first 'Elbow' goes to the..." I point to an older student in the front.

"Right!"

"And after the second 'Elbow Elbow' comes..." I cup my hand behind my ear to indicate that everyone can answer.

"Splash!" they say.

"If you 'Elbow' to the left first, or try anything besides 'Splash' at the end, like the chicken dance—" I fit my fists under my elbows and flap my arms like wings, "or the moonwalk, or you talk or make noise, then you are eliminated and you go to the 'I need to practice wall' and practice there," I point to a long white wall at the back of the room. The dancers nod excitedly and prepare their right arms for the first move, gluing both eyes on me for the cue.

"Go!"

As they perform the steps, I point to dancers who goof. "Marcos! Other elbow! You're late Jennifer! Oh my! The whole front row turned the wrong way!" By the time we've finished the step, almost half of the class has moved to the "I need to practice wall," and are laughing at the funny faces I make to eliminate dancers, while the remaining students sigh with relief. They survived round one!

* * *

Elimination helps me maintain the energy of a class, especially when teaching complicated steps. Children like to tackle the challenge of executing choreography without making a mistake, and are excited by the opportunity to shine. To preserve its appeal and avoid discouraging students who are eliminated multiple times, I play Elimination sparingly. Additionally,

I offer the option to opt out and watch from the "I need to practice wall" for more sensitive children who prefer not to play. These kids are usually just as excited to watch and often can't help themselves from dancing along with the rest of the group from the side. I am not thrilled by the competitive nature of the game, but Elimination almost always generates a positive energy shift in the class, and students ask to play again and again.

While games and challenges, such as Group-by-Group and Elimination, reenergize students, dancers don't need games or competition to enjoy dance class, as long as the class structure varies. Partner dancing, for example, always inspires smiles and playfulness, while simultaneously allowing dancers to mix and mingle. Sometimes, a direction as simple as, "say the words for me while sitting" energizes students by allowing them time to rest and build the desire to try the step again.

After years of testing, scrapping, and revising fun-infused strategies, I have witnessed thousands of smiles, jitters, and nods that confirm the truth: young dancers actually rehearse and perform better and achieve that sense of accomplishment if the process is engaging and fun.

Praise More Than Discipline ...

It is possible that teaching makes sense to me because learning never came easily to me. Reading and writing were especially troublesome obstacles in elementary school; I dreaded the moment that the teacher would call on me to read. It was as if my teachers had tossed me into a sea of alphabet soup. I doggie paddled from letter to letter, while my peers swam among them with smoothness and grace. "Sound the word out," everyone told me, but I did not even know where to begin sounding out that floating mess of letters.

When I started teaching dance classes in New York City's elementary schools, I recognized that doggie-paddling sensation among my students. Some public schools function at a distinctly thunderous noise level, perhaps because the wide hallways echo, or maybe because the schools are overflowing with students. Whatever the cause, the kids' responses to school reflected the commotion and anxious atmosphere around them. I empathized with the students, many of whom shared my struggles with literacy.

For me, every poor reading score, or paper handed back smothered in red pen marks, ate away at my confidence to the point that I did not enjoy reading or writing at all. Many of the students I taught in New York City struggled to attend school every day, and, on the days they are present, the catch up work was tedious and frustrating. Their frustration often manifested in disruptive behavior. I watched several exhausted public school teachers, worn by the ubiquitous, infinite emergencies and precarious circumstances inherent to their jobs, explode at a student for talking without permission: "Why are you talking? And what happened to your hair? Did you brush your hair today before you came to school? Boy you need to brush your hair because it is a *mess*. And stop talking!"

I discovered early on while teaching in elementary schools that teachers and parents respond to student misbehavior in wildly different ways. Some teachers would tell a disruptive child he or she had messy hair, and some parents would teach the lesson with a bathroom whipping. I was a huge advocate of classroom management and safety from the beginning, but I recognized the difference between discipline that made the kid seem like the worst person in the world, and discipline that told the child that he or she had misbehaved while simultaneously offering the child an opportunity to demonstrate good behavior. Whatever the potential of dance to intimidate and discourage students, I knew that I wanted my dance classes to be a place to succeed and enjoy learning. By simultaneously challenging physicality, concentration, and teamwork skills, dancing can connect students' bodies, minds, and hearts, and unhinge a deep sense of accomplishment.

Through my goal to uplift confidence, I also strive to create an atmosphere where I praise more students than I discipline them. The worst reason to discipline a child is misbehavior that I could have prevented with better class structure. Kids generally do not misbehave because they are bad kids, but because they need attention and do not know ways to attract it besides causing big enough trouble to necessitate teacher intervention. I make it as easy as possible to be a good student. I create formations that separate talkative friends. To ensure my dancers know what to expect, I always strive for consistency: I start and end every class the same way, insist on a safe dance space by controlling noise level and the number of students dancing at once, and follow through with consequences. For example, if I tell the dancers to dance silently, and Charlie makes farting noises, I point to him, say, "You're not dancing silently," and ask him to sit in the remember chair—where we go when we need to remember rules—until he is ready to join the class again, which will be soon if the dance class looks fun! All schools, parents, and teachers have different opinions about the efficacy and benefits of remember chairs, time-outs, or any other form of discipline that separates students from the group. The remember chair works well for me, but I have varied what I call it and how I use it based on the teaching environment and the students. My point is that whatever disciplinary action I use, consistency allows the dancers to rely on a system in which they can hear and see me (due to my barely five-foot stature, this sometimes means standing on a table), and know that I can hear and see them. Students shouldn't need to act out to attract my attention. They can rely on my praise for following directions, and the remember chair or my disapproval for disruptive behavior.

* * *

One of the greatest changes I ever made to my teaching was an almost instant fix. I taught at P.S. 189 in Washington Heights, New York City, for seven years, and built wonderful relationships with the students there. Those kids, most of whom spoke Spanish as their first language, taught me so much, inspiring me to visit the Dominican Republic twice! One day, the second year I taught there, I was walking to the grocery store a few blocks from P.S. 189 when I recognized one of my students from the school walking home with her mom. I waved and smiled, and she was so happy to see me that she dropped her lunch bag, hopped from her perch and skipped to me for a hug, pigtails bouncing.

"Ms. Nagata!" she said. "Hola, Ms. Nagata!" I set my bags on the ground, knelt down, squeezed her, and said, "Oh, hola!" I waved at her mom, who grinned at us while picking up the lunch box. I searched my mind for the student's name. I knew that she danced big, stood at the front, and remembered the choreography. Though I could recall the name of the boy who sat in the remember chair for tripping another student the week before during dance class, and the girl who could not say a nice word to anyone, frequently exclaiming comments like "You dance so bad!" this superstar student's name was a mystery.

So, without addressing her by name, I said, "Wow, I cannot believe you're here so early! Is that your nice mama? You are so lucky to have a nice mama!" and walked away perplexed. I had spent too much attention and time disciplining the students who didn't want to be there or follow directions when I could have been praising exceptional classroom behavior, and challenging the students who loved to dance.

I returned to P.S. 189 the next week with a bag full of name tags, determined to memorize the names of the superstar students. Instead of saying, "Jamal, no talking," "Emily, no talking," "Raquel, no talking," I said, "Wow. Look how beautiful. Tommy," who was sitting where everyone could see, "is sitting so quietly." The entire class shuffled on their bottoms to sit just like Tommy, legs crossed, hands on knees, eyes on me. "Tommy looks like he is ready for the next dance step. Tommy, stand please." Some students in the front row lifted their chests. They wanted me to choose them to dance next.

From then on, I made name tags for all of my students, and took special care to say the names of cooperative, motivated, enthused students more often. By focusing on those children who wanted to dance, my messages and directions became more positive, and the dancing environment brightened. I left classes happy with the students' progress, and I imagine they could confidently sense my appreciation for their dancing.

... *But Don't Praise Too Much*

One of the worst mistakes I observe in enthusiastic beginner teachers is the word "good." "Arabelle, that was so good," "Good!" "Good!" "GOOD!"

Overuse of good is especially prevalent during creative movement or improvisational activities, perhaps because improvisation seems personal and teachers are uncomfortable commenting on personal work. However, if the direction is to dance like a wet noodle, and Eric is walking along like a tall-backed businessman, a "good" directed to the entire class is simply not true. An effective teacher in this situation could continue to have the group dance like a wet noodle and ask Eric to try something else, or divide the class into two groups so that every student could learn their peers' wet-noodle dancing, or tell Eric to pick a friend to help him demonstrate wet noodle dancing. If the teacher congratulates with good too often, or uses good as a filler word to stall while brainstorming the next activity, praise loses its meaning. Conversely, authentic reactions build trust with students. If they know that when the teacher applauds the teacher means it, they will know that when a whole audience applauds, the audience means it, too.

I was always impressed by the way d'Amboise approached corrections with equal earnestness and humor. "That was almost right," he would say. "The only mama huhu was the kick kick turn around step. I only saw one dancer turn the right way!" The kids would point and laugh at Jacques as he scrunched up his eyebrows and puckered his lips in an overly dramatic disappointed expression. D'Amboise's phrase, "mama huhu" is a Mandarin saying that means so-so or mediocre. Along with his funny faces, mama huhu sent a clear message: the dancer goofed. But no one felt targeted or shamed, because everyone was too busy laughing at his mama huhu comments. D'Amboise demonstrated the incredible power of humor to gently motivate dancers to rise to high standards of excellence while only praising when he meant it.

Teach in Baby Steps ...

One of the most effective confidence-building strategies I honed, informed by my personal floundering in that alphabet soup sea, was steady, step-by-step teaching. For example, I never deliver all of the information at once when teaching a tricky step. Instead of asking students to dive into the alphabet soup, I do my best to let them wade into the broth, and add only one or two letters at a time. For instance, say the first four counts of a 32-count step involve crossing right foot over left, turning in a full circle, jumping both legs wide, and then closing the feet back together. After acknowledging that the step is complex by labeling it "the hard step," I face the dancers and first help them identify their right foot.

"Shake your right foot," I say, mirroring the students. "Stomp it!" A popcorn-like chorus of stomps echoes throughout the room. "Remember: Your right foot is the foot closest to the windows." I demonstrate the first four counts—"Cross." I point down to my foot closest to the window. "Window foot in front!" Then I continue, "Turn. Open. Close," first in slow motion, then in a silly voice with exaggerated big hips, then with the students following. "Once again, dancers," I say. But this time, we do not complete the step: "Cross, freeze!"

I saunter around the student statue garden for a feet check. "Does everyone have the window foot crossed in front?" I ask. Some of the kids, frozen with hands on their hips and noses pointing forward, dart their eyes from side to side, checking their position against their neighbors. Once 100 percent of the students cross the window foot in front, and end with feet together, I move on to the next four counts.

Some dancers in the class do not need all of these steps to learn the choreography. They already know which foot to cross in front, and memorize the movements after trying them only once or twice. But the step-by-step approach is still interesting and fun for those more experienced students. They laugh at my silly version and are thrilled when they remember to cross the right foot in front as I walk around for the feet check. Variation—in speed, challenges (e.g., eyes closed, eyes on ceiling, without words, whispering words), groups (e.g., boys, girls, stage right, stage left), direction the students face when dancing the step, even my teaching voice (e.g., low, high, silly, whispered)—allows me to keep the class fun and interesting while helping the students grasp the step, little by little, as a team.

By teaching in baby steps, every small accomplishment—memorizing the steps, making the dancing as big as possible, fitting the steps to the music—represents an achievement. Even if the child has low test scores, or only ends up taking one class, or we dance in the hallway because all the other spaces are occupied, or the school loses after-school funding, I want each student to walk out the door feeling authentically proud and successful, even if the task at which he or she succeeded was as small as remembering to cross the window foot in front.

... *But Know That You're Teaching More Than Just Steps*

From the first day I taught at public schools in Chinatown, my Chinese students wanted to know: "Ms. Nagata, are you Chinese?" The answer is no, no I am not. Like most Asians, I am often confused as Chinese, but I am a fourth generation Japanese American. The truth was always so disappointing to them. Students would often corner me in a group to ask, and, when they discovered I was Japanese, their little shoulders slumped forward and their eyes drooped toward the ground. So I started embellishing my responses, saying. "No, I am Japanese, but my *very best* friend is Chinese." This was not a complete fabrication. I do have a very good friend who happens to be Chinese, and one day, over an especially chocolaty mocha, I expressed frustration about the Chinese question with her. "They all want me to be Chinese," I said. "It's exhausting to explain myself again and again."

My friend, who had patiently and compassionately listened to my speech, gazed down at her blue, ceramic coffee mug, and traced its rim with the tip of her index finger. "Corrine," she said, "is it really that bad to be Chinese?"

I thought I was teaching the kids to be careful when making assumptions about ethnicity by explaining that I was Japanese. But the kids were not asking if I was Chinese just because they were curious. Rather, they wanted me to be Chinese because they were trying to imagine themselves in my position; they were looking to me as a Chinese role model. At the same time I was demonstrating grapevines, I was also a living illustration of an Asian dancer and teacher. Perhaps the experience of being inspired by a powerful leader who looked Chinese was a lot more important than the choreography I was demonstrating.

I still struggle with the best way to respond to students who think I am Chinese. It is complicated, because I am not, but the full response is not always worth the time, or relevant or important in the context of the class. This question is among many that continue to perplex me as a teacher: How do I keep boys interested in dance, when T-Ball and Karate are considered more masculine options? How do I continue to generate new activities and ideas and avoid becoming stale? What is the best way to support new teachers while challenging them to improve quickly? How do I hire and encourage a diverse group teachers to reflect more of the cultures with which our students identify (including race, ethnicity, LGBT, and religious cultures)?

The dance teachers at the front of the room and the ways those teachers respond to the unique needs of each class is profoundly reflective of our culture. How do I expect to attract and retain boys in dance class when nearly all of the dance teachers I hired are women? Or empower the diverse, young women we teach to become leaders when white men still dominate the choreography I see on stage?

I want my students to hear the word "dance" and react with smiles because they had a great, positive, and fun experience that challenged their brains and bodies and left them feeling successful. So I make dance class fun and I praise students as they accomplish each baby step along the way.

I want my students to discover that, if they think hard, sweat, express themselves, and dance with confidence, they can move audiences. So I insist that they dance big, with lots of energy, and I show them with my kindness, praise, and poise that confidence is unrelated to status or the control of others.

I also want my students to be proud of their unique backgrounds and bodies and welcoming of others. I want them to be able to imagine themselves as professional dancers or teachers or choreographers and I want them to have access to more dance classes than the ones I might teach in the hallways and stairwells of their schools.

Invest in Student Success

My teaching style has evolved in many ways since I started twenty years ago, but the most radical difference, and the detail that distinguishes a new teacher from an experienced one, is the way I now tailor what and how I teach to the particular needs of each class. Lifting up my torso in a demi plié was an important lesson for me to learn from Mr. Savage because

I wanted to make dance my career, but for the children who will have only one or two classes with me and are not interested in becoming dancers, I am much better off telling them to bend their knees and moving on to something that interests them, like a cool dance move or a clap combination they can show off in the yard. It is tempting for us teachers to give students the same steps in the same way our teachers taught us. But leading students to success means being invested in their success. To do that, we need to consider what success means to them, and that is something largely influenced by the cultures with which they identify. Ultimately, students cannot succeed outside their cultural identity—their cultural identity (including LGBTQ and religious communities) is a component of their being. All the strategies that I have developed—playing games, and slow and animated step-by-step instruction—are effective when they support the cultural context of the school community and the goals of the students. Whatever tools teachers discover for helping their students feel successful, when we catch our students smile because they finally mastered a challenging phrase choreographed from us for them and their unique interests—then we have fun and feel successful, too.

Epilogue

The chapters in this text vary greatly in style and topic, yet what is consistent throughout is an understanding that our bodies cannot move through space irrespective of our culture. The work stands on the shoulders of many Dance Education scholars and educators. Some of the most closely related work in this area is that of Dance Education scholar Sherry Shapiro. In her discourse of critical pedagogy and the body she writes of the significance of "recognizing the nature of the postmodern body; understanding how it is inscribed by culture, mediates power, and expresses resistance to the normalizing practices of society."[1] This understanding of the body can reflect a pedagogy where the lived experience of the body "becomes part of the curriculum."[2]

As I move forward in my journey as an artist, scholar, educator, I reflect on how the body is an invaluable and often dismissed repository of embodied cultural knowledge. The body can be used in the classroom to impact student success and esteem.

Today one of my colleagues shared a sad teaching moment with me.

> I walked in this morning at 9:30 p.m. and Brittney (a recent graduate from our program who was working with the summer high school program—and our only black graduate) was leading the entire group (students of the summer high school dance intensive) in a Beyonce warm-up. All of the black students were grouped together. When I walked in all of the students acted as if they were caught in something bad, wrong or criminal. It made me feel sad and like I failed (and fail often) at creating a safe space for students of color and for blackness to be welcomed and celebrated in the dance program. I don't want anyone to feel like they have to sneak in what they care about outside of the margins and undercover.

What was sad for me was that I have had similar experiences, more times than I care to count; and that in these past experiences, I did not realize how problematic the scene was. These eye-opening moments remind me that yes, there is still more work to be done.

In the summer of 2015, I attended a dance studies seminar that served as a think tank for academicians with interests in or relating to dance. Many discussions around a pedagogy of disruption took place. Discomfort in the learning process was affirmed. Yes, we learn from discomfort. But this idea of discomfort was also challenged. How much discomfort is too much? How many obstacles must a student overcome to succeed in his or her learning environment? There is no simple answer and there is no way for students to have equal experiences. But I do seek balance, and it is my goal that students do not feel alienated, confronted, or rejected in my classroom.

To be sure, transformative education is not the easy road. It is hard to disrupt and question the way people view dance and the world. But for me, the work is worthwhile. For me, if I am not going to face the challenges of my field then I question why I am here—I do not want to be the complicit participant.

Students appreciate culturally relevant teaching, with teachers quickly seeing the results. But let me be clear, there is a lot of work involved with cultural relevant teaching, an approach to teaching rooted in the theoretical frame of critical pedagogies. As highlighted in Julie Kerr-Berry's chapter on teaching dance history, critical dance pedagogy is also a powerful teaching method that can be challenging for students and teachers alike to deconstruct many of the power structures embedded in our way of knowing the world. It is challenging and, for me, can often be "unfun." I have left class totally depleted by the relentless resistance of my students. I have felt "pushback" to the point that I wanted to throw in the towel. I had talked to my students a lot about my hetero-normative privilege and my educational privilege—owning my own privilege and explaining how we all have privilege. But there was no way to get around the "me" versus "them" dichotomy with my white students. I had one student tell me, in an annoyed tone, "I never thought about race before I met you," as if I was the bearer of bad news. I was not sure if I should be honored or dismayed. I do not think she realized the irony of her statement. The fact that she had never had to think about race demonstrated her privilege. But, I stayed the course, supported by my colleagues and friends. My mother shared with me many times, that for her, it took a lot of time and a lot of processing to deconstruct and reconstruct her understanding of the world as it related to social constructs. So I persevered, knowing I probably would not have the best teaching evaluations in the world, but I was quite possibly making a lifelong impact.

Recently, I got an email from a student I taught critical dance pedagogy in a class where I challenged students to question power structures. I can't say I connected with this student at the time, although I did not think she was the most resistant either. Her email read:

Dr. Nya,

I wanted to email you because this has been on my mind for a while. I have not really known how to explain what I had been thinking but I figured you would appreciate hearing it either way. I amongst a lot of my classmates did not take the idea of white privilege very well. I was very much turned off by what we read in class and I wanted to apologize. Since briefly being in the professional world, even as just an intern, I have learned a lot about male privilege. I will not go into the why or how but as a successful professional women I am sure you know what male privilege is all too well. I wanted to apologize for not being open minded to what we learned about white privilege in class. You said something about how the privileged cannot be told that they are so by the underprivileged. I have learned this with being a female and feeling what male privilege is as the underprivileged. Thanks to you I realized in that same moment what you were trying to explain to us about white privilege. I know this is not my most eloquent epiphany ever but I wanted you to know that I really appreciate all that you taught us in your class. Thank you so much for everything and hope you have a great summer!

In addition, I saw this video and thought that it was an interesting activity to really see privilege through their own eyes and just figured it was worth sharing.

"What is privilege?" Buzzfeed (available on YouTube)

See you next year!
Sophomore 2015

I was delighted to receive this email, but I was also reflective about the teaching experience. In hindsight, I must say that I focused so much on explaining to students what privilege is, that I did not empower students. I see privilege as a gift and a responsibility. For with privilege comes the opportunity to widen spaces for others. No doubt the significant changes in this country were never made solely by those oppressed, allies and those who held privilege were active in many pursuits of civil rights—from abolitionists to the recent victory that legalized gay marriage. I realize that framing privilege as an opportunity makes it easier for students to come to terms with it.

Today the American dancing body comes in all sizes, shapes, genders, non-genders, sexual orientations, and abilities. We, as dance educators, must teach to the American dancing body about the American dancing body. For if we don't, we perpetuate the limited idea of what this body looks like—and tell a lie. I recently saw a movie where dancer and actor Channing Tatum performed a duet with Stephen "Twitch" Boss, a dancer who established himself on *So You Think You Can Dance?* I was delighted to see the white and black dancers perform a mirror/twin dance with ease. The two mirrored each other, divided by a large frame set up like a mirror. Race was not a factor in this dance. Similarly, I am excited to see how many children will grow up seeing Misty Copeland performing leading roles as a principal ballerina with the American Ballet Theatre and not even conceiving of a day when such was not a reality. Yesterday a theater colleague told me he was changing his staging of *The Colored Museum* (a play written for a black cast) because he just cast a white student in a black role. He explained, "She was so good, I had to cast her." Each of these acts creates cracks in the glass ceilings above us and in the foundation below us. It is our time to decenter, disrupt, and change the world.

Chapter Notes

Preface

1. Prudence L. Carter, *Keepin' It Real: School Success Beyond Black and White* (New York: Oxford University Press, 2005).

2. James Banks, "Cultural Pluralism and the Schools," *Educational Leadership* 32.3 (1974): 163–66; Lisa Delpit, *Other People's Children: Culture Conflict in the Classroom*, (New York: The New Press, 1995); Geneva Gay, *Culturally Responsive Teaching: Theory, Research, and Practice*, 2d ed. (New York: Teachers College Press, 2010); Asa G. Hilliard, *The Reawakening of the African Mind* (Boston: Beacon Press, 1998); and Christine E. Sleeter, *Professional Development for Culturally Responsive and Relationship-Based Pedagogy* (New York: Peter Lang, 2011).

Chapter One

1. Vusi Ngema, personal interview, University of Cape Town, South Africa, 2002.

2. Menah A. E. Pratt-Clarke, *Critical Race, Feminism, and Education: A Social Justice Model* (New York: Palgrave Macmillan, 2010), 19.

3. Sharon Gewirtz, "Conceptualizing Social Justice in Education: Mapping the Territory," *Journal of Educational Policy* 13.4 (1998): 469–484; and George Theoharis, "Social Educational Leaders and Resistance: Toward a Theory of Social Justice Leadership," *Educational Administration Quarterly* 43.2 (2007): 221–258.

4. Paulo Freire, *Pedagogy of the Oppressed* (New York: Continuum, 1986).

5. Gloria Ladson-Billings, *The Dreamkeepers* (San Francisco: Jossey-Bass, 1994), 18.

6. *Ibid.*

7. Banks, "Cultural Pluralism and the Schools"; Gay, *Culturally Responsive Teaching*; and Ladson-Billings, *The Dreamkeepers*.

8. Banks, "Cultural Pluralism and the Schools," 165.

9. Gay, *Culturally Responsive* Teaching, 31.

10. Barry Kanpol, *Critical Pedagogy: An Introduction* (Westport, CT: Bergin & Garvey, 1994), 27.

11. Margaret W. Sallee, Moreen E. Logan, Susan Sims, and W. Paul Harrington, "Challenges to Engaging White Students on a Multicultural Programming," in *Student Engagement in Higher Education: Theoretical Perspectives and Practical Approaches for Diverse Populations* (New York: Routledge, 2009).

12. Arne Duncan, "A Call to Teaching," speech presented at the University of Virginia (Charlottesville, Virginia, October 9, 2009).

13. Wayne Au, Bill Bigelow, and Stan Karp, *Rethinking Our Classrooms, Volume 1: Teaching for Equity and Justice*, new ed. (Milwaukee: Rethinking Schools, 2007), X.

14. Ladson-Billings, *The Dreamkeepers*; Hilliard, *The Reawakening of the African Mind*; Delpit, *Other People's Children*; Gay, *Culturally Responsive Teaching*; Banks, "Cultural Pluralism and the Schools"; Sleeter, *Professional Development for Culturally Responsive and Relationship-Based Pedagogy*.

209

15. This was cited in Judith Lynne Hanna, *Partnering Dance and Education: Intelligent Moves for Changing Times* (Champaign, IL: Human Kinetics, 1999), 79.

16. Richard Kraus, Sarah Chapman Hilsendager, and Brenda Dixon (Gottschild), *History of the Dance in Art and Education*, 3d ed. (Englewood Cliffs, NJ: Prentice Hall, 1991); Hanna, *Partnering Dance and Education*; and Thomas Hagood, *Legacy in Dance Education* (Amherst, NY: Cambria Press, 2008).

17. Sherry B. Shapiro, *Dance, Power, and Difference: Critical Feminist Perspectives on Dance Education* (Champaign, IL: Human Kinetics, 1998); and Sherrie Barr and Doug Risner, "Weaving Social Foundations Through Dance Pedagogy: A Pedagogy of Uncovering," *Journal of Dance Education* 14.4 (2014): 136–145.

18. Barr and Risner cite resistance from white students, but this is an important issue as many dance educators teach predominately white populations. More on resistance to CDP in Chapter 7 and Epilogue.

19. Shapiro, *Dance, Power, and Difference*, 15.

20. *Ibid.*

21. Mary Stone Hanley, "Introduction," in *Culturally Relevant Arts Education for Social Justice: A Way Out of No Way*, ed. George W. Noblit, Gilda L. Sheppard, Tom Barone, and Lee Anne Bell (New York: Routledge, 2013), 7.

22. *Ibid.*, 9.

23. *Ibid.*, 8.

24. *Ibid.*

25. *Ibid.*, 10.

26. Donna M. Davis and Shirley Marie McCarther, "Following the Drinking Gourd: Culturally Relevant Pedagogy and Curriculum Development Through the Arts," *The Educational Forum* 79.1 (2015): 68–80; Kathryn J. Azevedo, Sonia Mendoza, María Fernández, K. Farish Haydel, Michelle Fujimoto, Evelyn C. Tirumalai, and Thomas N. Robinson, "Turn Off the TV and Dance! Participation in Culturally Tailored Health Interventions: Implications for Obesity Prevention Among Mexican American Girls," *Ethnicity & Disease* 23.4 (2013): 452–461.

27. Ofotsu W. Adinku, *African Dance Education in Ghana: Curriculum and Instructional Materials for a Model Bachelor of Arts (hons.) Dance in Society* (Accra: Ghana niversities Press, 1994).

28. Maureen F. Legge, "Te Ao Kori as Expressive Movement in Aotearoa New Zealand Physical Education Teacher Education (PETE): A Narrative Account," *Asia Pacific Journal of Health, Sport and Physical Education* 2.3/4 (2011): 81–95.

29. Elizabeth Melchior, "Culturally Responsive Dance Pedagogy in the Primary Classroom," *Research in Dance Education* 12.2 (2011): 119–135.

30. *Ibid.*

31. Kerry Chappell, "Creativity in Primary Level Dance Education: Moving Beyond Assumption," *Research in Dance Education* 8.1 (2007): 27–52.

32. Kyra Danielle Gaunt, *The Games Black Girls Play: Learning the Ropes from Double-Dutch to Hip-Hop* (New York: New York University Press, 2006).

33. Nyama McCarthy-Brown, "'The Proof Is in The Pudding': An Examination of Three Elected Dance Department Curricula and How Cultural Diversity Is Valued," PhD diss. (Temple University, 2011).

34. *Ibid.*

35. *Ibid.*

36. Geneva Gay, *Culturally Responsive Teaching: Theory, Research, and Practice*, 2d ed. (New York: Teachers College Press, 2010), 13.

37. Herbert R. Hohl, *I Won't Learn from You: And Other Thoughts on Creative Maladjustment* (New York: New Press, 1994), 6.

38. Mary C. Waters, *Ethnic Options: Choosing Identities in America* (Berkeley: University of California Press, 1990).

39. Pierre Bourdieu, "Cultural Reproduction and Social Reproduction," in *Power and Ideology in Education*, ed. J. Karabel and A. H. Halsey (New York: Oxford University Press, 1977).

40. Rachelle Winkle-Wagner, Kelly Ward, and Lisa Wolf-Wendel, *Cultural Capital: The Promises and Pitfalls in Educational Research* (San Francisco: Jossey-Bass, 2010), 6.

41. *Ibid.*, 8.

42. *Ibid.*, 5.

43. Carter, *Keepin' It Real*, 138.

44. *Ibid.*, 139.

45. Lisa Delpit, *Other People's Children: Culture Conflict in the Classroom* (New York: The New Press, 1995).

46. Ruth Gustafson, *Race and Curriculum: Music in Childhood Education* (New York: Palgrave Macmillan, 2009).

47. *Ibid.*

Chapter Two

1. The terms, culturally relevant teaching and culturally relevant pedagogy are used interchangeably throughout this text.
2. Bonnie M. Davis, *How to Teach Students Who Don't Look Like You* (Thousand Oaks: Corwin Press, 2006), 4.
3. Ruby Payne, *A Framework for Understanding Poverty* (Highlands, TX: Aha! Process, 2001).
4. Elizabeth Melchior, "Culturally Responsive Dance Pedagogy in the Primary Classroom," *Research in Dance Education* 12.2 (2011):119–135 and D. Holt, "Hidden Strengths: The Case for the Generalist Teacher of Art," in *Primary Arts Education,* ed. David Holt (London: Falmer Press, 1997), 84–95.
5. Gay, *Culturally Responsive Teaching,* 45.
6. Ladson-Billings, *The Dreamkeepers*; Gay, *Culturally Responsive Teaching*; Carmen Mercado, "Caring as Empowerment: School Collaboration and Community Agency," *The Urban Review* 25.1 (1993); Deborah Eaker-Rich and Jane Van Galen, *Caring in an Unjust Room* (Albany: State University of New York, 1996); Michele Foster, *Black Teachers on Teaching* (New York: Norton, 1998).

Chapter Three

1. Harry K. Wong and Rosemary T. Wong, *The First Days of School* (Mountain View, CA: Harry K. Wong, 2004), 179.
2. Barbara Glass, *African American Dance: An Illustrated History* (Jefferson. NC: McFarland, 2007).
3. David Dorfman, personal conversations and class observations, in Lewiston, Maine, and Bloomington, Indiana, 2014 and 2015, respectively.
4. Ruth Gustafson's research supports my argument that many African Americans understanding of music and dance as inseparable. Gustafson conducted research on African American students and their kinesthetic relationship to music as an explanation for their poor performance in many music education courses throughout the United States, wherein a kinesthetic experience is detached from music listening.

Ruth Gustafson, *Race and Curriculum: Music in Childhood Education* (New York: Palgrave Macmillan, 2009).
5. Ann Haas Dyson and Celia Genishi, eds., *The Need for a Story: Cultural Diversity in Classroom and Community* (Urbana: National Council for Teachers of English, 1994).
6. Lisa Stulberg and Sharon Lawner Weinberg, *Diversity in American High Education* (New York: Routledge, 2011).

Chapter Four

1. Nyama McCarthy-Brown, "'The Proof Is in The Pudding': An Examination of Three Selected Dance Department Curricula and How Cultural Diversity Is Valued," PhD diss. (Temple University, 2011).
2. Angela McRobbie, "Dance Narratives and Fantasies," in *Meaning in Motion: New Cultural Studies of Dance,* ed. Jane Desmond (Durham: Duke University Press, 1997).
3. *Ibid.,* 208.
4. Marion E. Gridley, *Maria Tallchief: the Story of an American Indian* (Minneapolis: Dillon Press, 1973).
5. Maria Tallchief and Larry Kaplan, *Maria Tallchief: America's Prima Ballerina* (New York: Henry Holt, 1997).
6. Lili C. Livingston, *American Indiana Ballerinas* (Norman: University of Oklahoma Press, 1997).
7. Nora Boustany, "Prominent Ballet Dancer Rosella Higher," *Washington Post* (November 8, 2008).
8. Livingston, *American Indiana Ballerinas.*
9. *Ibid.*
10. *Ibid.*
11. Allen Hughes, "Without Regard for Color," *New York Times* (Feburary 21, 1965).
12. Dance Theatre of Harlem Website 2015 available at http://www.dancetheatre ofharlem.org. Accessed on June 8, 15.
13. Melanye White Dixon, *Marion Cuyjet and the Judimar School of Dance: Training Ballerinas in Black Philadelphia 1948–1971* (Lewiston, NY: Edwin Mellon Press, 2011).
14. Joselli Deans, "Black Ballerinas Dancing on the Edge: An Analysis of the Cultural Politics in Delores Browne's and Raven Wilkinson's Careers, 1954–1985," EdD diss. (Philadelphia, Temple University, 2001).

15. Penny Ward, *Classic Black, Classic Black*, videotaped at Bruno Walter Auditorium (New York: The New York Public Library for the Performing Arts, February 12, cassette 2, 1996).

16. Dixon, *Marion Cuyjet and the Judimar School of Dance*.

17. Deans, "Black Ballerinas Dancing on the Edge."

18. *I'll Make Me a World: A Century of African American Arts*, documentary [VHS], directed by Denise A. Greene and Sam Pollard (PBS, 1999).

19. Margalit Fox, "Albert Evans, Ebullient City Ballet Dancer, Is Dead at 46," *New York Times* (June 24, 2015).

20. Meryl L. Lodge presented at the Mellon Dance Studies Summer Seminar at Northwestern on Ballet in South Africa. She noted that a large number of the dancers of color in the South African ballet companies were recruited from Cuba (Evanston, IL, 2015).

21. Dorion Weichmann, "Choreography and Narrative: The *Ballet d'Action* of the Eighteenth Century," in *Cambridge Companion to Ballet*, ed. Marion Kant (New York: Cambridge University Press, 2007), 53.

22. *Ibid.*, 55.

23. *Ibid.*

24. Alvin Ailey and Peter A. Bailey, *Revelations* (New York: Birch Lane Press, 1997), 128.

25. Karyn Collins, "Does Classism Have Color?" *Dance Magazine* (June 2005).

26. Anne Haas Dyson and Celia Genishi, *The Need for Story: Cultural Diversity in Classroom and Community*, National Council of Teachers (1994), 2.

27. Linda Goss and Marion Barnes, eds., *Talk That Talk: An Anthology of African American Story Telling* (New York: Simon & Schuster, 1989), 10.

28. Rafaela G. Castro, *Chicano Folklore: A Guide to the Folktales, Traditions, Ritual and Religious Practices of Mexican Americans* (New York: Oxford University Press, 2001), 74.

29. Sue Stinson, "Hidden Curriculum of Hidden Gender," *The Journal of Dance Education* 5.2 (2005): 51–57.

30. Carrie Gaiser, "Caught Dancing: Hybridity, Stability, and Subversion in Dance Theatre of Harlem's Creole Giselle," *Theatre Journal* 58.2 (May 2006): 269–289.

31. Anna B. Scott, "What's It Worth to Ya? Adaptation and Anachronism: Rennie Harris's Pure Movement and Shakespeare," in *The Routledge Dance Studies Reader*, ed. Alexander Carter and Janet O'Shea (New York: Routledge, 2010).

32. Brenda Dixon Gottschild, *Digging the Africanist Presence in American Performance* (Westport, CT: Praeger, 1996).

Chapter Five

1. Robert Sternberg, ed., *Handbook of Creativity* (New York: Cambridge University Press, 1999).

2. Alma Hawkins, *Creating Through Dance* (Englewood Cliffs, NJ: Prentice-Hall, 1964), 5.

3. *Ibid.*, 4–5.

4. Lucia Matos, "Writing in the Flesh Body, Identity, Disability, and Difference," in *Dance in a World of Change: Reflections of Globalization and Cultural Difference*, ed. Sherry Shapiro (Raleigh: Human Kinetics, 2008), 79.

5. Jacqui Malone, *Steppin' on the Blues* (Urbana: University of Illinois Press, 1996), 10.

6. Kathak is an Indian classical dance style from North India, popularity for the dance dates as far back as the sixteenth century; Pallabi Chakravorty, *Bells of Change: Kathak Dance, Women and Modernity in India* (New York: Seagull Books, 2008).

7. Pratishtha Saraswat, *Essential Elements of Kathak* (Kuningan, Indonesia: Embassy of India, 2014), 8.

8. Chakravorty.

9. Bagashree Vaze, personal interview, recorded, March 2015.

10. *Ibid.*

11. *Ibid.*

12. *Ibid.*

13. Marian Barnes and Linda Goss, *Talk That Talk: An Anthology of African American Storytelling* (New York: Simon & Schuster Touchstone, 1989).

14. Kariamu Welsh, personal interview, June 2015.

15. *Ibid.*

16. *Ibid.*

17. *Ibid.*

18. Adrienne Kaeppler, "An Introduction to Dance Aesthetics," *Yearbook for Traditional Music* 35 (2003): 154.

19. *Ibid.*
20. Shana, personal interview, Philadelphia, Pennsylvania, 2009.
21. Welsh.
22. Larry Neal, "The Black Arts Movement," *The Drama Review* 12.4 (1968): 29.
23. Barbara Glass, *African American Dance: An Illustrated History* (Jefferson, NC: McFarland, 2007).
24. Kaeppler, "An Introduction to Dance Aesthetics."
25. Liz Lerman, *Liz Lerman's Critical Response Process: A Method for Getting Useful Feedback on Anything You Make, from Dance to Dessert* website available at: http://dance-exchange.org/projects/critical-response-process/. Accessed July 13, 2015.
26. Liz Lerman, *Liz Lerman's Critical Response Process: A Methods for Getting Useful Feedback on Anything You Make, From Dance to Dessert* (Dance Exchange, 2003).

Chapter Six

1. This study was approved by the IRB Board at Indiana University.
2. All students in the contemporary dance program were selected for a minimum of one repertory course. Two of these courses focused on socio-political themes and are examined in this case study. Students attended rehearsals two times each week over the course of one academic semester. Upon completion, students performed the works four times over the course of a weekend in January of 2015.
3. Joan Wink, *Critical Pedagogy: Notes from the Real World* (Boston: Pearson Education, 2005), 67.
4. Myles, Horton, and Paulo Freire, *We Make the Road by Walking: Conversations on Education and Social Change* (Philadelphia: Temple University Press, 1990); Ira Shor, *Empowering Education: Critical Teaching for Social Change* (Chicago: University of Chicago Press, 1992).
5. Lisa Scherff and Karen Spector, *Culturally Relevant Pedagogy: Clashes and Confrontations* (Lanham, MD: Rowman and Littlefield Education, 2011), 63.
6. Charles Mills, *The Racial Contract* (Ithaca: Cornell University Press, 1997).
7. Mica Pollock, *Colormute: Race Talk Dilemmas In An American School* (Princeton: Princeton University Press, 2004).

8. Eduardo Bonilla-Silva, *Racism Without Racists: Color-Blind Racism and the Persistence of Racism in America* (Lanham, MD: Rowman & Littlefield, 2014).
9. Dance Ability International, http://www.danceability.com/. Accessed July 13, 2015.
10. Liz Lerman, http://www.lizlerman.com/ and http://danceexchange.org/. Accessed July 13, 2015.
11. I learned *Mapping* in 2000 from performance artist, activist and educator Guillermo Gomez Pena and Bonnie Brooks, associate professor and lead curator of the Dance Center of Columbia College, Chicago. Guillermo Gomez Pena and Pocha Nostra, http://www.pochanostra.com. Accessed July 13, 2015.
   Choreographer Doug Varone led *Mapping* during his Devices: Choreographic Mentorship Project, 2014, http://www.dougvaroneanddancers.org/. Accessed July 13, 2015.
12. Steve Paxton, Nancy Stark-Smith, Karen Nelson and K.J. Holmes, http://www.contactquarterly.com/contact-improvisation/about/index.php
13. Dance for PD is a trademarked dance movement training curriculum founded in partnership with the Mark Morris Dance Group and the Brooklyn (New York) Parkinson Group. http://danceforparkinsons.org/. Accessed July 13, 2015.
14. bell hooks, *Teaching to Transgress* (New York: Routledge, 1994), 8.
15. *Ibid.*, 39.
16. *Ibid.*, 14.

Chapter Seven

1. Thomas DeFrantz, *Dancing Revelations: Alvin Ailey's Embodiment of African American Culture* (Oxford: Oxford University Press, 2004).
2. Brenda Dixon Gottschild, *Digging the Africanist Presence in American Performance: Dance and Other Contexts* (Westport, CT: Greenwood, 1996).
3. Brenda Dixon Gottschild, *The Black Dancing Body: A Geography from Coon to Cool* (New York: Palgrave Macmillian, 2003).
4. Brenda Dixon Gottschild, *Joan Myers Brown & the Audacious Hope of the Black Ballerina: A Biohistory of American Performance* (New York: Palgrave Macmillan, 2011).

5. Susan Manning, *Modern Dance, Negro Dance: Race in Motion* (Minneapolis: University of Minnesota Press, 2004).

6. John O. Perpener, III, *African-American Concert Dance: The Harlem Renaissance and Beyond* (Urbana: University of Illinois Press, 2001).

7. Peggy Schwartz and Murray Schwartz, *The Dance Claimed Me: A Biography of Pearl Primus* (New Haven: Yale University Press, 2011).

8. Maria Tallchief and Larry Kaplan, *Maria Tallchief: America's Prima Ballerina* (New York: Henry Holt, 1997).

9. Dayna Goldfine, et al., dir. *Ballets Russes* [DVD] (New York: Zeitgeist Films, 2006).

10. Native American Encyclopedia, *Native American Encyclopedia*, NAE, 2010. Web. June 7, 2015.

11. Paulo Freire and Myra Bergman Ramos, excerpt from *Pedagogy of the Oppressed*, in *The Institution of Education*, ed. H. Svi Shapiro, Kathe Latham, Sabrina N. Ross, 5th ed. (Boston: Pearson Custom, 2006), 155–162.

12. For example, Freire specifically references peasant classes as those oppressed.

13. Pierre Bourdieu and Jean Claude Passeron, *Reproduction in Education, Society and Culture* (London: Sage, 1977).

14. Lynne M. Webb, Myria W. Allen, and Kandi L. Walker, "Feminist Pedagogy: Identifying Basic Principles," *Academic Exchange Quarterly* 6.1 (2002): 67.

15. *Ibid.*

16. Lisa D. Delpit. *Other People's Children: Cultural Conflict in the Classroom* (New York: New Press, 1995).

17. Geneva Gay, *Culturally Responsive Teaching: Theory, Research and Practice* (New York: Teachers College Press, 2000).

18. Gloria Ladson-Billings, *The Dreamkeepers: Successful Teaching of African American Children*, 2d ed. (San Francisco: Jossey-Bass, 2009).

19. Richard Delgado and Jean Stefancic, *Critical Race Theory: An Introduction*, 2d ed. (New York: New York University Press, 2012), 3.

20. *Ibid.*, p. 6.

21. Edward Taylor, David Gillborn, and Gloria Ladson-Billings, *Foundations of Critical Race Theory in Education* (New York: Routledge, 2009).

22. Julie Kerr-Berry, "Dance Education in an Era of Racial Backlash: Moving Forward as We Step Backwards," *Journal of Dance Education* 12.2 (2012): 48–53.

23. Jessica M. Charbeneau, "Enactments of Whiteness in Pedagogical Practice: Reproducing and Transforming White Hegemony in the University Classroom," PhD diss. (University of Michigan, 2009), viii, ProQuest (AAT 304929724).

24. Timothy A. Berry, personal communication to author, February 15, 2015.

25. Frances A. Maher and Mary Kay Thompson Tetreault, "Learning in the Dark: How Assumptions of Whiteness Shape Classroom Knowledge," in *Race and Higher Education: Rethinking Pedagogy in Diverse College Classrooms*, ed. Annie Howell and Franklin A. Tuitt (Cambridge: Harvard Educational Review, 2003), 72.

26. Glenn E. Singleton and Curtis Linton, *Courageous Conversations about Race: A Field Guide for Achieving Equity in the Schools* (Thousand Oaks: Corwin Press, 2006), 160.

27. Ruth Frankenberg, *White Women, Race Matters: The Social Construction of Whiteness* (Minneapolis: University of Minnesota Press, 1993), 1.

28. *Ibid.*, 6.

29. Liz Lerman, workshop with artist, Perpich Center for Arts Education (Golden Valley, MN, June 18, 2014).

30. Molefi Kete Asante, *The History of Africa: A Quest for Eternal Harmony* (New York: Routledge, 2015).

31. Tribal African Art: Benin style, available at http://www.zyama.com/benin/pics..htm. Accessed February 19, 2015.

32. Julia L. Foulkes, *Modern Bodies: Dance and American Modernism from Martha Graham to Alvin Ailey* (Chapel Hill: University of North Carolina Press, 2002).

33. *Ibid.*, 22.

34. Perpener, *African-American Concert Dance*, 18, 19.

35. *Free to Dance: What Do You Dance?*, Episode 1, dir. Madison Davis Lacy, [DVD] (Thirteen/WNET New York, 2001).

36. Perpener, *African-American Concert Dance*, 1–24.

37. *Free to Dance: What Do You Dance?*

38. Susan Leigh Foster, *Worlding Dance* (New York: Palgrave Macmillan, 2009), 2.

39. This table is based on a synthesis several scholarly works. They include the following: Brenda Dixon Gottschild, *Digging the Africanist Presence in American Perform-*

ance: Dance and Other Contexts (Westport, CT: Greenwood, 1996); Robert Farris Thompson, *African Art in Motion: Icon and Act* (Berkeley: University of California Press, 1979); Marshall Stearns and Jean Stearns, *Jazz Dance: The Story of American Vernacular Dance* (New York: Schirmer Books, 1968); Kariamu Welsh-Asante, *African Dance: An Artistic, Historical, and Philosophical Inquiry* (Trenton: Africa World Press, 1996), and Peter H. Wood, "'Gimme de Knee Bone Bent': African Body Language and the Evolution of American Dance Forms." *Free to Dance*, web, last modified February 27, 2015, http://www.pbs.org/wnet/freetodance/.

40. Peter Wood, "'Gimme de Knee Bone Bent': African Body Language and the Evolution of American Dance Forms." *Free to Dance*, web, last modified February 27, 2015, http://www.pbs.org/wnet/freetodance/.

41. *Ibid.*

42. Singleton and Linton, *Courageous Conversations*, 169.

43. *Ibid.*, 170.

44. Perpener, *African-American Concert Dance*, 13.

45. Singleton and Linton, *Courageous Conversations*, 173.

46. Elizabeth F. Barkley, K. Patricia Cross, Claire Howell Major, *Collaborative Learning Techniques: A Handbook for College Faculty* (San Francisco: Jossey-Bass, 2005).

47. *Ibid.*

48. *Ibid.*, 193–204.

49. Foulkes, *Modern Bodies.*

50. James Allen, *Without Sanctuary: Photographs and Postcards of Lynching in America* (Santa Fe: Twin Palms, 2000).

51. *Dancing in the Light: Six Dances by African American Choreographers*, dir. Madison Davis Lacy [DVD] (West Long Beach, NJ: Kultur, 2007).

52. Dixon Gottschild, *Digging the Africanist Presence*, 60.

53. *Ibid.*

54. Thomas A. Angelo and K. Patricia Cross, *Classroom Assessment Techniques: A Handbook for College Teachers*, 2d ed. (San Francisco: Jossey-Bass, 1993), 126–131.

55. *Ibid.*, 126–131.

56. Dixon Gottschild, *Digging the Africanist Presence*, 60.

57. *Ibid.*, 60.

58. *Ibid.*, 78.

59. John C. Bean, *Engaging Ideas: The Professor's Guide to Integrating Writing, Critical Thinking, and Active Learning in the Classroom*, 2d ed. (San Francisco: Jossey-Bass, 2011), 120–145.

60. *Ibid.*, 133.

61. *Ibid.*, 133–134.

62. Tim Wise, *White Like Me: Reflections on Race from a Privileged Son* (Berkeley: Soft Skull Press, 2011), vii.

63. Nyama McCarthy-Brown, "Dancing in the Margins: Experiences of African American Ballerinas," *Journal of African American Studies* 15.3 (2011): 385–408.

64. Peggy McIntosh, "White Privilege: Unpacking the Invisible Knapsack," in *The Institution of Education*, ed. H. Svi Shapiro, Kathe Latham, Sabrina N. Ross, 5th ed., 242 (Boston: Pearson Custom, 2006).

65. Brenda Dixon Gottschild, *Joan Myers Brown & the Audacious Hope of the Black Ballerina: A Biohistory of American Performance* (New York: Palgrave Macmillan, 2011).

66. Joann Kealiinohomoku, "An Anthropologist Looks at Ballet as an Ethnic Form of Dance," in *Moving History/Dancing Cultures: A Dance History Reader*, ed. Ann Dils and Ann Cooper Albright (Middletown, CT: Wesleyan University Press, 2001), 33–43.

67. Frankenberg, *White Women*, 6.

Chapter Eight

1. Joseph Aguilar, "The Archaeology of the Pueblo Revolt and Spanish Reconquest at Tunyo, San Ildefonso Pueblo, New Mexico" (presentation, School for Advanced Research colloquium, Santa Fe, New Mexico, October 22, 2014).

2. Clyde Ellis, Luke Lassiter, and Gary H. Dunham, *Powwow* (Lincoln: University of Nebraska Press, 2005).

3. Jacqueline Shea Murphy, *The People Have Never Stopped Dancing: Native American Modern Dance Histories* (Minneapolis: University of Minnesota Press, 2007), 33.

4. CIA Report, as quoted in Murphy, 32.

5. *Ibid.*, 31.

6. *Ibid.*

7. As quoted in Murphy, 38.

8. *Ibid.*, 38.

9. *Ibid.*, 39.

10. *Ibid.*

11. *Ibid.*, 40.

12. *Ibid.*, 43.

13. *Ibid.*, 45.

14. As quoted in Murphy, 48.

15. Clyde Ellis, *A Dancing People: Pow-wow Culture on the Southern Plains* (Lawrence: University Press of Kansas, 2003), 77.

16. Adrienne Keene, "Native Appropriations: Representations, Pop Culture, and Cultural Resistance in Cyber Space" (presentation at University of California–Berkeley, 2015).

Chapter Nine

1. Judith Hanna, *Partnering Dance and Education* (Champaign, IL: Human Kinetics, 1999), 79.

2. Pegge Vissicaro, *Studying Dance Cultures Around the World: An Introduction to Multicultural Dance Education* (Dubuque: Kendall Hunt, 2004).

3. John Perpener, III, "Cultural Diversity and Dance History Research," in *Researching Dance: Evolving Modes of Inquiry*, ed. S. H. Fraleigh and P. Hanstein (Pittsburgh: University of Pittsburgh Press, 1999), 341.

4. *Ibid.*, 342.

5. Drid Williams, *Anthropology and the Dance: Ten lectures* (Urbana: University of Illinois Press, 2004), 170–171.

6. Brenda Dixon Gottschild, *Digging The Africanist Presence in American Performance* (Westport, CT: Praeger, 1996).

7. *Ibid.*, 61.

8. *Dance Magazine College Guide 2012–2013*, http://www.dancemagazine.com/the collegeguide?templateless=du. Accessed August 2013.

9. Pierre Bourdieu, *Language and Symbolic Power* (Cambridge: Harvard University Press, 1991).

10. *Ibid.*

11. David Newman, *Identities and Inequalities* (Columbus, OH: McGraw-Hill Higher Education, 2011), 81.

12. Marta E. Savigliano, "Worlding Dance and Dancing Out There in the World," in *Worlding Dance,* ed. Susan L. Foster (New York: Palgrave Macmillan, 2009).

13. Nancy Reynolds, ed., *The Dance Catalog* (New York: Harmony Books 1979).

14. Savigliano, 179.

15. Pierre Bourdieu, *Language and Symbolic Power* (Cambridge: Harvard University Press, 1991),167.

16. Privilege as used in this document refers to: the hierarchical positioning of dance forms in American higher education, financial funding, and social status.

17. Savigliano,165.

18. *Ibid.*

19. I use the word authenticity to mean, as close to the source and origin of creation as possible. This is not to say that there is no value in dance that is inauthentic, removed from the source, or out of context for that matter. However, there is, in my opinion, a need for context to be explained to viewers so that inauthentic and/or hybrid dance forms are not mistaken for authentic dance forms representing a specific group of people.

20. Manfred Steger, *Globlization: A Very Short Introduction* (Oxford: Oxford University Press, 2003), 8.

21. Sociologist Roland Robertson explains globalization as a process and globality as the result (Robertson 1992), 10.

22. Sara Kugler, "'Harlem Shake' Craze Needs Historical, Cultural Context," http://www.msnbc.com/melissa-harris-perry/harlem-shake-craze-needs-historical-cultur. Accessed December 2013.

23. *Ibid.*

24. Williams, 212.

25. Eric Lott, *Blackface Minstrelsy and the American Working Class* (New York: Oxford University Press, 1995).

26. Savigliano.

27. John Martin, "Dance Recital Given by Negro Artists," *New York Times* (April 27, 1931); John Martin, *Introduction to the Dance* (New York: Norton, 1939); Lincoln Kirstein, *The Book of Dance: A Short History of Classic Theatrical Dancing* (Garden City: Garden City Publishing Co., 1935); Pearl Primus, "African Primitive Dance," in *The Dance Encyclopedia*, comp. and ed. Anatole Chujoy (New York: A.S. Barnes, 1949); La Meri, "Ethnic Dance," in *The Dance Encyclopedia*, comp. and ed. Anatole Chujoy (New York: Simon & Schuster, 1967).

28. Richard Kraus, Sarah C. Hilsendager, and Brenda Dixon (Gottschild), *History of the Dance in Art and Education* (Englewood Cliffs, NJ: Prentice Hall, 1991).

29. Martin.

30. Edward Said, *Orientalism* (New York:

Pantheon Books, 1978). Jane Desmond, "Dancing Out the Difference: Cultural Imperialism and Ruth St. Denis's *Radha* of 1906," in *Moving History/Dancing Cultures*, ed. Ann Cooper Albirght and Ann Dils (Middletown, CT: Wesleyan University Press, 2001); Priya Srinvasan, *Sweating Saris* (Philadelphia: Temple University Press, 2011).

31. Srinvasan, 58.

32. Said, 3.

33. "Orientalism can be discussed and analyzed as the corporate institution for dealing with the Orient—dealing with it by making statements about it, authorizing views of it, describing it, by teaching it, settling it, ruling over it: in short, Orientalism as a Western style for dominating, restructuring, and having authority over the Orient."

33. Desmond, 263.

34. *Ibid.*

35. *Ibid.*

36. Sunaina Maira, "Belly Dancing: Arabface, Orientalist Feminism, and the U.S. Empire," *American Quarterly* 60.2 (2008): 317–345; Donnalee Dox, "Dancing Around Orientalism," *The Drama Review* 50.4 (2006): 52–71.

37. Lincoln Kirstein, *The Book of Dance: A Short History of Classic Theatrical Dancing* (Garden City: Garden City Publishing Co., 1935).

38. John Martin, Dance recital given by Negro artists, *New York Times* (April 27, 1931, 30).

39. Pearl Primus, "African Primitive Dance," in *The Dance Encyclopedia*, ed. Anatole Chujoy (New York: A.S. Barnes, 1949).

40. La Meri, *Total Education in Ethnic Dance* (New York: Marcel Dekker, 1977), 1.

41. La Meri, "Ethnic Dance," in *The Dance Encyclopedia*, ed. Anatole Chujoy (New York: Simon & Schuster, 1967), 338–339.

42. *Ibid.*

43. Julie Kerr-Berry, "Progress and Complacency a 'Post-racial' Dance in Higher Education," *Journal of Higher Education* 10 (2010): 3–5.

44. Joann Kealiinohomoku, "An Anthropologist Looks at Ballet as a Form of Ethnic Dance," in *Moving History/Dancing Cultures: A Dance History*, ed. Ann Albright and Ann Dils (Middletown, CT: Wesleyan University Press, 1970), 33.

45. Kariamu Welsh, *Zimbabwe Dance: Rhythmic Forces, Ancestral Voices, and Aesthetic Analysis* (Trenton: Africa World Press, 2000), 12.

46. Matteo, "Ethnic Dance," in *The Dance Catalog*, ed. N. Reynolds (New York: Harmony Books, 1979).

47. Lynne Fauley Emery, *Black Dance From 1619 to Today* (Highstown, NJ: Princeton Book Company, 1988).

48. Frank Rey, "Jazz: America's Ethnic Dance," in *Anthology of American Jazz Dance*, ed. G Giordano (Evanston: Orion Publishing House, 1971).

49. Richard Long, *The Black Tradition in American Dance* (New York: Smithmark, 1989).

50. Rey.

51. Barbara Glass, *African American Dance: an Illustrated History* (Jefferson, NC: McFarland, 2006).

52. Judith L. Hanna, "Ethnic Dance Research Guide: Relevant Data Categories," *CORD NEWS* 6.1 (1973): 42–44.

53. Judith L. Hanna, *To Dance Is Human* (Chicago: University of Chicago Press, 1979), 54.

54. Selma Jeane Cohen, ed., "Ethnic Dance," in *The International Encyclopedia of Dance* (Oxford Reference published online, 2005).

55. Foster.

56. Karen Clemente, and Luke Kahlich, eds., *Dance Directory: Program of Professional Preparation in Colleges and Universities, and Performing Arts Schools in the United States and Canada* (Reston, VA: American Alliance for Health, Physical Education and Recreation, 1992).

57. Janice Ross, *Moving Lessons: Margaret H'Doubler and the Beginning of Dance in Higher Education* (Madison: University of Wisconsin Press, 2000), 13.

58. *Ibid.*

59. Margaret H'Doubler, *The Dance and its Place in Education* (New York: Harcourt, Brace, 1925), 26.

60. Thomas Hagood, *Legacy in Dance Education* (Amherst: Cambria Press, 2008).

61. *Ibid.*, 56.

62. University of Cape Town, Dance Department website, "School of Dance Undergraduate Syllabus," http://www.dance.uct.ac.za/. Accessed August 2013.

63. New World School of the Arts Dance Department Website, New World School of the Arts, Dance Department. 2013. "BFA Degrees." http://nwsa.mdc.edu/col_deg_

dance/program_info/program_info.html. Accessed August 2013.

64. Pomona College, Dance Department website, "Dance Courses." http://catalog. pomona.edu/preview_program.php?catoid= 3&poid=180. Accessed August 2013.

65. Nyama McCarthy-Brown, "'The Proof Is in The Pudding': An Examination of Three Selected Dance Department Curricula and How Cultural Diversity Is Valued," PhD diss. (Temple University, 2011).

66. University of Georgia, Dance Department website, Topical Outline 2013, University of Georgia, Dance Department. 2013 "Programs." http://www.dance.uga.edu/. Accessed August 2013.

67. University of Hawaii Manoa, Department of Theatre and Dance website, "Program Overview." http://manoa.hawaii.edu/ dance/futurestudent/index.php. Accessed March 2014.

68. Arizona State University, Herberger Institute for Design and the Arts, School of Film, Dance, and Theatre, "About." https://

filmdancetheatre.asu.edu/about. Accessed November 2015.

69. Onye Ozuzu, personal conversation, June 25, 2015, Columbia College in Chicago, Illinois.

70. Denison University, Dance, "Degree essentials" http://denison.edu/academics/ dance/degree-essentials. Accessed December 2013.

71. Vissicaro.

72. Foster.

73. Nyama McCarthy-Brown.

74. Welsh.

75. *Ibid.* Foster; and McCarthy-Brown.

76. Savigliano.

Epilogue

1. Sherry B. Shapiro, *Pedagogy and the Politics of the Body: A Critical Praxis* (New York: Garland, 1999), 141.

2. *Ibid.*

Bibliography

Adinku, W. Ofotsu. *African Dance Education in Ghana: Curriculum and Instructional Materials for a Model Bachelor of Arts (hons.) Dance in Society.* Accra: Ghana Universities Press, 1994.

Aguilar, Joseph. "The Archaeology of the Pueblo Revolt and Spanish Reconquest at Tunyo, San Ildefonso Pueblo, New Mexico." Presentation, School for Advanced Research colloquium, Santa Fe, New Mexico, October 22, 2014.

Aliey, Alvin. *Revelations.* New York: Birch Lane Press, 1995.

Allen, James. *Without Sanctuary: Photographs and Postcards of Lynching in America.* Santa Fe: Twin Palms, 2000.

Asante, Molefi Kete. *The History of Africa: A Quest for Eternal Harmony,* 2d ed. New York: Routledge, 2015.

Asante, Molefi Kete. "Race in Antiquity: Truly Out of Africa." Race Web. Last modified May 19, 2009. http://www.asante.net/articles/19/race-in-antiquity-truly-out-of-africa/.

Au, Wayne, Bill Bigelow, and Stan Karp. *Rethinking Our Classrooms, Volume 1: Teaching for Equity and Justice,* new ed. Milwaukee: Rethinking Schools, 2007.

Azevedo, Kathryn J., Sonia Mendoza, María Fernández, K. Farish Haydel, Michelle Fujimoto, Evelyn C. Tirumalai, and Thomas N. Robinson. "Turn Off the TV and Dance! Participation in Culturally Tailored Health Interventions: Implications for Obesity Prevention Among Mexican American Girls," *Ethnicity & Disease* 23.4 (2013): 452–461.

Banks, James. "Cultural Pluralism and the Schools," *Educational Leadership* 32.3 (1974): 163–66.

Barkley, Elizabeth F., K. Patricia Cross, and Claire Howell Major. *Collaborative Learning Techniques: A Handbook for College Faculty.* San Francisco: Jossey-Bass, 2005.

Barnes, Marian, and Linda Goss, eds. *Talk that Talk: An Anthology of African-American Storytelling.* New York: Simon & Schuster Touchstone, 1989.

Barr, Sherrie, and Doug Risner. "Weaving Social Foundations Through Dance Pedagogy: A Pedagogy of Uncovering," *Journal of Dance Education* 14. 4 (2014): 136–145.

Bean, John C. *Engaging Ideas: The Professor's Guide to Integrating Writing, Critical Thinking and Active Learning in the Classroom,* 2d ed. San Francisco: Jossey-Bass, 2011.

Bonilla-Silva, Eduardo. *Racism Without Racists: Color-blind Racism and the Persistence of Racism in America.* Lanham, MD: Rowman & Littlefield, 2014.

Bourdieu, Pierre. "Cultural Reproduction and Social Reproduction." In *Power and Ideology in Education,* eds. J. Karabel and A. H. Halsey. New York: Oxford University Press, 1977.

Bourdieu, Pierre. *Distinction: A Social Critique on the Judgment on Taste.* Cambridge: Harvard University Press, 1984.

Bourdieu, Pierre. *Language and Symbolic Power.* Cambridge: Harvard University Press, 1991.
Bourdieu, Pierre, and Jean Claude Passeron. *Reproduction in Education, Society and Culture.* London: Sage, 1977.
Boustany, Nora. "Prominent Ballet Dancer Rosella Higher." *Washington Post,* November 8, 2008.
Carter, Prudence L. "'Black' Cultural Capital, Status Positioning, and Schooling Conflicts for Low-Income African American Youth," *Social Problems,* 50, Vol. 1 (2003): 136–55.
Carter, Prudence L. *Keepin' It Real: School Success Beyond Black and White.* New York: Oxford University Press, 2005.
Castro, Rafaela G. *Chicano Folklore: A Guide to the Folktales, Traditions, Ritual and Religious Practices of Mexican Americans.* New York: Oxford University Press, 2001.
Chappell, Kerry. "Creativity in Primary Level Dance Education: Moving Beyond Assumption." *Research in Dance Education* 8.1 (2007): 27–52.
Charbeneau, Jean M. "Enactments of Whiteness in Pedagogical Practice: Reproducing and Transforming White Hegemony in the University Classroom." PhD diss., University of Michigan, 2009. ProQuest (AAT 304929724).
Clark, Herbert H. *Using Language.* New York: Cambridge University Press, 1996.
Classic Black. Videotaped at Bruno Walter Auditorium. New York: The New York Public Library for the Performing Arts. By Penny Ward, on February 12, Cassette 2 [VHS]. 1996.
Clemente, Karen, and Luke Kahlich, eds. *Dance Directory: Program of Professional Preparation in Colleges and Universities, and Performing Arts Schools in the United States and Canada.* Reston, VA: American Alliance for Health, Physical Education and Recreation, 1992.
Collins, Karyn. "Does Classism Have Color?" *Dance Magazine,* June 2005.
Copeland, Misty. *Life in Motion: An Unlikely Ballerina.* New York: Touchstone, 2014.
Dance Ability International, 2012. Available at http://www.danceability.com/. Accessed July 13, 2015
Dance Magazine College Guide 2012–2013, Denison University, Dance, "Degree Essentials." Available at http://denison.edu/academics/dance/degree-essentials. Accessed December 2013.
Dance Theatre of Harlem Website, 2015. Available at http://www.dancetheatreofharlem.org. Accessed June 8, 2015.
Dancing in the Light: Six Dances by African American Choreographers. DVD. Directed by Madison Davis Lacy. West Long Beach, NJ: Kultur, 2007.
Davis, Bonnie M. *How to Teach Students Who Don't Look Like You.* Thousand Oaks: Corwin Press, 2006.
Davis, Donna M., and Shirley Marie McCarther. "Following the Drinking Gourd: Culturally Relevant Pedagogy and Curriculum Development Through the Arts," *The Educational Forum* 79.1 (2015):8–80.
Deans, Joselli. "Black Ballerinas Dancing on the Edge: An Analysis of the Cultural Politics in Delores Browne's and Raven Wilkinson's Careers, 1954–1985." EdD Dissertation, Temple University, 2001.
DeFrantz, Thomas. *Dancing Revelations: Alvin Ailey's Embodiment of African American Culture.* New York: Oxford University Press, 2004.
Delgado, Richard, and Jean Stefancic. *Critical Race Theory: An Introduction.* New York: New York University Press, 2012.
Delpit, Lisa. *Other People's Children: Culture Conflict in the Classroom.* New York: The New Press, 1995.
Desmond, Jane. "Dancing Out the Difference: Cultural Imperialism and Ruth St. Denis's *Radha* of 1906." In *Moving History/Dancing Cultures,* ed. A. Cooper Albirght and A. Dils, 256–287. Middletown, CT: Wesleyan University Press, 2001.
Desmond, Jane. "Embodying Difference." In *Meaning in Motion,* ed. Jane Desmond. Durham: Duke University Press, 1997.

Dixon, Melanye White. *Marion Cuyjet and the Judimar School of Dance: Training Ballerinas in Black Philadelphia 1948–1971.* Lewiston, NY: Edwin Mellon Press, 2011.

Dox, Donnalee. "Dancing Around Orientalism." *The Drama Review* 50.4 (2006): 52–71.

Duncan, Arne. "A Call To Teaching." Speech presented at the University of Virginia, Charlottesville, Virginia, October 9, 2009.

Dyson, Ann Haas, and Celia Genishi, eds. *The Need for a Story: Cultural Diversity in Classroom and Community.* Urbana: National Council for Teachers of English, 1994.

Eaker-Rich, Deborah, and Jane Van Galen. *Caring in an Unjust World: Negotiating Borders and Barriers in Schools.* Albany: SUNY Press, 1996.

Ellis, Clyde. *A Dancing People: Powwow Culture on the Southern Plains.* Lawrence: University Press of Kansas, 2003.

Ellis, Clyde, Luke Lassiter, and Gary H. Dunham. *Powwow.* Lincoln: University of Nebraska Press, 2005.

Emery, Lynne F. *Black Dance: From 1619 to Today.* Highstown, NJ: Princeton Book Company, 1988.

Foster, Michele. *Black Teachers on Teaching.* New York: Norton, 1998.

Foster, Susan L. ed. *Worlding Dance.* New York: Palgrave Macmillan, 2009.

Foulkes, Julia. *Modern Bodies: Dance and American Modernism form Martha Graham to Alvin Ailey.* Chapel Hill: University of North Carolina, 2002.

Frankenberg, Ruth. *White Women, Race Matters: The Social Construction of Whiteness.* Minneapolis: University of Minnesota Press, 1993.

Free to Dance: What Do You Dance? Episode 1, directed by Madison Davis Lacy. DVD. 2001; Thirteen/WNET New York, NY, 2001.

Freire, Paulo. *Pedagogy of the Oppressed.* New York: Continuum, 1986.

Freire, Paulo, and Myra Bergman Ramos. "Excerpt from *Pedagogy of the Oppressed.*" In *The Institution of Education,* ed. H. Svi Shapiro, Kathe Latham, Sabrina N. Ross, 5th ed., 155–162. Boston: Pearson Custom, 2006.

Friedlander, Diane, and Linda Darling-Hammond (with A. Andre, H. Lewis-Charp, L. McClosky, N. Richardson, O. Araiza, S. Sandler, and V. Velez-Rocha). *High Schools for Equality: Policy Supports for Student Learning in Communities of Color.* Available at http://www.edlawcenter.org/assets/files/pdfs/secondary%20reform/hsfe_policy_report.pdf. Accessed June 3, 2015.

Gaunt, Kyra Danielle. *The Games Black Girls Play: Learning the Ropes from Double-Dutch to Hip-Hop.* New York: New York University Press, 2006.

Gay, Geneva. *Culturally Responsive Teaching: Theory, Research, and Practice,* 2d ed. New York: Teachers College Press, 2010.

Gewirtz, Sharon. "Conceptualizing Social Justice in Education: Mapping the Territory." *Journal of Educational Policy* 13.4 (1998): 469–484.

Glass, Barbara. *African American Dance: An Illustrated History.* Jefferson, NC: McFarland, 2007.

Goldfine, Dayna, et al., dir. *Ballets Russes.* DVD. New York: Zeitgeist Films, 2006.

Gottschild, Brenda Dixon. *The Black Dancing Body: A Geography from Coon to Cool.* New York: Palgrave MacMillian, 2003.

Gottschild, Brenda Dixon. *Digging the Africanist Presence of American Performance.* Westport, CT: Praeger, 1996.

Gottschild, Brenda Dixon. *Joan Myers Brown and the Audacious Hope of the Black Ballerina: A Biohistory of American Performance.* New York: Palgrave Macmillan, 2012.

Gottschild, Brenda Dixon. "Stripping the Emperor." In *Digging the Africanist Presence in American Performance: Dance and Other Contexts.* Westport, CT: Greenwood, 1996.

Green, Diana. *Choreographing from Within: Developing the Habit of Inquiry as an Artist.* Champaign, IL: Human Kinetics, 2010.

Gustafson, Ruth. *Race and Curriculum: Music in Childhood Education.* New York: Palgrave Macmillan, 2009.

Hagood, Thomas. *Legacy in Dance Education.* Amherst, NY: Cambria Press, 2008.

Hagood, Thomas K. *Legacy in Dance Education: Essays and Interviews on Values, Practices, and People: An Anthology.* Amherst, NY: Cambria Press, 2008.

Hanley, Mary Stone. "Introduction." In *Culturally Relevant Arts Education for Social Justice: A Way Out of No Way,* ed. George W. Noblit, Gilda L. Sheppard, Tom Barone, and Lee Anne Bell. New York: Routledge, 2013.

Hanna, J.L. "Ethnic Dance Research Guide: Relevant Data Categories," *CORD NEWS,* Vol. 6, No. 1, 1973.

Hanna, Judith Lynne. *Partnering Dance and Education: Intelligent Moves for Changing Times.* Champaign, IL: Human Kinetics, 1999.

Hanna, Judith Lynne. *To Dance is Human.* Chicago: University of Chicago Press, 1979.

Hawkins, Alma. *Creating Through Dance.* Englewood Cliffs, NJ: Prentice-Hall, 1964.

H'Doubler, Margaret. *The Dance and Its Place in Education.* New York: Harcourt, Brace, 1925.

Hilliard, Asa G. *The Reawakening of the African Mind.* Boston: Beacon Press, 1998.

Holt, David. "Hidden Strengths: The Case for the Generalist Teacher of Art." In *Primary Arts Education,* ed. David Holt. London: Falmer Press, 1997.

hooks, bell. *Teaching to Transgress.* New York: Routledge, 1994.

Horton, Myles, and Paulo Freire. *We Make the Road by Walking: Conversations on Education and Social Change.* Philadelphia: Temple University Press, 1990.

Hughes, Allen. "Without Regard for Color." *New York Times,* February 21, 1965.

I'll Make Me a World: A Century of African American Arts. Documentary [VHS], directed by Denise A. Greene and Sam Pollard, PBS, 1999.

Kaeppler, Adrienne. "An Introduction to Dance Aesthetics." *Yearbook for Traditional Music* 35 (2003).

Kanpol, Barry. *Critical Pedagogy: An Introduction.* Westport, CT: Bergin & Garvey, 1994.

Katrak, Ketu. H. *Contemporary Indian Dance.* New York: Palgrave Macmillan, 2011.

Kealiinohomoku, Joann. "An Anthropologist Looks at Ballet as a Form of Ethnic Dance." In *Moving History/Dancing Cultures: A Dance History,* ed. Albright, Ann Cooper and Ann Dils, 33–42. Middletown, CT: Wesleyan University Press, 2001.

Keene, Adrienne. "Native Appropriations: Representations, Pop Culture, and Cultural Resistance in Cyber Space." Presentation, Native Perspectives on Representation, Berkeley, California, February 20, 2015.

Kerr-Berry, Julie. "Dance Education in an Era of Racial Backlash: Moving Forward as We Step Backwards." *Journal of Dance Education* 12.2 (2012): 48–53.

Kerr-Berry, Julie. "Progress and Complacency a 'Post-racial' Dance in Higher Education." *Journal of Higher Education* 10.1 (2010):3–5.

Kirstein, Lincoln. *The Book of Dance: A Short History of Classic Theatrical Dancing.* Garden City: Garden City Publishing Co., 1935.

Kohl, Herbert R. *I Won't Learn from You: And Other Thoughts on Creative Maladjustment.* New York: New Press, 1994.

Kraus, Richard, Sarah Chapman Hilsendager, and Brenda Dixon (Gottschild). *History of the Dance in Art and Education,* 3d ed. Englewood Cliffs, NJ: Prentice Hall, 1991.

Kugler, Sara. "'Harlem Shake' Craze Needs Historical, Cultural Context." Available at www.msnbc.com/melissa-harris-perry/harlem-shake-craze-needs-historical-cultur. Accessed December 2013.

Ladson-Billings, Gloria. *The Dreamkeepers: Successful Teachers of African American Teachers.* San Francisco: Jossey-Bass, 2009.

La Meri. "Ethnic Dance." In *The Dance Encyclopedia,* ed. Anatole Chujoy. New York: Simon & Schuster, 1967.

Legge, Maureen F. "Te Ao Kori as Expressive Movement in Aotearoa New Zealand Physical Education Teacher Education (PETE): A Narrative Account." *Asia Pacific Journal of Health, Sport and Physical Education* 2.3/4 (2011): 81–95.

Lerman, Liz. *Liz Lerman's Critical Response Process: Methods for Getting Useful Feedback on Anything You Make, from Dance to Dessert.* Available at http://danceexchange.org/projects/critical-response-process/. Accessed July 13, 2015.

Lerman, Liz, and John Borstel. *Liz Lerman's Critical Response Process: A Methods for Getting Useful Feedback.* Dance Exchange, 2003.

Lerman, Liz. Workshop with artist, June 18, 2014, Perpich Center for Arts Education, Golden Valley, MN.

Livingston, Lili C. *American Indiana Ballerinas.* Norman: University of Oklahoma Press, 1997.

Long, Richard. *The Black Tradition in American Dance.* New York: Smithmark, 1989.

Lott, Eric. *Love and Theft: Blackface Minstrelsy and the American Working Class.* New York: Oxford University Press, 1995.

Maher, Frances A., and Mary Kay Thompson Tetreault. "Learning in the Dark: How Assumptions of Whiteness Shape Classroom Knowledge." In *Race and Higher Education: Rethinking Pedagogy in Diverse College Classrooms,* ed. Annie Howell and Franklin A. Tuitt, 69–96. Cambridge: Harvard Educational, 2003.

Maira, Sunaina. "Belly Dancing: Arab-face, Orientalist Feminism, and the U.S. Empire." *American Quarterly* 60. 2 (2008): 317–345.

Maletic, Vera. *Body—Space—Expression: Development of Rudolf Laban's Movement and Dance Concepts.* Berlin: Walter de Gruyter, 1987.

Malone, Jacqui. *Steppin' on the Blues.* Urbana: University of Illinois Press, 1996.

Manning, Susan. *Modern Dance, Negro Dance: Race in Motion.* Minneapolis: University of Minnesota, 2004.

Martin, John. "Dance Recital Given by Negro Artists." *New York Times,* April 27, 1931.

Martin, John. *Introduction to the Dance.* New York: Norton, 1939.

Matos, Lucia. "Writing in the Flesh Body, Identity, Disability, and Difference." In *Dance in a World of Change: Reflections of Globalization and Cultural Difference,* ed. Sherry Shapiro. Raleigh: Human Kinetics, 2008.

Matteo. "Ethnic Dance." In *The Dance Catalog,* ed. N. Reynolds, 146–153. New York: Harmony Books, 1979.

McCarthy-Brown, Nyama. "Dancing in the Margins: Experiences of African American Ballerinas." *Journal of African American Studies* 15.3 (2011): 385–408.

McCarthy-Brown, Nyama. "Poverty of Culturally Diverse Dance Resources: Its Impact in Our Classrooms and Beyond," *Arts Education Policy Review* 116.1 (2015): 30–42.

McCarthy-Brown, Nyama. "'The Proof Is in The Pudding': An Examination of Three Selected Dance Department Curricula and How Cultural Diversity Is Valued." PhD dissertation, Temple University, 2011.

McCutchen, Brenda P. *Teaching Dance as Art in Education.* Champaign, IL: Human Kinetics, 2006.

McIntosh, Peggy. "White Privilege: Unpacking the Invisible Knapsack." In *The Institution of Education,* ed. H. Svi Shapiro, Kathe Latham, Sabrina N. Ross, 5th ed., 239–242. Boston: Pearson Custom, 2006.

McRobbie, Angela. "Dance Narratives and Fantasies," in *Meaning in Motion: New Cultural Studies of Dance,* ed. Jane Desmond. Durham: Duke University Press, 1997.

Melchior, Elizabeth. "Culturally Responsive Dance Pedagogy in the Primary Classroom." *Research in Dance Education* 12.2 (2011): 119–135.

Mercado, Carmen. "Caring as Empowerment: School Collaboration and Community Agency." *The Urban Review* 25.1 (1993).

Meyer Spacks, Patricia. "The Difference It Makes." In *A Feminist Perspective in the Academy: The Difference It Makes,* ed. Walter R. Gove and Elizabeth Langland, 7–24. Chicago: University of Chicago Press, 1983.

Mica Pollock, *Colormute: Race Talk Dilemmas in an American School.* Princeton: Princeton University Press, 2004.

Mills, Charles. *The Racial Contract.* Ithaca: Cornell University Press, 1997.

Murphy, Jacqueline Shea. *The People Have Never Stopped Dancing: Native American Modern Dance Histories.* Minneapolis: University of Minnesota Press, 2007.

Native American Encyclopedia. *Native American Encyclopedia.* NAE, 2010. Web. 7 June 2015.

Neal, Larry. "The Black Arts Movement." *The Drama Review* 12.4 (1968): 29.
New World School of the Arts, Dance Department. 2013. "BFA Degrees." Available at http://nwsa.mdc.edu/col_deg_dance/program_info/program_info.html. Accessed August 2013.
Newman, David. *Identities and Inequalities.* Columbus, OH: McGraw-Hill Higher Education, 2011.
Ngema, Vusi. Recorded personal interview. University of Cape Town, South Africa, 2002.
Pai, Young. *Cultural Foundations of Education.* Columbus, OH: Merrill, 1990.
Payne, Ruby. *A Framework for Understanding Poverty.* Aha! Process 2001.
Perpener, John. O. III. *African-American Concert Dance: The Harlem Renaissance and Beyond.* Urbana: University of Illinois Press, 2001.
Perpener III, John. "Cultural Diversity and Dance History Research." In *Researching Dance: Evolving Modes of Inquiry,* ed. S. H. Fraleigh and P. Hanstein, 334–351. Pittsburgh: University of Pittsburgh Press, 1999.
Peterson, Anya Royce. "Ethnic Dance." In *The International Encyclopedia of Dance, Reference Edition,* ed. S. J. Cohen and Dance Perspectives Foundation. Oxford University Press. Accessed June 23, 2010.
Pomona College, Dance Department, 2013. "Dance Courses." Available at http://catalog.pomona.edu/preview_program.php?catoid=3&poid=180. Accessed August 2013.
Pratt-Clarke, Menah A.E. *Critical Race, Feminism, and Education: A Social Justice Model.* New York: Palgrave Macmillan, 2010.
Primus, Pearl. "African Primitive Dance." In *The Dance Encyclopedia,* ed. Anatole Chujoy. New York: A.S. Barnes, 1949.
Renta, Priscilla. "Salsa Dance: Latino/a History in Motion," *CENTRO Journal* 16 (2004): 139–157.
Rey, Frank. "Jazz: America's Ethnic Dance." In *Anthology of American Jazz Dance,* ed. Giordano. Evanston: Orion Publishing House, 1971.
Reynolds, Nancy, ed. *The Dance Catalog.* New York: Harmony Books, 1979.
Risner, Doug and Susan Stinson. "Moving Social Justice: Challenges, Fears and Possibilities in Dance Education," *International Journal of Education & the Arts* 11.6 (2010): 1–26.
Robertson, Roland. *Globalization, Social Theory and Global Culture.* London: Sage, 1992.
Ross, Janice. *Moving Lessons: Margaret H'Doubler and the Beginning of Dance in American Education.* Madison: University of Wisconsin Press, 2000.
Said, Edward. *Orientalism.* New York: Pantheon Books, 1978.
Sansom, Adrienne N. "Mindful Pedagogy in Dance: Honoring the Life of the Child." *Research in Dance Education* 10.3 (2009): 161–176.
Saraswat, Pratishtha. *Essential Elements of Kathak.* Kuningan, Indonesia: Embassy of India, 2014.
Savigliano, Marta. E. "Worlding Dance and Dancing out there in the World." In *Worlding Dance,* ed. Susan L. Foster, 163–190. New York: Palgrave Macmillan, 2009.
Scherff, Lisa, and Karen Spector. *Culturally Relevant Pedagogy: Clashes and Confrontations.* Lanham, MD: Rowman & Littlefield, 2011.
Schwartz, Peggy, and Murray Schwartz. *The Dance Claimed Me: A Biography of Pearl Primus.* New Haven: Yale University Press, 2011.
Shapiro, Sherry B. *Pedagogy and the Politics of the Body: A Critical Praxis.* New York: Garland, 1999.
Shapiro, Sherry B., ed. *Dance, Power, and Difference: Critical Feminist Perspectives on Dance Education.* Champaign, IL: Human Kinetics, 1998.
Shor, Ira. *Empowering Education: Critical Teaching for Social Change.* Chicago: University of Chicago Press, 1992.
Singleton, Glenn E. and Curtis Linton. *Courageous Conversations about Race.* Thousand Oaks: Corwin Press, 2006.
Sleeter, Christine E. *Professional Development for Culturally Responsive and Relationship-Based Pedagogy.* New York: Peter Lang, 2011.

Sleeter, Christine E., and Catherine Cornbleth. *Teaching with Vision: Culturally Responsive Teaching in Standards-Based Classrooms.* New York: Teachers College Press, 2011.

Sleeter, Christine E., and Peter McLaren. *Multicultural Education, Critical Pedagogy, and the Politics of Difference.* Albany: SUNY Press, 1995.

Srinivasan, Priya. *Sweating Saris.* Philadelphia: Temple University Press, 2011.

Stearns, Marshall, and Jean Stearns. *Jazz Dance: The Story of American Vernacular Dance.* New York: Schirmer, 1968.

Steger, Manfred. *Globilization: A Very Short Introduction.* Oxford: Oxford University Press, 2003.

Sternberg, Robert, ed. *Handbook of Creativity.* New York: Cambridge University Press, 1999.

Stinson, Sue. "Seeking a Feminist's Pedagogy for Children's Dance." In *Dance, Power, and Difference: Critical and Feminist Perspective on Dance Education*, ed. Sherry Shapiro. Champaign, IL: Human Kinetics, 1998.

Stulberg, Lisa, and Sharon Lawner Weinberg. *Diversity in American High Education.* New York: Routledge, 2011.

Tallchief, Maria, and Larry Kaplan. *Maria Tallchief: America's Prima Ballerina.* New York: Henry Holt, 1997.

Taylor, Edward, David Gillborn, and Gloria Ladson-Billings. *Foundations of Critical Race Theory in Education.* New York: Routledge, 2009.

Theoharis, George. "Social Educational Leaders and Resistance: Toward a Theory of Social Justice Leadership." *Educational Administration Quarterly* 43.2 (2007): 221–258, 2007.

Thornton, Samuel. *Laban's Theory of Movement; A New Perspective.* Boston: Plays Inc., 1971.

Thompson, Robert Farris. *African Art in Motion: Icon and Act.* Berkeley: University of California Press, 1974.

Tribal African Art: Benin Style. Available at http://www.zyama.com/benin/pics.htm. Accessed February 19, 2015.

Treuer, Anton. *Everything You Ever Wanted to Know about Indians but Were Afraid to Ask.* St. Paul: Borealis Press, 2012.

University of California at Irvine, Dance Department. "Dance Coursework." Available at http://dance.arts.uci.edu/dance-coursework. Accessed August 2013.

University of Cape Town, Dance Department. "School of Dance Undergraduate Syllabus." Available at http://www.dance.uct.ac.za/. Accessed August 2013.

University of Georgia, Dance Department. "Programs." Available at http://www.dance.uga.edu/. Accessed August 2013.

University of Hawaii Manoa, Department of Theatre and Dance. 2014. "Program Overview." Available at http://manoa.hawaii.edu/dance/futurestudent/index.php. Accessed March 2014.

University of Surrey, dance department. "Studying Dance at Surrey." Available at http://www.surrey.ac.uk/dft/study/dance/danceatsurrey/index.htm. Accessed August 2013.

Vaze, Bagashgree. Personal interview, recorded. 2015

Vissicaro, Pegge. *Studying Dance Cultures around the World: an Introduction to Multicultural Dance Education.* Dubuque: Kendall Hunt, 2004.

Waters, Mary C. *Ethnic Options: Choosing Identities in America.* Berkeley: University of California Press, 1990.

Webb, Lynne, Myria W. Allen, and Kandi L. Walker. "Feminist Pedagogy: Identifying Basic Principles." *Academic Exchange Quarterly* 6.1 (2002): 67–72.

Welsh, Kariamu. *Zimbabwe Dance: Rhythmic Forces, Ancestral Voices, and Aesthetic Analysis.* Trenton: Africa World Press, 2000.

Welsh-Asante, Kariamu., ed. *African Dance: An Artistic, Historical, and Philosophical Inquiry.* Trenton: African World Press, 1997.

Williams, Drid. *Anthropology and the Dance: Ten Lectures.* Urbana: University of Illinois Press, 2004.

Williams, Raymond. "Culture Is Ordinary." In *Resources of Hope: Culture, Democracy, Socialism*, ed. Robin Gale, 3–14. London: Verso, 1989.

Wink, Joan. *Critical Pedagogy: Notes from the Real World*. Boston: Pearson Education, 2005.
Winkle-Wagner, Rachelle, Kelly Ward, and Lisa Wolf-Wendel. *Cultural Capital: The Promises and Pitfalls in Educational Research*. San Francisco: Jossey-Bass, 2010.
Wise, Tim. *White Like Me: Reflections on Race from a Privileged Son*. Berkeley: Soft Skull Press, 2011.
Wong, Harry, and Rosemary T. Wong. *The First Days of School*. Mountain View, CA: Harry K. Wong, 2004.
Wood, Peter. "'Gimme de Knee Bone Bent': African Body Language and the Evolution Of American Dance Forms." *Free to Dance* Web. Last modified February 27, 2015. http://www.pbs.org/wnet/freetodance/.

About the Contributors

Selene **Carter** is an assistant professor of contemporary dance at Indiana University. Her choreographic work integrates improvisational scores and historic compositional approaches.

Kelly **Fayard** is the assistant dean and director of the Native American Cultural Center at Yale College. She is a member of the Poach Band of Creek Indians, in southern Alabama, and has attended and participated in many powwows throughout the United States.

Julie **Kerr-Berry** is a professor and director of the dance program at Minnesota State University at Mankato. Her teaching practice, creative and scholarly research are centered on social justice through the theoretical frameworks of critical pedagogy and critical race theory.

Nyama **McCarthy-Brown** is an educator, scholar, and artist committed to widening spaces for people of color in dance. She has been writing and developing teaching strategies in the area of dance education for more than ten years.

Corrine **Nagata** is the owner and director of Nagata Dance in San Francisco and focuses a great deal of attention on community engagement and teacher training.

Index

aborigine 155
abstraction 85, 86, 91
Adams, Diana 146
aesthetic criteria 94, 95
African dance aesthetic 32, 93, 98, 180
African music and dance 58, 92
Africanisms 127, 134, 136, 138, 140, 141, 142, 144, 146, 147
Afrocentrism 133
Afro-modern 178
Ailey, Alvin 72, 137, 147
Alessi, Alito 115
Alvin Ailey American Dance Theater 69, 70
Aman Folk Ensemble 173
American Ballet Theatre 70
American Negro Ballet Company 69, 80
American School of Ballet 69
ancestry 67, 92, 141, 150
Anderson, Lauren 70, 84
anti-dance regulations 157
Arizona State University 185
Asante, Molefi Kete
Ash, Aesha 72
Asians 8, 14, 31, 36, 38, 71, 79, 87, 108, 110, 128, 177, 182, 184, 185, 189, 201
assessment 9, 61, 62, 63, 82, 83, 84, 90, 91, 95, 99, 100, 102; objectivity 82; peer 83; self 83
audience 56, 72, 93, 98, 101, 103, 112, 115, 119, 120, 123, 126, 199
authenticity 148, 174, 216
authoritarian model 128, 129, 132; see also Freire, Paulo
autobiographical movement poem 60, 61, 62

Balanchine, George 67, 68, 79, 144, 145, 146, 147

ballet 2, 4, 7, 8, 9, 10, 14, 20, 31, 32, 37, 51, 53, 56, 65–84, 128, 133, 134, 136, 140, 142, 145, 146, 147, 149, 151, 169, 171–191, 207
Ballet Hispanico 81, 17
Ballet Russe de Monte Carlo 67, 68, 69
"banking model" and "anti-banking" 16, 25, 129, 143, 151
Banks, James 17, 209
Barr, Sherrie 20
Bean, John 148
belly dancing 177
Benin (kingdom) 133, 134
Bharatanatyam 174, 181, 189
Big Apple 55
Black Arts Movement 97
black dance 28, 142, 146, 147, 151, 170, 179, 217, 221
black dancing body 142, 146, 150
Black Power 97
Blackfoot tribe 164
blackness 142, 144, 147, 148, 150, 153, 204
Body Techniques 188
bollywood 178
Borstel, John 101
Bourdieu, Pierre 30, 172, 173
Brown, Joan Myers 69, 79, 151
Browne, Delores 69, 77
"brownface" 177; see also Indian dancers
Bureau of Indiana Affairs (BIA) 154, 155, 167
bustle (Native dress) 162, 163, 164

Canadian tribes (First Nation) 154
canon 47, 187
capoeira 47, 76, 132
caring 43, 44
Charbeneau, Jean 130
Chiang Ching Dance Company 173

Chicano 47
chicken 164; *see also* native dances
China 54, 66, 77, 201, 202
Choctaw Tribe 67, 168
choreography 85, 90, 91, 95, 100, 101, 102, 106, 108, 110, 110, 117, 125
Chouteau, Yvonne 67, 68
Chuck Davis Dance Company 173
Chung, Frances 79
church 93, 94, 159, 178
circle(s) 31, 55, 59, 76, 106, 165, 200
class 3, 4, 7, 9, 16, 18, 104, 138, 169, 173, 180, 187, 188; middle class 29, 96, 129
classical stories 73, 77
classism 172, 173, 180, 185
Cole, Jack 180
colorblind 105, 113
colorism 69, 70
Columbia College in Chicago 185
commodification of dance 173, 174, 186
communal experience 59, 98
community 59, 61, 64, 72, 92, African American dance 94, 97, 98, 180; Native American 160
competition dance 28, 29, 37, 47, 87
Complexions 70
contact improvisation 59, 60, 115, 118, 181
contemporary dance 13, 14, 37, 70, 78, 89, 90, 91, 100, 115, 179, 183, 184, 185, 213
Copeland, Misty 70, 77, 79, 80, 207
Corporeal Lineages 188
costume 23, 36, 91, 101, 136, 162, 168
course offerings 177, 185
creative process 23, 85, 86, 88, 91, 105, 125
Creek (Indians) 156
Creek Nation 155
Creole Giselle 69, 78, 80
critical dance pedagogy (CDP) 5, 10, 11, 16, 18, 19, 20, 27, 45, 65, 66, 68, 70, 72, 74, 76, 78, 80, 82, 84, 86, 87, 88, 90, 92, 94, 96, 98, 100, 102, 103, 104, 106, 108, 109, 110, 111, 112, 114, 116, 118, 122, 124, 125, 126, 128, 130, 132, 156, 158, 160, 162, 164, 166, 168, 169, 170, 172, 174, 176, 178, 180, 182, 184, 185, 186, 188, 189, 192, 194, 196, 198, 200, 202, 204, 205.
critical pedagogy 3, 10, 18, 20, 103, 104, 129, 204.
critical race theory 16, 18, 20, 129
Critical Response Process (CRP) 101
Cuba 66, 71, 76, 81
Cubism 136
cuentos (stories) 73
cultural aesthetics 94
cultural appropriation 66, 78, 138, 140, 146, 152, 154, 155, 160, 175, 177

cultural capital 30, 31
cultural currency 31, 32
cultural dominance 152, 170; *see also* Eurocentric and ethnocentric
cultural identity 66, 78, 92, 175, 203
cultural informants 99; *see also* cultural referents
cultural knowledge 2, 18, 22, 24, 102, 204
cultural mapping 116, 117, 122
cultural marker 95
cultural orientation 57, 58, 60, 72, 85, 90, 129
cultural reference 17, 34, 47, 48, 58, 101
cultural sensitivity 9, 15, 19, 95, 98, 154, 180, 181
cultural superiority (only culture that matters) 27, 87; *see also* Eurocentric
culturally relevant teaching 3, 4, 5, 8, 10, 11, 13–29, 31, 33, 34, 35, 37, 38, 39, 40, 41, 43, 44, 45, 46, 47, 48, 49, 51, 56, 57, 58, 65, 66, 68, 70, 71, 72, 74, 75, 76, 78, 80, 82, 84, 86, 88, 90, 92, 94, 96, 97, 98, 100, 102, 104, 106, 108, 110, 112, 114, 116, 118, 120, 122, 124, 126, 129, 185, 205
culturally responsive teaching 5, 10, 17, 18, 24, 26, 64, 97, 98
culture (explanation of) 35–36
culture clash 95
curriculum 9, 10, 11, 17, 20, 23, 24, 25, 26, 34, 37, 38, 39, 40, 47, 48, 63, 64, 66, 68, 71, 72, 76, 81, 84, 88, 127, 130, 155, 171, 172, 183, 184, 185, 186, 188, 204; equity 184, 183, 185
customs 22, 26, 35, 36, 37, 42, 43, 51, 53, 75, 51, 178
Cuyjet, Marion 69

d'Amboise, Jacques 191, 193, 199
dance accent 57, 58
dance as language 57, 58, 140
dance attire 10, 13, 52, 74
The Dance Catalog 173, 179
dance composition 85, 86, 87, 88, 91, 92, 95, 99, 101, 102, 184; Africanist approach 92; Tongan informed approach 94, 95, 100; Western compositional approach 85, 101
dance ethnography 94
dance hierarchies 188
dance history 5, 10, 63, 65, 70, 127, 128, 130, 131, 132, 133, 134, 136, 138, 140, 148, 149, 150, 152, 153, 154, 155, 157, 161, 163, 165, 167, 183, 184, 187, 205
Dance History Walk 132
dance imperialism 66, 174, 177, 186
dance-making 137

dance organizations (culturally informed) 15
Dance Theatre of Harlem (DTH) 69, 78, 81, 194
Danceability 115
dancing stick 163
Darling-Hammond, Linda 23
Delpit, Lisa 3, 33, 34, 129
deMille, Agnes 72
Denison University 185
dobalè 51
Dorfman, David 55
Diaghilev, Serge 136; Diaghilev's Ballet Russe 136
disability (differently abled physically) 52, 120, 121, 122, 123
diverse content 20, 39, 40
diversifying curriculum and content: 11, 19, 20, 26, 27, 38, 40, 63, 64, 82, 84, 154, 156, 158, 160, 162, 164, 166, 168, 170, 172, 174, 176, 178, 180, 182, 184, 186, 188, 192, 194, 196, 198, 200, 202
diversity of a class 52
drum groups 162
Duncan, Isadora 136, 182
Dunham, Katherine 138, 140, 146

Egungun (mask from Nigeria) 135
embodied cultural markers 21, 204
embodied histories 58
embodied storytelling 60
embodiment 14, 33, 58, 88
Ethnic Dance 79, 170, 171, 173, 176, 178, 179, 180, 181, 182, 184
ethnocide 156, 157, 166
Eurocentricity 20, 31, 32, 63, 66, 72, 89, 92, 93, 98, 127, 131, 169, 170, 172, 174, 183
Europeanism 138, 139, 140, 141, 142, 146
Evans, Albert 70

fancy 163; *see also* native dances
fancy shawl 165; *see also* native dances
feather fan 161, 164
feminist pedagogy 104, 129
feminist theory 16, 20, 21, 104
Five Moons 67, 68, 128
Flamenco dance 95, 179, 185
Flight of Spirit 68
formative feedback 101
Foster, Susan 138, 185
Foulkes, Julia 137, 143, 144, 148
Frankenburg, Ruth 131, 152
Freire, Paulo 16, 25, 104, 125, 128, 129, 151
Friedlaender, Diane 23
fusion 75, 134, 136, 138, 140, 145, 146, 147, 176

Gathering of Nations Powwow 154
Gay, Geneva 3, 17, 23, 26, 43, 129
gender 3, 4, 14, 16, 18, 19, 20, 21, 25, 29, 42, 44, 45, 52, 60, 73, 74, 75, 80, 87, 97, 104, 130, 138, 139, 144, 161, 177, 206
Gennaro, Peter 180
genocide 157, 158
Ghost Dance 158
Giordano, Gus 180
Giselle 67, 69, 72, 78
global dance 20, 175, 176
globality 171, 175, 180, 181
Gottschild, Brenda Dixon 20, 79, 127, 144, 145, 146, 147, 151, 171
Graham, Martha 128, 137, 140, 141, 150, 187, 189, 182
grass dance 163; *see also* native dances
Griffin, Charlotte 188
Guy, Edna 137, 138, 148

hair 15, 51, 128, 163, 194, 197,
Hanley, Mary 23, 24
Harlem shake 175
Harris, Rennie 78
Hawkins, Alma 20, 85, 86, 182
H'Doubler, Margaret 20, 182
head roach 164
high art 32, 66, 171, 187
higher education 2, 11, 15, 20, 28, 38, 39, 40, 63, 64, 63, 64, 65, 85, 171, 172, 176, 181, 182, 183, 185, 188
Hightower, Rosella 67, 80
Hilsendager, Sarah 20, 169
hip-hop 7, 8, 9, 22, 25, 32, 37, 47, 66, 100, 132, 174, 185, 187, 188
"hipster headdress" 160
homosexuality 14, 28, 32, 44; *see also* LGBTQ
honor beats 161
hooks, bell 125
hoop dance 165; *see also* native dances
horizontal plane 57
Houston Ballet 70, 84

identity markers 156, 169
improvisation 57, 58, 59, 98, 101, 118
Indian agents 156, 157
Indian classical dance 37, 90, 181, 212
Indian dancers 176; *see also* "brownface"
Indigenous 155
inscriptions of the body 86, 87

Jamison, Judith 69
Jansinski, Roman 68
jazz dance 22, 141, 147, 179, 180, 182, 183, 184, 188

jingle 164; *see also* native dances
Joburg Ballet 71, 81
Joint Forces Dance Company 115

K-12 19, 36, 40, 42, 63, 113
kabiesi 51
Kaeppler, Adrienne 94
Kathak 90, 183, 189
Kealinohomoku, Joan 79, 151, 178, 179
Kikuchi, Yuriko 128
"kill the Indian and save the man" 157
Ku Klux Klan 70

Ladson Billings, Gloria 3, 16, 17, 23, 44, 129
language 6, 18, 25, 26, 36, 39, 42, 48, 54, 56, 57, 58, 65, 77, 79, 82, 91, 95, 113, 119, 130, 140, 141, 147, 161, 162, 168, 169, 171, 172, 173, 181, 182, 185, 188, 189, 193, 194, 195, 198
lapa 51
Larkin, Moscelyne 67, 68
Larsen, Mike 68, 80
Latino 8, 58, 71, 79, 98
LGBTQ 21, 28, 44, 45, 47, 203; *see also* homosexuality
Lerman, Liz 101, 115, 132; *see also* Critical Response Process
lexicon 186, 188; *see also* language
Limón, José 128
The Little Mermaid 118
low art 66, 93, 188
Luigi 180
lyrics 88, 89, 90, 92

Maher, Frances 130
Malone, Jacqui 92
mama huhu 199
Maria Alba Spanish Company 173
Martin, John 67, 178
Mattox, Matt 180
meaning making (in relation to dance-making) 24, 25, 34
Mexican folklore 73
Mitchell, Arthur 68, 69, 70, 146
moccasin 164
modern (dance) 2, 8, 9, 14, 20, 23, 31, 89, 122, 128, 136, 137, 138, 139, 140, 143, 147, 150, 151, 152, 156, 169, 170, 171, 172, 174, 178, 179, 181, 182–189, 192
modernism 128, 134, 136, 137, 138
mono-cultural values 182
movement: affinities 36, 43, 56, 57, 58, 64; history 56, 82; invention 90, 98, 101; language 82; practices 98, 186, 187; traditions 188

multiculturalism 38, 46, 48
multi-nation 156
multiple cultures (students identify with) 46
Murphy, Jacqueline Shea 156

naming exercises 56, 76
National Ballet Company of Iran 71
National Dance Institute (NDI) 191, 200
National Dance Standards 85, 91
national identities 66
Native American community 5, 36, 55, 58, 67, 68, 73, 76, 97, 128, 137, 150, 152, 154, 155, 156, 157, 159, 160, 161, 163, 165, 166, 167, 168
native beadwork 162, 163
native dances: chicken 164; grass dance 163; fancy 163; fancy shawl 165; hoop dance 165; jingle 164; northern traditional 163; round dance 165; southern straight 163; traditional buckskin 164; traditional southern cloth 164; two-step 165
native initiation 160
native mascots 160
native nations 157
native regalia 160
native religion 157
neighborhood soundscape 93
Nelson, Karen 115
Neuro-Kinesthetic Practices 188
New York City Ballet (NYCB) 65 67, 68, 69, 72, 79
New York Negro Ballet 69
northern traditional 163; *see also* native dances

Ojibwe 164
Oklahoma 67, 68, 128, 163, 164, 168
opera 66
Orientalism 176, 177
Osage Tribe 67
othering 9, 147, 174, 177, 186

pagan 176, 188
Paris Opera Ballet 67
Pedagogy of the Oppressed, 104, 128
Perpener, John, III 137, 141, 170
personal dance history 63
Peter Pan 160
Philadanco 69, 144
physical abilities (and disability) 16, 116, 118, 119, 121, 122, 123
physical or kinesthetic response 93
Picasso, Pablo 135, 136, 140
La Pietà (Michelangelo) 133, 135

"Pioneers in Negro Concert Dance" 143
Plains Indian 154
Pocahontas 160
Ponca tribe 163
powwow 55, 154, 155, 156, 157, 159–168;
  contests 161; grand entry 161; head man
  161; head woman 161; powwow music,
  "pushups" and honor beats 162; *see also*
  native dances
prima ballerina 67, 77, 128
Primus, Pearl 138, 140, 141, 142, 143, 144, 178
primitive dance 178
privilege 2, 6, 8, 9, 13, 14, 15, 17, 18, 19, 27,
  65, 66, 105, 112, 121, 122, 131, 137, 138,
  147, 148, 149, 150, 152, 169, 172, 173, 174,
  178, 185, 187, 189, 205, 206
Puerto Rico 71
"pushups" 162

queer 14, 29, 44, 75

race 3, 4, 5, 6, 7, 14, 16, 18, 19, 20, 21, 23,
  32, 39, 55, 58, 78, 79, 80, 81, 87, 89, 90,
  97, 104, 105, 106, 107, 109, 110, 111, 112,
  113, 114, 119, 123, 128, 129, 130, 131, 137,
  138, 141, 142, 144, 149, 150, 163, 169, 172,
  177, 178, 180, 182, 187, 196, 201, 202,
  205, 207
racism 67, 72, 105, 106, 107, 111, 114, 128,
  129, 131, 134, 135, 136, 137, 143, 144, 148,
  149, 150, 151, 152, 155, 169, 172, 173, 178,
  180, 185
Radha 177; *see also* St. Denis, Ruth
The Red Detachment of Women 66
Renaissance Italy 65, 133, 137
resistance 20, 24, 36, 89, 97, 132, 150, 155,
  204, 205
reverence 53, 55, 76, 84
Rey, Frank 179, 180
Rhoden, Dwight 70
rhythm 51, 54, 58, 59, 89, 90, 91, 93, 98, 99,
  139, 144, 175
Richardson, Desmond 70
ring shout 55
Risner, Doug 20
rituals 22, 24, 26, 51, 52, 53, 54, 55, 64, 75,
  76, 94, 97, 117, 133, 134, 138, 157, 158, 178,
  189
Rome and Jewels 78
Romeo and Juliet 73, 78
round dance 165; *see also* native dances
Royal Academy of Dance 66
rubric 61, 62, 63, 83, 84, 99, 100

sagittal plane 57
St. Denis, Ruth 128, 137, 148, 176, 177

salsa 28, 37, 76, 178
San Francisco Ballet 8, 79, 173, 187
San Iidefonso 156; *see also* Tewa
Savage, Reginald 190, 191, 192, 202
Savigliano, Marta 173, 174
Scott, Anna B. 78
segregation 6, 7, 69
sexual orientation 29
sexuality 3, 60, 177
Shapiro, Sherry 19, 20, 21, 204
Shawn, Ted 128, 148, 150
Shawnee tribe 68
social responsibility 97
South Africa 13, 71, 77
southern straight 163; *see also* native
  dances
southern cloth 164, 168; *see also* native
  dances
stereotypes 155, 160, 161, 177
Stinson, Susan 20, 73
storytelling 58, 60, 71, 72, 73, 76, 89, 90,
  91, 92
Strange Fruit 142, 143, 144
stratification (of dance) 188
student culture 78
student sharing (of culture) 30
subordinate groups 170
Swan Lake 72, 74
symphony 93

Tallchief, Maria 67, 77, 128, 211, 214, 225
Tallchief, Marjorie 67
Tamiris, Helen 138, 140
Tan, Yuan Yuan 79
tap 141, 179, 184, 188
Tektonika Ondine 103, 115, 120, 124
Tetreault, Mary Kay Thompson 130
Tewa 156; *see also* San Iidelfonso
Tokyo Ballet 71
touch 59, 60, 61, 118, 165
traditional buckskin 164; *see also* native
  dances
traditional southern cloth 164; *see also*
  native dances
traditional Western dance communities
  28, 38, 76
transgender 14, 29, 44
tribal dances 154; *see also* native dances;
  powwows
tribal princess 154, 161
Tudor, Anthony 69
two-step 165; *see also* native dances

U.S. military 161
University of California, Irvine 185, 188,
  225

University of Cape Town 183
University of New Mexico 185
University of Surrey 183
Urban Movement Practices 185

vertical plane 57
vintage jazz 180
Vissicaro, Pegge 170

Wanted 103, 105, 107, 114
Watson, Dawn Marie 144
Webb, Lynne 129
Weinstein, Ellen 191, 192, 193
Welsh, Kariamu 92, 97, 179
West Africa 98, 133, 134, 139, 146, 178, 181, 185, 189

Western-based dance 7, 9, 27, 32, 39, 54, 58
Western cultural aesthetic 97
Western superiority 87
whiteness 127, 128, 129, 130, 131, 132, 133, 136, 137, 138, 147, 148, 149, 150, 152, 153, 157
Wilkinson, Raven 69, 70, 77, 128
Williams, Drid 170
Wood, Peter H. 140
world dance 4, 5, 39, 138, 139, 146, 169, 171, 173, 174, 175, 176, 177, 178, 179, 180, 181, 182, 183, 184, 185, 186, 187, 188, 189